THE NOVELS OF
SAMUEL RICHARDSON

With a Life of the Author, and Introductions by
WILLIAM LYON PHELPS
M.A. (Harvard), Ph.D. (Yale)
Professor of English Literature at Yale College

COMPLETE IN NINETEEN VOLUMES

SAMVEL RICHARDSON'S NOVELS

Publishers' Guarantee

EDITION DE LUXE

This edition is limited to twelve hundred and thirty-two numbered and registered copies. It is printed from type on American deckle edge paper, and the type has been distributed.

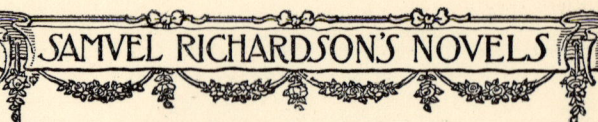

Croscup & Sterling Co.

THIS IS COPY NO. 592

Stothard del.

THE NOVELS
OF
Samuel Richardson

COMPLETE AND UNABRIDGED

The Pantiles.

Illustrated

NEW YORK: CROSCUP & STERLING COMPANY

PR
3661
.P5
v.16

BARD COLLEGE LIBRARY
Annandale-on-Hudson, N.Y. 12504

THE HISTORY

OF

Sir Charles Grandison

BY

MR. SAMUEL RICHARDSON

WITH AN INTRODUCTION BY
WILLIAM LYON PHELPS
Professor of English Literature at Yale College

COMPLETE IN SEVEN VOLUMES
VOLUME FOUR

Printed from type for Subscribers only by
CROSCUP & STERLING COMPANY
NEW YORK

COPYRIGHT, 1901
BY CROSCUP & STERLING COMPANY.

SYNOPTICAL TABLE OF CONTENTS

LETTER I.

PAGE

Miss Byron to Miss Selby.—A seventh letter from Dr. Bartlett: Sir Charles Grandison receives a visit from Clementina's friendly servant Camilla, in disguise, unknown to all the Porretta family, except the marchioness and Signor Jeronymo: receives a friendly letter from Jeronymo. Tender scene between Clementina and her mother the marchioness.—The doctor's eighth letter: describing the interview of Sir Charles Grandison and Clementina, in presence of the marchioness.— The doctor's ninth letter describes Clementina's conference with her brother Jeronymo; and another visit from Camilla to Sir Charles Grandison. Father Marescotti likewise visits and counsels him. Letter from the Marquis della Porretta to Sir Charles Grandison; and Sir Charles's reply to it. Affectionate letter from Signor Jeronymo to Sir Charles . 1—40

LETTER II.

Miss Byron to Miss Selby.—A tenth letter from Dr. Bartlett: Description of a formal visit Sir Charles Grandison paid to the whole of the Porretta family assembled: their different characters clearly displayed on this occasion; and the affectionate parting of Sir Charles and his friend Jeronymo 41—51

LETTER III.

Miss Byron to Miss Selby.—An eleventh letter from Dr. Bartlett: Signor Jeronymo writes to Sir Charles Grandison an account of what farther passed in conversation between the family after his departure . . . . 52—60

LETTER IV.

Miss Byron to Miss Selby.—Dr. Bartlett's twelfth letter: Sir Charles Grandison takes leave of his friends at Bologna, and is setting out for Florence; when he receives a friendly

Vol. IV—2.

CONTENTS.

letter from Signor Jeronymo, by which he learns that Clementina had earnestly entreated her father to permit her to see him once again before his departure; but that she had met with an absolute refusal: Jeronymo also describes the ill-treatment of his sister by her aunt, and her resignation under her trials. Sir Charles arrives at Naples, and there visits Clementina's brother, the general: account of his reception, and of the conversation that passed between them . 60—71

LETTER V.

Miss Byron to Miss Selby.—Dr. Bartlett's thirteenth letter; containing an account of Sir Charles Grandison's final departure from Italy; and various matters relative to the Porretta family; the persecutions Clementina endured from her relations; and a letter Sir Charles Grandison received from Mrs. Beaumont. Dr. Bartlett concludes with an apostrophe on the brevity of all human affairs . . . . 71—78

LETTER VI.

Miss Harriet Byron to Miss Lucy Selby.—Explanation of the causes of Sir Charles Grandison's uneasiness, occasioned by intelligence lately brought him from abroad. Miss Byron wishes that Sir Charles was proud and vain, that she might with the more ease cast off her acknowledged shackles. She enumerates the engagements that engross the time of Sir Charles; and mentions his tender regard toward the two sons of Mrs. Oldham, the penitent mistress of his father Sir Thomas. A visit from the Earl of G—— and his sister Lady Gertrude . . . . 79—86

LETTER VII.

Miss Byron to Miss Selby.—Sir Charles Grandison dines with Sir Hargrave Pollexfen and his gay friends; his reflections on the riots and excesses frequently committed at the jovial meetings of gay and thoughtless young men. Sir Charles negotiates a treaty of marriage for Lord W——; and resolves to attempt the restoring of the oppressed Mansfield family to their rights . . . . 86—95

LETTER VIII.

Miss Byron to Miss Selby.—Farther traits in the character of Sir Charles Grandison . . . . 95—96

CONTENTS.

LETTER IX.

Sir Charles Grandison to Dr. Bartlett.—Sir Charles describes the interview he had with Sir Harry Beauchamp and his lady; and how he appeased the anger of the imperious lady. His farther proceedings in favour of the Mansfields . . 96—113

LETTER X.

Miss Byron to Miss Selby.—A visit from the Countess of D—— and the earl her son. Account of the young earl's person and deportment. Miss Byron confesses to the countess that her heart is already a wedded heart, and that she cannot enter into a second engagement. Reflections on young men being sent by their parents on travel to foreign countries . 113—121

LETTER XI.

Miss Byron to Miss Selby.—Various self-debatings and recriminations that passed through the young lady's mind on the expectation of breakfasting with Sir Charles Grandison 121—123

LETTER XII.

Miss Byron to Miss Selby.—Sir Charles Grandison communicates to Miss Byron the farther distressing intelligence he has received from Bologna:—His friend Signor Jeronymo dangerously ill, his sister Clementina declining in health, and their father and mother absorbed in melancholy. This communication comes from the Bishop of Nocera, Clementina's second brother; who entreats Sir Charles to make one more visit to Bologna. Farther affecting information from Mrs. Beaumont respecting Lady Clementina's cruel treatment at the palace of Milan, and her removal from thence to Naples. Sir Charles resolves on going to Bologna. Miss Byron's dignified and generous conduct on the occasion . . 123—137

LETTER XIII.

Miss Byron to Miss Selby.—Informs her of the generosity and kind condescension of Sir Charles to Mrs. Oldham and her family, as related by Miss Grandison: their difference of opinion on that subject . . . . . 138—142

CONTENTS.

LETTER XIV.

PAGE

Miss Byron to Miss Selby.—An early visit from Miss Jervois, who communicates with much pleasure the particulars of a late interview she had with her mother: relates a conversation that passed between her guardian, Mrs. O'Hara, and Captain Salmonet: describes the affectionate behaviour of Sir Charles to her, on introducing her to her mother; and his kind instructions concerning her deportment on the occasion . . . . 142—149

LETTER XV.

Miss Byron to Miss Selby.—Sir Charles solicits his sister to fix the day for her marriage before he leaves England. Visit from Lord G——, the Earl, and Lady Gertrude. Miss Grandison unusually thoughtful all the time of dinner. The Earl of G—— and Lady Gertrude request a conference with Sir Charles after dinner. Purport of it. Miss Grandison's reluctance to so early a day as her brother names, but at length accedes to his powerful entreaties; though wholly unprepared, she says . . . . 149—157

LETTER XVI.

Miss Byron to Miss Selby.—Serious conversation between Miss Byron and Miss Grandison concerning the approaching marriage. The latter expresses her indifference for Lord G——; compares his character with that of her brother; entreats Miss Byron to breakfast with her the next day, and to remain with her till the event takes place . . 157—160

LETTER XVII.

Miss Grandison to Miss Byron.—Ludicrous description of three marriages given by Miss Grandison, with the anticipation of her own . . . . 161—163

LETTER XVIII.

Miss Byron to Miss Selby.—Great preparations for Miss Grandison's marriage: her generous offer to Miss Byron of her share of her mother's jewels, who refuses to accept of them, and gives her opinion as to their disposal. Miss Grandison

CONTENTS.   ix

PAGE

is pleased with the hint, and acts accordingly. Account of Dr. Bartlett's interesting conversation with Miss Byron on the subject of Sir Charles going to Italy, and his attachment to Miss Byron. The young lady's emotions: her alternate hopes and fears: she resolves on relinquishing Sir Charles in favour of Lady Clementina . . . . . 163—167

LETTER XIX.

Miss Byron to Miss Selby.—Debate concerning the place where the marriage ceremony is to be performed. Conversation between Miss Byron and Miss Grandison interrupted by Lady Gertrude. Miss Byron expresses much concern for Lord G——, from Miss Grandison's present conduct to him; but is inclined to hope that an alteration may be effected . 167—174

LETTER XX.

Miss Byron to Miss Selby.—Account of Sir Charles's return from Windsor: his joy on restoring the worthy family of the Mansfields from oppression: his interview with his friend Beauchamp at Sir Harry's; and cheerful behaviour at his sister's wedding, though his own heart is torn with uncertainty. Farther proofs of his esteem for Miss Byron . . . . 174—180

LETTER XXI.

Miss Byron to Miss Selby.—Sir Charles briefly lays before his sister the duties of a married life: some remarks on her behaviour. Lord W——'s generosity to his nieces on Lady G——'s marriage. Painful reflections on the departure of Sir Charles. Opinions on the proper age for the marrying of women . . . . 181—193

LETTER XXII.

Miss Byron to Miss Selby.—Conversation with Dr. Bartlett. Artless remarks of Miss Jervois, and her censures on the conduct of Lady G—— to her lord. Mr. Galliard proposes an alliance for Sir Charles. Contrast between Lady G—— and Lady L—— in disposing of their uncle's present. Miss Byron's perturbed state of mind: the cause of it. Her noble resolution in favour of Lady Clementina . . . 193—200

CONTENTS.

LETTER XXIII.

PAGE

Miss Byron to Miss Selby.—Conference between Lord W—— and Sir Charles on the management of servants: their conduct frequently influenced by example. Remarks on the helpless state of single women. Plan proposed for erecting Protestant Nunneries in England, and places of refuge for penitent females . . . . 200—209

LETTER XXIV.

Lady G—— to Miss Byron.—Invitation to dinner. Account of a matrimonial altercation, and of the arrival of Lady Olivia . . . . 209—211

LETTER XXV.

Miss Byron to Miss Selby.—Encloses Lady G——'s letter, and describes her concern for Lord G—— . . . 211—213

LETTER XXVI.

Miss Byron to Miss Selby.—Lady Olivia is introduced to Miss Byron. Some traits in that lady's character related by Dr. Bartlett. She declares her passion for Sir Charles to Lady L——. She endeavours to prevail on him to defer his voyage, and is indignant at meeting with a refusal. Miss Byron's exalted behaviour . . . . 214—224

LETTER XXVII.

Miss Byron to Miss Selby.—Conversation with Sir Charles concerning Lord and Lady G——. His anxiety for their happiness; but hopes much from Miss Byron's influence over his sister . . . . 224—227

LETTER XXVIII.

Miss Byron to Miss Selby.—Sir Charles departs unexpectedly, from the kindest motives. The concern and solicitude of his friends. Miss Byron's mind much agitated. The eldest of Mrs. Oldham's sons presented with a pair of colours by Sir Charles . . . . 227—232

CONTENTS. xi

LETTER XXIX.

PAGE

Miss Byron to Miss Selby.—Account of Lady Olivia's behaviour. Her horrid attempt to stab Sir Charles. Miss Byron describes the state of her own mind, and resolves to return to Northamptonshire . . . . 232—237

LETTER XXX.

Miss Byron to Miss Selby.—Particulars of a very interesting conversation with Mrs. Reeves and Lady D——. Miss Byron's ingenuous reply to Lady D——'s interrogation. Her explanation of some of Sir Charles's expressions in the library. Conference which had formerly embarrassed her . 237—245

LETTER XXXI.

Miss Byron to Miss Selby.—Preparations for her journey into Northamptonshire. Regrets at parting with friends. Lady Olivia is desirous of visiting Miss Byron. Remarks on politeness. Unpleasant consequences sometimes resulting from it. Remarks on the conduct of Sir Charles . 245—247

LETTER XXXII.

Miss Byron to Miss Selby.—Lady G—— quarrels with her lord, who entreats Miss Byron's assistance in effecting a reconciliation. That lady's kind advice and opinion. Lady G—— resumes her good humour; but will not acknowledge herself to have been in the wrong . . . . 247—255

LETTER XXXIII.

Miss Byron to Miss Selby.—Relates what passed on a visit to Lady Olivia. Miss Byron pities the impetuosity of her temper, and admires her many amiable qualities. Pays another visit to Lady G——; and gives an account of the reconciliation between her and her husband . . 255—262

LETTER XXXIV.

Miss Byron to Miss Selby.—Mr. Fowler brings a letter from Sir Rowland Meredith, most affectionately soliciting the hand of Miss Byron in favour of his nephew . . . 263—266

xii   CONTENTS.

LETTER XXXV.

PAGE

Miss Byron to Sir Rowland Meredith.—She regards Sir Rowland as her father; avows her affection for Sir Charles, notwithstanding his engagements with another lady, and disclaims the generous intentions of Sir Rowland in her favour, in his will . . . . 266—268

LETTER XXXVI.

Miss Byron to Miss Selby.—Arrangements for her journey. Thoughts on public amusements. Retrospect. Tender parting with Dr. Bartlett . . . . . . 269—272

LETTER XXXVII.

Miss Byron to Lady G——.—Description of her journey: account of those friends who accompanied her to Dunstable and of those who met her there, from Northamptonshire; of Mr. Greville and Mr. Fenwick's collation for her at Stratford; of Mr. Orme again saluting her by the highway-side, as the coach passed his park-wall; and of her kin reception at Selby House . . . . 272—278

LETTER XXXVIII.

Lady G—— to Miss Byron.—The opinions of the Dunstable party respecting Miss Byron. Charms of the mind superior to those of person. Lady G——'s opinion of Miss Byron's aunt Selby, and of her cousins Lucy and Nancy; thinks her uncle's wit too much studied; defends her own character, and the attack made by herself and sister on Miss Byron at Colnebrooke. Lord G—— proposes parting with his collection of moths and shells: gives the latter to Miss Jervois, at his lady's request, and presents Lady G—— with a set of old Japan china . . . . . 278—286

LETTER XXXIX.

Miss Jervois to Miss Byron.—Her regret at parting with Miss Byron at Stratford: encomiums on her guardian and Mr. Beauchamp: censures the conduct of Lady G—— to her lord. Instance of her dutiful behaviour to her mother, on accidentally meeting with her. . . . . 287—291

CONTENTS.

LETTER XL.

Miss Byron to Lady G——.—Reproves Lady G—— for her levity. Does not find the society of her country friends relieve the anxiety of her mind; laments the absence of those she has just left: is visited by Mr. Fenwick, Mr. Greville, and Mr. Orme. Mr. Greville's rudeness, and her own magnanimity. Hears of Sir Hargrave Pollexfen's return . . . 291—296

LETTER XLI.

Lady G—— to Miss Byron.—Ideas of female delicacy. Report of Sir Hargrave's return confirmed. Sir Charles meets with an adventure on the road to Paris. Delivers Sir Hargrave and Mr. Merceda from the chastisement of an enraged husband. Sir Charles's firmness and temper on the occasion . . . . 296—304

LIST OF ILLUSTRATIONS

SIR CHARLES GRANDISON, VOLUME IV.

SHE HEARD THEM, AND SCREAMED, AND LEAVING THE LADDER, RAN, TO AVOID THEM, TILL SHE CAME IN SIGHT OF THE GREAT CASCADE. (p. 62) . . . . . . *Frontispiece*
Engraved by Heath from a drawing by Stothard.

SIR HARRY CLEARED UP AT ONCE—MAY I HOPE, MADAM—AND OFFERED TO TAKE HER HAND 105
Engraved by Walker from a drawing by Stothard.

SHE PULLED OUT OF HER STAYS, IN FURY, A PONIARD, AND VOWED TO PLUNGE IT INTO HIS HEART 236
Drawn and engraved by R. Vinkeles, 1799.

ANNE SAW HER FIRST, I ALIGHTED, AND ASKED HER BLESSING IN THE SHOP 289
Engraved by Walker from a drawing by Stothard.

THE HISTORY
of
SIR CHARLES GRANDISON

LETTER I.

Miss Byron.—In continuation.

London, Friday Morning, March 31.

HERE, my Lucy, once more I am. We arrived yesterday in the afternoon.

Lady Betty Williams and Miss Clements have been already to welcome me on my return. My cousin says they are inseparable. I am glad of it, for Lady Betty's sake.

Dr. Bartlett is extremely obliging. One would think that he and his kinsman gave up all their time in transcribing for us. I send you now his seventh, eighth, and ninth letters. In reading the two latter, we were struck (for the two sisters and my lord were with us) with the nobleness of Clementina. Her motive, through her whole delirium, is so apparently owing to her concern for the soul of the man she loved (entirely regardless of any interest of her own), that we all forgot what had been so long our wishes, and joined in giving preference to her.

Dr. Bartlett's seventh letter.

I HAD another visit paid me, proceeds Mr. Grandison, two hours after the general left me, by the kind-hearted Camilla, disguised as before.

I come now, chevalier, said she, with the marchioness's connivance, and, I may say, by her command; and, at the same time, by the command of Signor Jeronymo, who knows of my last attendance upon you, though no one else does, not even the marchioness. He gave me this letter for you.

But how does the noblest young lady in Italy, Camilla? How does Lady Clementina?

More composed than we could have hoped for, from the height of her delirium. It *was* high; for she has but a very faint idea of having seen you this morning.

The marchioness had bid her say, that although I had now given her despair instead of hope, yet that she owed it to my merit, and to the sense she had of the benefits they had actually received at my hands, to let me know that it was but too likely that resentments might be carried to an unhappy length; and that therefore she wished I would leave Bologna for the present. If happier prospects presented, she would be the first to congratulate me upon them.

I opened the letter of my kind Jeronymo. These were the contents:

I AM infinitely concerned, my dear Grandison, to find a man equally generous and brave as my brother is, hurried away by passion. You *may* have acted with your usual magnanimity in preferring your religion to your love, and to your glory. I, for my part, think you to be a distressed man. If you are not, you must be very insensible to the merits of an excellent woman, and very ungrateful to the distinction she honours you with. I must write in this style, and think she does honour by it even to my Grandison. But should the consequences of this affair be unhappy for either of you; if, in particular, for my *brother,* what cause of regret would our family have that a *younger* brother was saved by the hand which deprived them of a more worthy *elder?* If for *you,* how deplorable would be the reflection, that you saved one brother, and perished by the hand of another? Would to God that his passion, and your spirit, were more moderate!

But let me request this favour of you; that you retire to Florence, for a few days, at least.

How unhappy am I, that I am disabled from taking part in a more active mediation!—Yet the general admires you. But how can we blame in him a zeal for the honour of his family, in which he would be glad at his soul to include a zeal for yours?

For God's sake, quit Bologna for a few days only. Clementina is more sedate. I have carried it, that her confessor shall not at present visit her; yet he is an honest and a pious man.

What a fatality! Every one to mean well, yet every one to be miserable! And can religion be the cause of so much unhappiness? I cannot *act*. I can only *reflect*. My dear friend, let me know by a line, that you will depart from **Bologna to-morrow**; and you will then a little lighten the heart of your JERONYMO.

I sent my grateful compliments to the marchioness by Camilla. I besought her to believe, that my conduct on this occasion should be such as should merit her approbation. I expressed my grief for the apprehended resentments. I was sure that a man so noble, so generous, so brave, as was the man from whom the resentments might be supposed to arise, would better consider of anything: but it was impossible for me, I bid Camilla say, to be far distant from Bologna; because I still presumed to hope for a happy turn in my favour.

I wrote to Signor Jeronymo to the same effect. I assured him of my high regard for his gallant brother; I deplored the occasion which had subjected me to the general's displeasure; bid him depend upon my moderation. I referred to my known resolution, of long standing, to avoid a meditated rencounter with *any* man; urging, that he might for that reason, the more securely rely upon my care to shun any acts of offence either to or from a son of the Marquis della Porretta; a brother of my dear friend Jeronymo, and of the most excellent and beloved of sisters!

Neither the marchioness nor Jeronymo were satisfied with

the answers I returned: but what could I do? I had promised the general that I would not leave Bologna till I had apprised him of my intention to do so; and I still was willing, as I bid Camilla tell the marchioness, to indulge my hopes of some happy turn.

The marquis, the bishop, and general went to Urbino; and there, as I learnt from my Jeronymo, it was determined, in full assembly, that Grandison, as well from difference in religion, as from inferiority in degree and fortune, was unworthy of their alliance: and it was hinted to the general, that he was equally unworthy of his resentment.

While the father and two brothers were at Urbino, Lady Clementina gave hopes of a sedate mind. She desired her mother to allow her to see me: but the marchioness, believing there were no hopes of my complying with their terms, and being afraid of the consequences, and of incurring blame from the rest of her family, now especially that they were absent, and consulting together on what *was* proper to be done, desired she would not think of it.

This refusal made Clementina the more earnest for an interview. Signor Jeronymo gave his advice in favour of it. The misfortune he had met with had added to his weight with the family. It is a family of harmony and love. They were hardly more particularly fond of Clementina than they were of one another, throughout the several branches of it: this harmony among them added greatly to the family consequence, as well in public as private. Till the attempt that was made upon their Jeronymo, they had not known calamity.

But the confessor strengthening the marchioness's apprehensions of what the consequence of indulging the young lady might be, all Jeronymo's weight would have failed to carry this point, had it not been for an enterprise of Clementina, which extremely alarmed them, and made them give in to her wishes.

Camilla has enabled me to give the following melancholy account of it, to the only man on earth to whom I could communicate particulars, the very recollection of which tears my heart in pieces.

The young lady's malady, after some favourable symptoms, which went off, returned in another shape; her talkativeness continued; but the hurry with which she spoke and acted, gave place to a sedateness that she seemed very fond of. They did not suffer her to go out of her chamber; which she took not well: but Camilla, being absent about an hour, on her return missed her, and alarmed the whole house upon it. Every part of it, and of the garden, was searched. From an apprehension, that they dared not so much as whisper to one another, they *dreaded* to find her whom they so carefully sought after.

At last, Camilla seeing, as she supposed, one of the maid-servants coming down stairs with remarkable tranquillity, as she thought, in her air and manner: Wretch! said she, how composed do you seem to be in a storm that agitates everybody else!

Don't be angry with me, Camilla, returned the supposed servant.

Oh, my lady! my *very* Lady Clementina, in Laura's clothes! Whither are you going, madam?—But let the marchioness know (said she, to one of the women-servants who then appeared in sight) that we have found my young lady.—What, dear madam, is the meaning of this?—Go, Martina (to another woman-servant), go this instant to my lady!—Dear Lady Clementina, what concern have you given us!

And thus she went on, asking questions of her young lady, and giving orders, almost in the same breath, till the marchioness came to them in a joyful hurry, from one of the pavilions in the garden, into which she had thrown herself, tortured by her fears, and dreading the approach of every servant with fatal tidings.

The young lady stood still, but with great composure. I *will* go, Camilla, said she; indeed I will. You disturb me by your frantic ways, Camilla. I wish you would be as sedate and calm as I am. What's the matter with the woman?

Her mother folding her arms about her—Oh, my sweet girl! said she, how could you terrify us thus? What's the meaning of this disguise? Whither were you going?

Vol. IV—3.

Why, madam, I was going on God's errand; not on my own —What is come to Camilla? The poor creature is beside herself!

Oh, my dear! said her mother, taking her hand, and leading her into her own apartment (Camilla following, weeping with joy for having found her), Tell me, said she, tell me, has Laura furnished you with this dress?

Why no, madam; I'll tell you the whole truth. I went and hid myself in Laura's room, while she changed her clothes: I saw where she put those she took off; and when she had left her room, I put them on.

And for what? For what, my dear? Tell me what you designed?

I am neither afraid nor ashamed to tell. It was God's errand I was going upon.

What *was* the errand?

Don't weep then, my dear mamma, and I'll tell you. Do let me kiss away these tears.—And she tenderly embraced her mother.

Why I have a great mind to talk to the Chevalier Grandison. I had many fine thoughts upon my pillow; and I believed I could say a great deal to the purpose to him; and you told me I must not see him: so I thought I would not. But then I had other notions come into my head; and I believed if I could talk freely to him, I should convince him of his errors. Now, thought I, I know he will mind what I say to him, more than perhaps he will my brother the bishop, or Father Marescotti. I am a simple girl, and can have no interest in his conversion; for he has refused me, you know: so there is an end of all matters between him and me. I never was refused before: *was* I, my mamma? I never will be twice refused. Yet I owe him no ill-will. And if one can save a soul, you know, madam, there is no harm in that. So it is God's errand I go upon, and not my own. And shall I not go? Yes, I shall. I know you will give me leave.—She courtesied. Silence is permission. Thank you, madam— and seemed to be going.

Well might her mother be silent. She could not speak;

but, rising, went after her to the door, and taking her hand, sobbed over it her denial (as Camilla described it); and brought her back, and motioned to her to sit down.

She whispered Camilla, What ails my mamma? Can you tell?—But see how calm, how composed, I am! This world, Camilla! what a vain thing is this world! and she looked up. And so I shall tell the chevalier. I shall tell him not to refuse heaven, though he has refused a simple girl, who was no enemy to him, and might have been a faithful guide to him thither, for what he knew. Now all these things I wanted to say to him, and a vast deal more; and when I have told him my mind, I shall be easy.

Will my precious girl be easy, broke out into speech her weeping mother, when you have told the chevalier your mind? You *shall* tell him your mind, my dear; and God restore my child to peace, and to me!

Well now, my mamma, this is a good sign—for if I have moved you to oblige me, why may I not move him to oblige himself?—that's all I have in view. He has been my tutor, and I want, methinks, to return the favour, and be his tutoress; and so you will let me go—won't you?

No, my dear, we will send for him.

Well, that may do as well, provided you will let us be alone together; for these proud men may be ashamed, before company, to own themselves convinced by a simple girl.

But, my dearest love! whither would you have gone? Do you know where the chevalier's lodgings are?

She paused.—She does not, surely, Camilla?

Camilla repeated the question, that the young lady might herself answer it.

She looked as if considering—then, Why no, truly, said she, I did not think of that: but everybody in Bologna knows where the Chevalier Grandison lives—don't you think so?—But when shall he come? That will be better; *much* better.

You shall go, Camilla, disguised as before. Probably he has not quitted Bologna yet. And let him know, to a tittle, all that has passed, on this attempt of the dear soul. If he can bring his mind to comply with our terms, it may not yet be too late: though it *will be* so after my lord and my two sons return from Urbino. But small are my hopes from him. If the interview makes my poor child easy, that will be a blessed event: we shall all rejoice in that. Meantime, come with me, my dear—but first resume your own dress—and then we will tell Jeronymo what we were determined upon. He will be pleased with it, I know.

You tell me, my good Miss Byron, that I cannot be too particular; yet the melancholy tale, I see, affects you too sensibly: as it also does my Lord and Lady L——, and Miss Grandison. No wonder, when the transcribing of them has the same effect upon me, as the reading had at my first being favoured with the letters that give the moving particulars.

Dr. Bartlett's eighth letter.

I PROCEED now to give an account of Mr. Grandison's interview with Lady Clementina.

He had no sooner heard the preceding particulars, than he hastened to her, though with a tortured heart.

He was introduced to the marchioness and Signor Jeronymo, in the apartment of the latter.

I suppose, said the marchioness, after first civilities, Camilla has told you the way we are now in. The dear creature has a great desire to talk with you. Who knows, but she may be easier after she has been humoured?—She is more composed than she was, since she knows she may expect to see you. Poor thing! she has hopes of converting you.

Would to heaven, said Jeronymo, that compassion for her disordered mind may have that effect upon my Grandison which argument has not had!—Poor Grandison! I can pity you at my heart. These are hard trials to your humanity! Your distress is written in your countenance!

It is deeper written in my heart, said I.

Indeed, Dr. Bartlett, it was.

The marchioness rang. Camilla came in. See, said she, if Clementina is disposed now to admit of the chevalier's visit; and ask her, if she will have her mamma introduce him to her.

By all means, was the answer returned.

Clementina, at our entrance, was sitting at the window, a book in her hand. She stood up. A great, but solemn composure, appeared in her air and aspect.

The marchioness went to the window, holding her handkerchief at her eyes. I approached with profound respect her Clementina; but my heart was too full to speak first—*She* could speak. She did, without hesitation——

You are nothing to me now, chevalier: you have refused me, you know; and I thank you: you are in the right, I believe. I am a very proud creature. And you saw what trouble I gave to the best of parents and friends. You are certainly in the right. She that can give so much concern to them, must make any man afraid of her. But religion, it seems, is your pretence. Now I am sorry that you are an obstinate man. You *know* better, chevalier. I think you *should* know better. But you have been my tutor. Shall I be yours?

I shall attend to every instruction that you will honour me with.

But let me, sir, comfort my mamma.

She went to her, and kneeled: Why weeps my mamma? taking a hand in each of hers, and kissing first one, then the other. Be comforted, my mamma. You see I am quite well. You see I am sedate.—Bless your Clementina!

God bless my child!

She arose from her knees; and stepping towards me—You are very silent, sir; and very sad—but I don't want you to be sad.—Silent I will allow you to be; because the tutored should be all ear. So I used to be to you.

She then turned her face from me, putting her hand to her forehead—I had a great deal to say to you; but I have forgot it all—why do you look so melancholy, chevalier? You know your own mind; and you did what you thought just and fit —did you not? Tell me, sir.

Then turning to her weeping mother—The poor chevalier cannot speak, madam—yet had nobody to bid him do this, or bid him do that—he is sorry, to be sure!—Well, but, sir, turning to me, don't be sorry.—And yet the man who once refused me.—Ah, chevalier! I thought that was very cruel of you: but I soon got over it. You see how sedate I am now. Cannot you be as sedate as I am?

What could I say? I could not sooth her: she boasted of her sedateness. I could not argue with her. Could I have been hers, could my compromise have been allowed of, I could have been unreserved in my declarations. Was ever man so unhappily circumstanced?—Why did not the family forbid me to come near them? Why did not my Jeronymo renounce friendship with me? Why did this excellent mother bind me to her, by the sweet ties of kindness and esteem; engaging all my reverence and gratitude?

But let me ask you, chevalier, how could you be so *unreasonable* as to expect that I should change my religion, when you were so very tenacious of yours? Were you not *very* unreasonable to expect this?—Upon my word, I believe you men think it is no matter for us women to have any consciences, so as we do but study your wills, and do our duty by you. Men look upon themselves as gods of the earth, and on us women but as their ministering servants!—But I did not expect that *you* would be so unreasonable. You used to speak highly of our sex. Good women, you used to say, were angels. And many a time have you made me proud that I *was* a woman. How could you, chevalier, be so unreasonable?

May I, Madam, to her mother, acquaint her with the proposals I made?—She seems to think that I insisted upon her change of religion.

It was not designed she should think so: but I remember now, that she would not let me tell all I had to say, when I was making my report to her of what had passed between the bishop and you. It was enough, she said, that she had been refused; she besought me to spare the rest: and since that, she has not been in such a way that we *could* talk to her on that part of the subject. We took it for granted that *she* knew it all, because *we* did. Could we have yielded to your proposals, we should have enforced them upon her.—If you acquaint her with what you had proposed, it may make her think she has not been *despised,* as she calls it; the notion of which changed her temper from over thoughtful to over lively.

No need of speaking low to each other, said the young lady. After your slight, sir, you may let me hear *anything.*—Madam! you see how sedate I am. I have quite overcome myself. Don't be afraid of saying *anything* before me.

Slight, my dearest Lady Clementina! Heaven is my witness, your honoured mamma is my witness, that I have not slighted you!—The conditions I had proposed, could they have been complied with, would have made me the happiest of men!

Yes, and me the unhappiest of women. Why, you refused me, did you not? And putting both her hands spread before her face; don't let it be told abroad that a daughter of that best of mothers was refused by any man less than a prince! —Fie upon that daughter! To be able to stand before the proud refuser! [She walked from me.] I am ashamed of myself!—O Mrs. Beaumont! but for *you,* my secret had been buried here! putting one hand on her bosom, holding still the other before her face.—But, sir, sir, coming towards me, don't speak! Let me have all my talk out—And then—everlasting silence be my portion!

How her mother wept! How was I affected!

I had a great deal to say to you, I thought: I wanted to convince you of your errors. I wanted *no* favour of you, sir: mine was a pure, disinterested esteem. A voice from Heaven, I thought, bid me convert you. I was setting out to convert you. I should have been enabled to do it, I doubt not: *Out of the mouths of babes and sucklings;* do you remember that text, sir?—Could I have gone, when I would have gone— I had it *all* in my head then—but now I have lost it—Oh that impertinent Camilla!—*she* must question me—the woman addressed me in a quite frantic way. She was vexed to see me so sedate.

I was going to speak—Hush, hush, when I bid you! and she put her hand before my mouth. With both my hands I held it there for a moment and kissed it.

Ah, chevalier! said she, not withdrawing it, I believe you

are a flattering man! How *can* you, to a poor *despised* girl——

Let me *now* speak, madam—use not a word that I cannot repeat after you. Let me beg of you to hear the proposals I made——

I mentioned them; and added, Heaven only knows the anguish of my soul—Hush, said she, interrupting, and turning to her mother—I know nothing of these men, madam! Do you think, my mamma, I may believe him? He *looks* as if one might!—Do you think I may believe him?

Her mother was silent, through grief.

Ah, sir! my mamma, though she is not your enemy, cannot vouch for you!—But I will have you bound by your own hand. She stept to her closet in a hurry, and brought out pen, ink, and paper.—Come, sir, you must not play tricks with me. Give me, under your hand, what you have now said—but I will write it, and you shall sign it.

She wrote, in an instant, as follows:

> The Chevalier Grandison solemnly declares that he did, in the most earnest manner, of his own accord, propose, that he would *allow* a certain young creature, if she might be *allowed* to be his wife, the free use of her religion; and to have a discreet man, at her choice, for her confessor: and that he would never oblige her to go to England with him: and that he would live in Italy with her every other year.

Will you sign this, sir?
Most willingly.
Do then.
I did.
And you *did* propose this?—Did he, madam?

My dear, he did. And I would have told you so; but that you were affected at his supposed refusal.

Why, to be sure, madam, interrupted she, it was a shocking thing to be *refused*.

Would you have wished us, my dear, to comply with these terms? Would you have chosen to marry a Protestant? A daughter of the house of Poretta, and of the house I sprung from, to marry an English Protestant?

Clementina took her mother aside; but spoke loud enough to be heard:

To be sure, madam, that would have been wrong: but I am glad I was not refused with contempt: that my tutor, and the preserver of my Jeronymo, did not *despise* me. To say truth, I was afraid he liked Olivia; and so made a pretence.

Don't you think, my dear, that you would have run too great a hazard of your own faith, had you complied with the chevalier's proposals?

Why no, surely, madam!—Might I not have had as great a chance of converting him, as he could have had of perverting me? I glory in my religion, madam.

So does he, my love, in his.

That is his *fault,* madam. Chevalier, stepping towards me, I think you a very obstinate man. I hope you have not heard our discourse.

Yes, my dear, he has: and I desire not but he should.

Would to God, madam, said I to the marchioness, that I had yours and my lord's interest! From what the dear Lady Clementina has hinted, I might presume——

But, sir, you are *mistaken,* perhaps, said the young lady. Though I answer for answering's sake, and to show that I have no doubt of my steadfastness in an article in which my soul is concerned; yet that is no proof of my attachment to an obstinate—I know what!—Heretic was, no doubt, in her head.

I took her mother aside: For God's sake, madam, encourage my presumptuous hopes. Do you not observe already an alteration in the lady's mind? Is she not more unaffectedly sedate than she was before? Is not her mind quieter, now she knows that everything was yielded up, that honour and conscience would permit to be yielded up? See that sweet serenity almost restored to those eyes, that within these few moments had a wilder turn!

Ah, chevalier! this depends not on me. And if it *did,* I cannot allow of my daughter's marrying a man so bigoted to his errors. Excuse me, sir! But if you were more indifferent in your religion, I should have more hopes of you, and less objection.

If, madam, I *could* be indifferent in my religion, the temptation would have been too great to be resisted. Lady Clementina, and an alliance with such a family——

Ah, chevalier! I can give you no hope.

Look at the sweet lady, madam! Behold her, as now, perhaps, balancing in my favour! Think of what she was, the joy of every heart; and what she may be! Which, whatever becomes of me, Heaven avert!—And shall not the noble Clementina have her mother for her advocate? God is my witness, that your Clementina's happiness is, more than my own, the object of my vows! Once more, for your Clementina's sake [What, alas! is *my* sake to that!] on my knee, let me request your interest: that, joined to my Jeronymo's, and, if the dear lady recede not, if she blast not these budding hopes, will, I doubt not, succeed.

The young lady ran to me, and offering to help me up with both her hands, Rise, chevalier!—Shall I raise the chevalier, madam?—I don't love to see him kneel. Poor chevalier!— See his tears!—What is the matter with everybody? Why do you weep?—My mamma weeps too!—What ails everybody?

Rise, chevalier, said the marchioness. Oh, this sweet prattler! She will burst my heart asunder!—You cannot, sir, prevail (I cannot *wish* that you should), but upon your own terms. And will not this sweet soul move you?—Hard-hearted Grandison!

What a fate is mine! (rising): with a soul penetrated by the disorder of this most excellent of women, and by the distress given by it to a family, every single person of which I both love and reverence, to be called hard-hearted! What is it I desire, but that I may not renounce a religion in which my conscience is satisfied, and be obliged to embrace for it, one, about which, though I can love and honour every worthy member of it, I have scruples, *more* then scruples, that my heart can justify, and my reason defend! You have not, madam, yourself, with a heart all mother and friend, a deeper affliction than mine.

Clementina, all this time, looked with great earnestness, now on me, now on her weeping mother—and at last, breaking silence [her mother could not speak], and taking her hand, and kissing it; I don't, said she, comprehend the reason of all this. This house is not the house it was: Who, but I, is the same person in it? My father is not the same: my brothers neither: my mamma never has a dry eye, I think: but I don't weep. I am to be the comforter of you all! And I *will*. Don't weep! Why now you weep the more for my comfortings!—Oh, my mamma? what would you say to your girl, if *she* refused comfort? Then kneeling down, and kissing her hand with eagerness; I beseech you, my dear mamma, I *beseech* you be comforted; or lend me some of your tears—what ails me that I cannot weep for you?—But, turning to me; See, the chevalier weeps too!—Then rising, and coming to me, her hand pressing my arm—Don't weep, chevalier, my tutor, my friend, my brother's preserver! What ails you?— Be comforted! Then taking her handkerchief out of her pocket with one hand, still pressing my arm with the other, and putting it to her eyes, and looking upon it.—No!—I thought I *could* have wept for you!—But why is all this!— You see what an example I, a silly girl, can set you—affecting a still sedater countenance.

O chevalier! said the weeping mother, and do you say your heart is penetrated?—Sweet creature! wrapping her arms about her; my own Clementina! Would to Heaven it were given me to restore my child!—O chevalier! if complying with your terms would do it—but *you* are immovable!

How can that be said, madam, when I have made concessions that a princely family should not, on a *beginning* address, have brought me to make? May I *repeat* before Lady Clementina——

What would he repeat to me? interrupted she. Do, madam, let him say all he has a mind to say. If it will make his poor heart easy, why let him say all he would say.—Chevalier, speak. Can I be any comfort to you? I would make you *all* happy, if I could.

This, madam, said I to her mother, is too much! Excellent young lady!—Who can bear such transcendent goodness of heart, shining through intellects so disturbed!—And think you, madam, that on earth there can be a man more unhappily circumstanced than I am?

Oh my Clementina! said the mother, dear child of my heart! And could you consent to be the wife of a man of a contrary religion to your own? A man of another country? You see, chevalier, I will put *your* questions to her. A man that is an enemy to the faith of his own ancestors, as well as to your faith?

Why, no, madam!—I hope he does not expect that I would.

May I presume, madam, to put the question in my own way?—But yet I think it may distress the dear lady, and not answer the desirable end, if I may not have hope of *your* interest in my favour; and of the acquiescence of the marquis and your sons with my proposals.

They will never comply.

Let me then be made to appear insolent, unreasonable, and even ungrateful, in the eyes of your Clementina, if her mind can be made the easier by such a representation. If I have no hopes of *your* favour, madam, I must indeed despair.

Had I any hope of carrying your cause, I know not what might be done: but I must not separate myself from my family, in this great article.—My dear (to Clementina), you said you should be easier in your mind, if you were to talk to the chevalier alone. This is the only time you can have for it. Your father and brothers will be here to-morrow—and then, chevalier, all will be over.

Why, madam, I did think I had a great deal to say to him. And as I thought I had no *interest* in what I had to say——

Would you wish, my dear, to be left alone with the chevalier? Can you recollect anything that you had intended to say to him, had you made him the visit you designed to make him?

I don't know.

Then I will withdraw. Shall I, my dear?

Ought I, sir (you have been my tutor, and many excellent lessons have you taught me—though I don't know what is become of them.—Ought I), to wish my mamma to withdraw? Ought I to have anything to say to you, that I could not say before her?—I think not.

The marchioness was retiring. I beg of you, madam, said I, to slip unobserved into that closet. You *must* hear all that passes. The occasion may be critical. Let me have the opportunity of being either approved or censured, as I shall appear to deserve, in the conversation that may pass between the dear lady and me, if you do withdraw.

O chevalier! you are equally prudent and generous! Why won't you be one of us? Why won't you be a Catholic?

She went out at the door. Clementina courtesied to her. I led her eye from the door, and the marchioness re-entered, and slipt into the closet.

I conducted the young lady to a chair, which I placed with its back to the closet door, that her mother might hear all that passed.—She sat down, and bid me sit by her.

I was willing she should lead the subject, that the marchioness might observe I intended not to prepossess her.

We were silent for a few moments. She seemed perplexed; looked up, looked down; then on one side, then on the other—At last: O chevalier! said she, they were happy times when I was your pupil, and you were teaching me English.

They were *indeed* happy times, madam.

Mrs. Beaumont was too hard for me, chevalier!—Do you know Mrs. Beaumont?

I do. She is one of the best of women.

Why, so I think. But she turned and winded me about most strangely. I think I was in a great fault.

How so, madam?

How so! Why to let her get out of me a secret that I had kept from my mother. And yet there never was a more indulgent mother. Now you look, chevalier! but I shan't tell you what the secret was.

I do not ask you, madam.

If you did, I would not tell you.—Well, but I had a great deal to say to you, I thought. I wish that frantic Camilla had not stopt me when I was going to you. I had a great deal to say to you.

Cannot you recollect, madam, any part of it?

Let me consider.—Why, in the first place, I thought you *despised* me. I was not sorry for that, I do assure you: that did me good. At first it vexed me—you cannot think how much. I have a great deal of pride, sir—But, well, I got over that; and I grew sedate—You see how sedate I am. Yet this poor man, thought I, whether he thinks so or not —(I will tell you all my thoughts, sir)—But don't be grieved.—You see how sedate *I* am. Yet I am a silly girl; you are thought to be a wise man. Don't disgrace your wisdom. Fie! a wise man to be weaker than a simple girl!— Don't let it be said.—What was I saying?

Yet this poor man, whether he thinks so or not, you said, madam.

True!—has a soul to be saved. He has taken great pains with *me,* to teach me the language of England: shall I not take some with *him,* to teach him the language of heaven!— No heretic can learn that, sir!—And I had collected abundance of fine thoughts in my mind, and many pertinent things from the fathers; and they were all in my head— But that impertinent Camilla—And so they are all gone— But this one thing I have to say—I designed to say something like it, at the conclusion of my discourse with you— So it is premeditated, you will say: and so it is. But let me whisper it—no, I won't neither—But turn your face another way—I find my blushes come already—But (and she put her spread hand before her face, as if to hide her blushes) don't look at me, I tell you.—Look at the window. [I did.] Why, chevalier, I did intend to say—But stay—I have wrote it down somewhere. [She pulled out her pocketbook.] Here it is. Look another way, when I bid you. —She read—'Let me beseech you, sir (I was very earnest, 'you see), to hate, to despise, to detest (now don't look this

'way), the unhappy Clementina with all my heart; but
'for the sake of your immortal soul, let me conjure you to
'be reconciled to our holy mother Church!'—Will you, sir?
—following my indeed averted face with her sweet face; for
I *could not* look towards her. Say you will. I heard you
once called an angel of a man: and is it not better to be an
angel in heaven?—Tender-hearted man! I always thought
you had sensibility—say you will—not for my sake—I told
you that I would content myself to be still despised. It
shall not be said that you did this for a wife!—No, sir,
your conscience shall have all the merit of it!—And I'll tell
you what; I will lay me down in peace—she stood up with
a dignity that was augmented by her piety; and I will say,
'Now do thou, O beckoning angel! (for an angel will be
'on the other side of the river—the river shall be death, sir!
'—Now do thou) reach out thy divine hand, O minister
'of peace! I will wade through these separating waters;
'and I will bespeak a place for the man who, many, many
'years hence, may fill it!—And I will sit next you for ever
'and ever!'—And this, sir, shall satisfy the poor Clementina; who will then be richer than the richest! So you see,
sir, as I told my mother, I was setting out on God's errand;
not on my own!

For hours might the dear lady have talked on, without
interruption from me!—My dear Doctor Bartlett! what did
I not suffer!

The marchioness was too near for herself: she could not
bear this speech of her pious, generous, noble daughter. She
sobbed; she groaned.

Clementina started—she looked at me. She looked round
her. Whence came these groans? Did you groan, sir?—
You are not a hard-hearted man, though they say you are.
But you will be a Catholic, sir? Say you will. I won't be
denied. And I will tell you what—if I don't resign to
my destiny in a few, a very few weeks, why then I will go
into a nunnery; and then I shall be God's child, you know,
even in this life.

What could I say to the dear lady? Her mind was raised

above an earthly love. Circumstanced as we were, how could I express the tenderness for her which overflowed my heart? Compassion is a motive that a woman of spirit will reject: and how could love be here *pleaded*, when the parties believed it to be in my own power to exert it? Could I endeavour to replace myself in her affection, when I refused to comply with their terms, and they with mine? To have argued against her religion, and in defence of my own, her mind so disturbed, could not be done: and ought I, in generosity, in justice to her family, to have attempted to unsettle her in a faith in which she, and all her family, were so well satisfied?

I could only, when I could speak, applaud her piety, and pronounce her an angel of a woman, an ornament of her sex, and an honour to her religion; and endeavour to waive the subject.

Ah, chevalier! said she, after a silence of some minutes, you are an obstinate man! Indeed you are—Yet, I think, you do not despise me.—But what says your paper?

She took it out of her bosom and read it. She seemed affected by it, as if she had not before considered it: and you *really* proposed these terms, sir? And would you have allowed me the full exercise of my religion? And should I have had my confessor? And would you have allowed me to convert you, if I could? And would you have treated my confessor kindly? And would you have been dutiful to my papa and mamma? And would you have loved my two other brothers as well as you do Jeronymo? And would you have let me live at Bologna?—You don't say, Yes.—But do you say, No?

To these terms, madam, most willingly would I have subscribed: and if, my dearest lady, they could have had the wished-for effect, how happy had I been!

Well!—She then paused; and resuming, What shall we say to all these things?

I thought her mother would take it well to have an opportunity given her to quit the closet, now her Clementina had changed her subject to one so concerning to the whole family. I favoured her doing so. She slipt out, her face bathed in tears, and soon after came in at the drawing-room door.

Ah, madam! said Clementina, paying obeisance to her, I have been arguing and pleading with the chevalier.

Then, speaking low, I believe he may, in time, be convinced: he has a tender heart. But hush, putting her finger to her mouth, and then speaking louder; I have been reading this paper again——

She was going on too favourably for me, as it was evident the marchioness apprehended (the first time that I had reason to think she was disinclined to the alliance), for she stopt her: My love, said she, you and I will talk of this matter by ourselves.

She rang. Camilla came in. She made a motion for Camilla to attend her daughter; and withdrew, inviting me out with her.

When we were in another room, Ah, chevalier! said she, how was it possible that you could withstand such a heavenly pleader? You cannot love her as she deserves to be loved: you cannot but act nobly, generously; but indeed you are an invincible man.

Not love her, madam! Your ladyship adds distress to my very great distress!—*Am* I, in your opinion, an ungrateful man?—But must I lose *your* favour, *your* interest? On that, and on my dear Jeronymo's, did I build my hopes, and *all* my hopes.

I know your terms can never be accepted, chevalier: and I have now no hopes of you. After this last conversation between you and the dear girl, I *can* have no hopes of you. Poor soul! she began to waver. Oh, how she loves you! I see you are *not* to be united: it is impossible. And I did not care to permit a daughter of mine further to expose herself, as it must have been to no manner of purpose.—You are concerned.—I should pity you, sir, if you had it not in your *power* to make yourself happy, and us, and ours too.

Little did I expect such a turn in my disfavour from the marchioness.

May I, madam, be permitted to take leave of the dear lady, to whose piety and admirable heart I am so much indebted?

I believe it may as well be deferred, chevalier.

Deferred, madam!—The marquis and the general come; and my heart tells me that I may never be allowed to see her again.

At *this* time it had better be deferred, sir.

If it must, I submit—God for ever bless you, madam, for all your goodness! God restore to you your Clementina! May you all be happy!—Time may do much for *me!* Time, and my own not disapproving conscience, may—but a more unhappy man never passed your gates!

I took the liberty to kiss her hand, and withdrew, with great emotion.

Camilla hastened after me. Chevalier, says she, my lady asks if you will not visit Signor Jeronymo?

Blessings attend my ever-valued friend! I cannot see him. I shall *complain* to him. My heart will burst before him. Commend me to that true friend. Blessings attend every one of this great excellent family! Camilla, obliging Camilla, adieu!

O Dr. Bartlett!—But the mother was right. She was to account for her conduct in the absence of her lord. She knew the determination of the family; and her Clementina was on the point of showing more favour to me, than, as things were circumstanced, it was proper she should show me: yet they had found out that Clementina, in the way she was in, was not easily diverted from anything she took strongly into her head; and they never had accustomed her to contradiction.

Well, Lucy, now you have read this letter, do you not own that this man and this woman can only deserve each other?—Your Harriet, my dear, is not worthy to be the handmaid of either. This is not an affectation of humility. You will be all of the same opinion, I am sure: and this letter will convince you, that *more* than his compassion, that his *love* for Clementina, was engaged. And so it *ought*.

And what is the inference but this—that your Harriet, were this great difficulty to be vincible, could pretend to hope but for half a heart? There cannot be that fervour, my dear, in a second love, that was in a first. Do you think there can?

Dr. Bartlett's ninth letter.

The young lady, proceeds Mr. Grandison, after I had left her, went to her brother Jeronymo. There I should have found her, had I, as her mother motioned by Camilla, visited my friend. But when I found he was likely to stand alone in his favour to me; when the marchioness had so unexpectedly declared herself against the compromise; I was afraid of disturbing his worthy heart by the grief which at the instant overwhelmed mine.

The following particulars Jeronymo sent me, within three hours after I left their palace:

His sister, making Camilla retire, showed him the paper which she had written, and made me sign, and asked him what he knew of the contents.

He knew not what had passed beteen his mother and me; nor did Clementina.

He told her that I had actually made those proposals. He assured her that I loved her above all women. He acquainted her with my distress.

She pitied me. She thought, she said, that I had not made any overtures, any concessions; that I despised her; and sensibly asked, Why the chevalier was sent for from Vienna? We all knew his mind as to religion, said she.

Then, after a pause, He never could have perverted me, proceeded she: he would have allowed me a confessor, would he not?

He would, answered Jeronymo.——

And he would have left me among my friends in Italy?— He would, replied he.

Well, brother, and I should have been glad, perhaps, to have seen England once; and he would, perhaps, have brought over his sisters and his father to visit us: and he praises them highly, *you know*. And if I were their sister, I could have gone over with them, *you know*. Do you think, if I had loved *them,* they would not have loved *me?* I am not an ill-natured creature, *you know;* and they *must* be courteous: are they not *his* sisters? And don't you think his father would love me? I should have brought no dishonour into his family, *you know*.—Well, but I'll tell you what, Jeronymo, he is really a tender-hearted man. I talked to him of his soul; and, upon my honour, I believe I could have prevailed, in time. Father Marescotti is a severe man, *you know;* and he has been always so much consulted, and don't love the chevalier, I believe: so that I fancy if I were to have a venerable sweet-tempered man for my confessor, between *my* love, and my *confessor's* prudence, we should gain a soul—don't you think so, Jeronymo?—And that would cover a great many sins. And all his family might be converted too, *you know!*

He encouraged her in this way of thinking. She believed, she said, that I was not yet gone. He is *so* tender-hearted, brother! *that* is my dependence. And you say he loves me. Are you sure of that?—But I have reason to think he does. He shed tears, as I talked to him, more than once; while my eyes were as dry as they are now. I did not shed one tear. Well, I'll go to him, and talk with him.

She went to the door; but came back on tiptoe; and in a whispering accent—My mamma is coming: Hush, Jeronymo! Let hush be the word!

The door opened—Here, madam, is your girl!—But it is not my mamma: the impertinent Camilla. She follows me as my shadow!

My lady desires to see you, Lady Clementina, in her dressing-room.

I obey. But where is the chevalier?

Gone, madam. Gone some time.

Ah, brother! said she, and her countenance fell.

What, gone! said Jeronymo, without seeing me! Unkind Grandison! He did not use to be so unkind.

This was the substance of the advices sent me by my friend Jeronymo.

I acquainted him in return, by pen and ink, with all that had passed between the marchioness and me, that he might not, by his friendship for me, involve himself in difficulties.

In the morning I had a visit from Camilla, by her lady's command, with excuses for refusing to allow me to take leave of Clementina. She hoped I was not displeased with her on that account. It was the effect of prudence, and not disrespect. She should ever regard me, even in a tender manner, as if the desired relation could have taken place. Her lord, and her brother the Conte della Porretta (as he is called), with the general and the bishop, arrived the night before, accompanied by the count's eldest son, Signor Sebastiano. She had been much blamed for permitting the interview; but regretted it the less, as her beloved daughter was more composed than before, and gave sedate answers to all the questions put to her. But, nevertheless, she wished that I would retire from Bologna, for Clementina's sake, as well as for my own.

Camilla added from Signor Jeronymo, that he wished to hear from me from the Trentine, or Venice: and as from herself, and in confidence, that her young lady was greatly concerned that I did not wait on her again before I went away: that she fell into a silent fit upon it; and that her mamma, on her not answering to her questions, for the first time chid her: that this gave her great distress, but produced what they had so much wished for, a flood of tears; and that now she frequently wept and lamented to her, What *should* she do? Her mamma did not love her, and her mamma talked against the chevalier. She wished to be allowed to see him. Nobody now would love her, but the chevalier and Jeronymo. It would be better for her to be in England, or anywhere, than to be in the sweetest country in the world, and hated.

Camilla told me that the marquis, the count his brother, and the general, had indeed blamed the marchioness for permitting the interview; but were pleased that I was refused taking leave of the young lady, when she seemed disposed to dwell on the contents of the note she had made me sign: they seemed now all of a mind, she said, that were I to comply with their terms, the alliance would not by any means be a proper one. Their rank, their degree, their alliances, were dwelt upon: I found that their advantages, in all these respects, were heightened; my degree, my consequence, lowered, in order to make the difference greater and the difficulties insuperable.

Clementina's uncle, and his eldest son, both men of sense and honour, who used to be high in her esteem, had talked to her, but could get nothing from her but No, and Yes,— Her father had talked to her alone; but they melted each other, and nothing resulted of comfort to either. Her mother joined him; but she threw herself at her mother's feet, besought her to forgive her, and not to *chide her again*. They had intended to discourage her from thinking of me upon any terms. The general and the bishop were to talk to her that morning. They had expressed displeasure at Signor Jeronymo, for his continued warmth in my favour. Father Marescotti was now consulted as an oracle: and I found, that, by an indelicacy of thinking, he imagined that the *husband* would set all right; and was for encouraging the Count of Belvedere, and getting me at distance.

Camilla obligingly offered to acquaint me, from time to time, with what occurred; but I thought it was not right to accept of a servant's intelligence out of the family she belonged to, unless some one of it authorised her to give it me. Yet you must believe I wanted not anxious curiosity on a subject so interesting. I thanked her; but said that it might, if discovered, lay her under inconveniences, which would grieve me for her sake. She had the good sense to approve of my declining her offer.

In the morning of the same day I had a visit made me which I little expected: it was from Father Marescotti. It is a common thing to load an enemy, especially if he be in holy orders, and comes to us in the guise of friendship, with the charge of hypocrisy: but partiality may be at the bottom of the accusation. Father Marescotti is a zealous Roman Catholic: I could not hope either for his interest or affection: he could not but wish to frustrate my hopes. As a man in earnest in his own principles, and who knew how steadfast I was in mine, it was his duty to oppose this alliance. He is perhaps the honester man for knowing but little of human nature, and of the tender passions. As to that of love, he seemed to have drawn his conclusions from general observations: he knew not how to allow for particular constitutions, nor to account for the delicacy of such a heart as Clementina's. Love, he thought, was always a poor blind boy, led in by a string, either by folly or fancy; and that once the impetus got over, and the lady settled into the common offices of life, she would domesticate herself, and be as happy with the Count of Belvedere, especially as he is a very worthy man, as if she had married the man once most favoured. On this presumption, it was a condescension in such a man to come to me, and to declare himself my friend; and advise me what to do for promoting the peace of a family which I professed to venerate; and you will hear that his condescension was owing to a real greatness of mind.

I was, from the moment of his entrance, very open, very frank: more so than he expected, as he owned. He told me that he was afraid I had conceived prejudices against him. The kinder then in him, I said, that he condescended to make me so friendly a visit. I assured him that I regarded him as a good man. I had indeed sometimes thought him severe; but that convinced me that he was very much in earnest in his religion. I was sensible, I said, that we ought always to look to the intention; to put ourselves in the situation of the persons of whose actions we presumed to judge; and even to think well of austerities, which had their foundation in virtue, in whatever manner they affected ourselves.

He applauded me; and said I wanted so little to be a Catholic, that it was a thousand pities I was not one: and he was persuaded that I would one day be a proselyte.

This father's business was to convince me of the unfitness

of an alliance between families so very opposite in their religious sentiments. He went into history upon it. You may believe that the unhappy consequence which followed the marriage between our Charles I. and the Princess Henrietta of France, were not forgotten. He expatiated upon them. But I observed to him that the monarch was the sufferer by the zeal of the queen for her religion, and not the queen, any otherwise than as she was involved in the consequenes of those sufferings which she had brought upon him. In short, father, said I, we Protestants, some of us have zeal; but let us alone, and it is not a persecuting one. Your doctrine of *merits* makes the zeal of your devotees altogether active, and perhaps the more flaming, in proportion as the person is more honest and worthy.

I lamented that I was sent for from Vienna, upon hopes, though my principles were well known, that otherwise I had never presumed to entertain.

He owned that that was a wrong step: and valued himself that he had not been consulted upon it; and that, when he knew it had been taken, he inveighed against it.

And I am *afraid,* father, said I——

He interrupted me—Why, I believe so!—You have made such generous distinctions in favour of the duty of a man acting in my function, that, I must *own,* I have not been an idle observer on this occasion.

He advised me to quit Bologna. He was profuse in his offers of service in any other affair; and I daresay was in earnest.

I told him that I chose not to leave it precipitately, and as if I had done something blameworthy. I had some hopes of being recalled to my father's arms. I should set out, when I left Bologna, directly for Paris, to be in the way of such a long-wished-for call: and then, said I, adieu to travelling! Adieu to Italy, for ever! I should have been happy, had I never seen it, but in the way for which I have been accustomed to censure the generality of my countrymen.

His behaviour at parting was such as will make me for ever revere him; and will *enlarge* a charity for all good men of his religion; which yet, before, was not a narrow one. For, begging my excuse, he kneeled down at the door of my ante-chamber, and offered up, in a very fervent manner, a prayer for my conversion. He could not have given me, any other way, so high as opinion of him: no, not had he offered me his interest with Clementina and her family. I embraced him, as he did me; tears were in his eyes. I thanked him for the favour of this visit; and recommending myself to his frequent prayers, told him that he might be assured of all the respectful services he should put it in my power to render him. I longed, Dr. Bartlett, to make him a present worthy of his acceptance, had I known what would have been acceptable, and had I not been afraid of affronting him. I accompanied him to the outward door. I never, said he, saw a Protestant that I loved before. Your mind is still more amiable than your person. Lady Clementina, I see, might have been happy with you: but it was not fit, on *our* side. He snatched my hand, before I was aware, and honoured it with his lips; and hastened from me, leaving me at a loss, and looking after him, and for him, when he was out of sight; my mind labouring as under a high sense of obligation to his goodness.

Religion and love, Dr. Bartlett, which heighten our relish for the things of both worlds, what pity is it that they should ever run the human heart either into enthusiasm or superstition; and thereby debase the minds they are both so well fitted to exalt!

I am equally surprised and affected by the contents of the following letter, directed to me. It was put within the door; nobody saw by whom. The daughter of the lady at whose house I lodge found it, and gave it to one of my servants for me.

Dont be surprised, chevalier; dont think amiss of me for my forwardness. I heard some words drop (so did Camilla, but she can't go out to tell you of them), as if somebody's life was in danger. This distracts me. I am not treated as I was accustomed to be treated. They don't love me now—they don't love their poor Clementina! Very true, chevalier! You, who are always telling me how dearly they all loved me, will hardly believe it, I suppose. Nothing now is said, but *You shall, Clementina*—from those who used to call me sister, and dear sister, at every word.

They said, I was well, and quite well, and ought to be treated with a high hand—I know from whom they have that. From myself. I said so to Mrs. Beaumont; but she need not to have told *them*. I won't go to her again, for that. They say I *shall*. God help me, I don't know where to go for a quiet mind. A *high hand* won't do, chevalier; I wish I knew what would; I would tell it to them. I once thought it would; else I had not said it to Mrs. Beaumont; but let them go on with their high hands, with all my heart; that heart will not hold always. It had been gone before now, had not Mrs. Beaumont got out of me—something— I won't tell you what—And then they sent for somebody— and somebody came.—And what then?—They need not threaten me so.—Somebody is not so much to blame as they will have it he is: and that somebody did make proposals—did you not, chevalier?—I had liked to have betrayed myself—I stopt just in time.

But, chevalier, I'll tell you a secret—Don't speak of it to anybody—May I depend upon you?—I know I may. Why, Camilla tells me that the Count of Belvedere is to come again.—Are you not sorry for your poor pupil? But I'll tell you another secret—And that is, what I intend to say to him—' Look you here, my lord, you are a very good sort ' of man; and you have great estates: you are very rich: ' you are, in short, a very good sort of man; but there is, ' however, a man in the world with whom I had rather live ' in the poorest hermitage in a wilderness, than with you in ' the richest palace in the world.' After this, if he be not the creeping mean man you said he was not, he will be answered—everything you said to me in former happy times I remember. You always said things to me, that were fit to be remembered. Yet I don't tell you who my hermit is, that I had rather live with. Perhaps there is no such man.

But this, you know, will be a sufficient answer to the Count of Belvedere. Don't you think so?

Here I have been tormented again!—Would you think it? I have been pleading for somebody, boldly, confidently, I said I could depend upon his honour! Ah, chevalier, don't you think I might?—I am to be locked up, and I can't tell what!—They won't let me see somebody—They won't let me see my poor Jeronymo!—You, and I, and Jeronymo are all put together!—I don't care, as I tell Camilla: I don't care: they will quite harden me.

But just now my mamma—Oh, she is the best of mothers! —My mamma tells me she will not persuade me, if I will be patient, if I will be good. My dear mamma, as I told her, I will be patient and good: but don't let them inveigh against the chevalier, then. What harm has he done?— Was he not—Ah! sir, now I blush!—Was he not sent for? —And did he not weep over me?—Yet is he none of your bold men, who look as proudly as if they were sure of your approbation!—Well, but what do you think my mamma said—Ah, Clementina! said she, would to God the chevalier, for *his own sake* (yes, she said for *his own sake;* and that made a great impression upon me; it was so good, you know, of my mamma), that the chevalier was in England, or a thousand miles off. So, sir, this is my advice—Pray take it; for I and Camilla heard some words; and Camilla, as well as I, is much troubled about them.—Get away to England as soon as you can—be sure do!—And some months hence bring your two sisters over with you; and by that time all our feuds will be ended, you know; and you shall take a house, and then I can go and visit your sisters, you know, and your sisters will visit us. You will come sometimes with them; won't you? Well, and I'll tell you how we will pass part of our time: they shall perfect me in my English: I will perfect them in Italian. They know as much of that, I suppose, at least, as I do of English: and we will visit every court, and every city. So, God bless you, sir, and get away as soon as you can. I put no name; for fear this should miscarry, and I should be found out.—Ah, sir! they are very severe with me! Pity me: but I know you will; for you have a tender heart. *It is all for you!*

These last five words were intended to be scratched out; and are but just legible.

How the contents of this letter afflict me! Words cannot express what I feel! I see, evidently, that they are taking wrong measures with the tenderest heart in the world; a heart that never has once swerved from its duty; and which is filled with reverence and love for all that boast a relation to it. Harsh treatment, and which is besides *new* to it, is *not* the method to be taken with such a heart. Shall I, thought I, when I had perused it, ask for an audience of a mother so indulgent, and give her my disinterested advice upon it? Once I could have done so; and even, in confidence, have shown her this very letter: but now she is one with the angry part of her family, and I dare not do it, for Clementina's sake. Talk of locking her up! Talk of bringing a lover to her!—*Threatening* her with going to Mrs. Beaumont, when they should *court* her to go thither!—Not suffer her to see her beloved Jeronymo!—*He* in disgrace too!—How hard, how wrong, is all this conduct!—I could have written to Jeronymo, thought I, and advised gentle measures, were he not out of their consultations.—As to the threatened *resentments,* they are as nothing to me. Clementina's sufferings are everything. My soul disdains the thought of fastening myself upon a proud family, that now looks upon me in a mean light. A proud heart undervalued will swell. It will be put upon *over*-valuing itself. You know, Dr. Bartlett, that I have a *very* proud heart: but when I am trampled upon, or despised, *then* it is most proud. I would call myself a *man,* to a prince, who should unjustly hold me in contempt; and let him know that I looked upon *him* to be no more. My pride is raised: yet against whom? Not Clementina! She has all my pity! She has seen, and I have found, that her unhappy delirium, though not caused by me (I bless God for that!), has made me tender as a chidden infant. And can I think of quitting Bologna, and not see if it be possible for me to gratify myself, and serve them in her restoration? Setting quite out of the question the general's causeless resentments, and the engagement I have laid myself under not to leave it without apprising him of my intention.

Upon the whole, I resolved to wait the issue of the new measures they have fallen upon. The dear lady has declared herself in my favour. Such a frank declaration must soon be followed by important consequences.

The third day after the arrival of her father and brothers from Urbino, I received the following billet from the marquis himself:—

CHEVALIER GRANDISON,—We are in the utmost distress. We cannot take upon us to forbid your stay at Bologna; but shall be obliged to you, if you will enable us to acquaint our daughter, that you are gone to England, or some far distant part of Italy.—Wishing you happy, I am, sir, your most obedient humble servant.

To this I wrote as follows:—

MY LORD,—I am excessively grieved for your distress. I make no hesitation to obey you. But as I am not conscious of having, in word or deed, offended you, or any one of a family to whom I owe infinite obligations; let me hope that I may be allowed a farewell visit to your lordship, to your lady, and to your three sons; that my departure may not appear like that of a criminal, instead of the parting, which, from the knowledge I have of my own heart, as well as of your experienced goodness, may be claimed by your lordship's,—Ever obliged, and affectionate humble servant,

GRANDISON.

This request, I understood, occasioned warm debates. It was said to be a very bold one: but my dear Jeronymo insisted that it was worthy of his friend, his deliverer, as he called me; and of an innocent man.

The result was, that I should be invited in form to visit and take leave of the family: and two days were taken, that some others of the Urbino family might be present, to see a man for the last time (and some of them for the first), who was thought, by his request, to have shown a very extraordinary degree of intrepidity; and who, though a Protestant, was honoured with so great an interest in the heart of their Clementina.

The day before I was to make this formal visit (for such it was to be), I received the following letter from my friend Jeronymo:—

MY DEAREST GRANDISON,—Take the particulars of the situation we are in here, that you may know what to expect, and how to act and comport yourself to-morrow evening.

Your reception will be, I am afraid, cold; but civil.

You will be looked upon by the Urbino family, who have heard more of you than they have seen, as a curiosity; but with more wonder than affection.

Of them will be present, the Count my father's brother, and his sons Sebastiano and Juliano, my aunt Signora Juliana de Sforza, a widow lady, as you know, and her daughter Signora Laurana, a young woman of my sister's age, between whom and my sister used to be, as you have heard, the strictest friendship and correspondence; and who insisted on being present on this occasion. They are all good-natured people; but love not either your country or religion.

Father Marescotti will be present. He is become your very great admirer.

My father thinks to make you his compliments; but if he withdraw the moment he has made them, you must not be surprised.

My mother says that as it is the last time that she may ever see you, and as she really greatly respects you, she shall not be able to leave you while you stay.

The general, I hope, will behave with politeness.

The bishop loves you; but will not, however, perhaps, be in high good humour with you.

Your Jeronymo will be wheeled into the same room. If he be more silent than usual on the solemn occasion, you will not do him injustice, perhaps, if you attribute it to his prudence; but much more to his grief.

And now let me tell you, as briefly as I can, the situation of the dear creature who must not appear, but who is more interested in the occasion of the congress than any person who will be present at it.

What passed between you and her at the last interview has greatly impressed her in your favour. The bishop, the general, and my father, soon after their return from Urbino, made her a visit in her dressing-room. They talked to her of the excellency of her own religion, and of the errors of the pretended reformed, which they called, and I *suppose* are, *damnable*. They found her steady in her abhorrence of the one, and adherence to the other. They were delighted with her rational answers and composed behaviour. They all three retired in raptures, to congratulate each other upon it; and returned with pleasure, to enter into farther talk with her; but when they mentioned you to her, she, led by their affectionate behaviour to her on their return, said it had given her great pleasure, and ease of mind, to find that she was not *despised* by a man whom every one of the family regarded for his merit and great qualities. The general had hardly patience: he walked to the farther end of the room: my father was in tears: the bishop soothed her, in order to induce her to speak her whole mind.

He praised you. She seemed pleased. He led her to believe that the whole family were willing to oblige her, if she would declare herself; and asked her questions, the answers to which must either be an avowal or a denial of her love; and then she owned that she preferred the Chevalier Grandison to all the men in the world: she would not, against the opinion of her friends, wish to be his; but never would be the wife of any other man.

What, said the general, though he continue a heretic?

He might be converted, he said. And he was a sweet-tempered and compassionate man: and a man of sense, as *he* was, must see his errors.

Would she run the risk of her own salvation?

She was sure she should never give up her faith.

It was tempting God to abandon her to her own perverseness.

Her reliance on His goodness to enable her to be steadfast was humble, and not presumptuous, and with a pious view to gain a proselyte; and God would not forsake a person so well intending. Was she not to be allowed her confessor? Her confessor should be appointed by themselves. She did not doubt but the chevalier would consent to that.

The bishop, you know, can be cool when he pleases. He bore to talk further with her.

My father was still in tears.

The general had no longer patience. He withdrew, and came to me, and vented on me his displeasure. It is true, Grandison, when it was proposed to send for you from Vienna, I, sanguine in my hopes, had expressed myself as void of all doubt but you would become a Catholic—your love, your compassion, your honour, as I thought, engaged by such a step taken on our side—I had no notion that on such a surprise, with such motives to urge your compliance, a young man like myself, and with a heart so sensible, could have been so firm: but these thoughts are all over—this, however, exposes me to the more reproaches.

We were high; and my mother and uncle came in to mediate between us.

I would not, I could not, renounce my friend; the friend of my *soul,* as in our first acquaintance; and the preserver of my life—miserable as that has been, the preserver of it, at a time when I was engaged in an *unlawful* pursuit, in which had I perished, what might I have now been, and where?

I ventured to give my opinion in favour of my sister's marriage with you, as the only method that could be taken to restore her; who, I said, loved you because you were a virtuous man; and that her love was not only founded in virtue, but was virtue itself.

My brother told me that I was as much beside myself with my notions of gratitude, as my sister was with a passion less excusable.

I bid him forbear wounding a wounded man.

Thus high ran words between us.

The bishop, meantime, went on with a true Church subtlety, to get out of the innocent girl her whole mind.

He boasted afterwards of his art. But what was there in it to boast of? A mind so pure and so simple as Clementina's ever was, and which only the pride of her sex, and motives of religion, had perhaps hindered her from declaring to all the world.

He asked her if she were willing to leave her father, mother, brothers, and country, to go to a strange land; to live among a hated people?

No, she said; you would not wish her to go out of Italy. You would live nine months out of twelve in Italy.

He told her, that she must, when married, do as her husband would have her.

She could trust to your honour.

Would she consent that her children should be trained up heretics?

She was silent to this question. He repeated it.

Well, my lord, if I must not be allowed to choose for myself; only let me not hear the chevalier spoken of disrespectfully: he does not deserve it. He has acted by me with as much honour as he did by my brother. He is an uniformly good man, and as generous as good—and don't let me have *other* proposals made me; and I will be contented. I had never so much distinguished him, if everybody had not as well as I.

He was pleased to find her answers so rational: he pronounced her quite well; and gave it as his opinion that you should be desired to quit Bologna. And your absence, and a little time, he was sure, would secure her health of mind.

But when her aunt Sforza and her cousin Laurana talked

with her next morning, they found her, on putting questions about you, absolutely determined in your favour.

She answered the objections they made against you with equal warmth and clearness. She seemed sensible of the unhappy way she had been in, and would have it that the last interview she had with you had helped to calm and restore her: and she hoped that she should be better every day. She praised your behaviour to her: she expatiated upon, and pitied, your distress of mind.

They let her run on till they too had obtained from her a confirmation of all that the bishop had reported; and upon repeating the conversation, would have it, upon experience, that soothing such a passion was not the way to be taken; but that a high hand was to be used, and that she was to be shamed out of a love so improper, so irreligious, so *scandalous,* to be encouraged in a daughter of their house with a heretic; and who had shown himself to be a determined one.

They accordingly entered upon their new measures. They forbade her to think of you: they told her that she should not upon any terms be yours; not now, even if you would change your religion for her. They depreciated your family, your fortune, and even your understanding; and brought to prove what they said against the latter, your obstinate adherence to your *mushroom* religion, so they called it; a religion that was founded in the wickedness of your eighth Henry; in the superstition of a child his successor; and in the arts of a vile woman, who had martyred a sister queen, a better woman than herself. They insisted upon her encouraging the Count of Belvedere's addresses, as a mark of her obedience.

They condemned, in terms wounding to her modesty, her passion for a foreigner, an enemy to her faith; and on her earnest request to see her father, he was prevailed upon to refuse her that favour.

Lady Juliana Sforza, and her daughter Laurana, the companion of her better hours, never see her, but they inveigh against you as an artful, an interested man.

Her uncle treats her with authority; Signor Sebastiano with a pity bordering on contempt.

My mother shuns her; and indeed avoids me: but as she has been blamed for permitting the interview, which they suppose the wrongest step that could have been taken, she declares herself neutral and resigns, to whatever shall be done by her lord, by his brother, her two sons, and Lady Juliana de Sforza: but I am sure, in her heart, that she approves not of the new measures; and which are also, as I have reminded the bishop, so contrary to the advice of the worthy Mrs. Beaumont; to whom they begin to think of once more sending my sister, or of prevailing on her to come hither: but Clementina seems not to be desirous of going again to her; we know not why; since she used to speak of her with the highest respect.

The dear soul rushed in to me yesterday. Ah, my Jeronymo! said she, they will drive me into despair. They hate me, Jeronymo—but I have written to somebody!—Hush! for your life, hush!

She was immediately followed in by her aunt Sforza, and her cousin Laurana, and the general; who, though he heard not what she said, insisted on her returning to her own apartment.

What! said she, must I not speak to Jeronymo? Ah, Jeronymo!—I had a great deal to say to you!

I raved; but they hurried her out, and have forbid her to visit me: they, however, have had the civility to desire my excuse. They are sure, they say, they are in the right way; and if I will have patience with them for a week, they will change their measures, if they find these new ones ineffectual. But my sister will be lost, irrecoverably lost; I foresee that.

Ah, Grandison! And can you still—but now they will not accept of your change of religion. Poor Clementina! Unhappy Jeronymo! Unhappy *Grandison!* I will say. If you are not so, you cannot deserve the affection of a Clementina.

But are *you* the somebody to whom she has written? *Has* she written to you? Perhaps you will find some opportunity to-morrow to let me know whether she has or not. Camilla is forbidden to stir out of the house, or to write.

The general told me, just now, that my gratitude to you showed neither more nor less, than the high value I put upon my own life.

I answered; That his observation *convinced* me, that he put a much less upon mine, than I, in the same case, should have put upon his.

He reconciled himself to me by an endearment. He embraced me. Don't say *convinced,* Jeronymo. I love not myself better than I love my Jeronymo.

What can one do with such a man? He *does* love me.

My mother, as I said, is resolved to be neutral: but it seems she is always in tears.

My mother stept in just now.—To my question after my sister's health; Ah, Jeronymo! said she, all is wrong! the dear creature has been bad ever since yesterday. They are all wrong!—But patience and silence, child! You and I have nothing to answer for.—Yet my Clementina, said she —Oh!—and left me.

I have no heart to write on. You will see, from the above, the way we are in. O my Grandison! what will you do among us?—I wish you would not come. Yet what hope, if you do not, shall I ever have of seeing again my beloved friend, who has behaved so unexceptionably in a case so critical?

You must not think of the dear creature: her head is ruined: for your *own* sake, you must not. We are all unworthy of you: yet not *all:* all, however, but Clementina, and (if true friendship will justify my claim to another exception) your afflicted JERONYMO.

LETTER II.

Miss Byron to Miss Selby.

O MY LUCY!—What think you!—But it is easy to guess what you must think. I will, without saying one word more, enclose

Dr. Bartlett's tenth letter.

THE next day (proceeds my patron) I went to make my visit to the family. I had nothing to reproach myself with; and therefore had no other concern upon me but what arose from the unhappiness of the noble Clementina: that indeed was enough. I thought I should have some difficulty to manage my own spirit, if I were to find myself insulted, especially by the general. Soldiers are so apt to value themselves on their knowledge of what, after all, one may call but their trade, but a private gentleman is often thought too slightly of by them. Insolence in a great man, a rich man, or a soldier, is a *call* upon a man of spirit to exert himself. But I hope, thought I, I shall not have this call from any one of a family I so greatly respect.

I was received by the bishop; who, politely, after I had paid my compliments to the marquis and his lady, presented me to those of the Urbino family to whom I was a stranger. Every one of those named by Signor Jeronymo, in his last letter, was present.

The marquis, after he had returned my compliment, looked another way, to hide his emotion: the marchioness put her handkerchief to her eyes; but withdrawing it again, looked upon me with tenderness; and I read in them her concern for her Clementina.

I paid my respects to the general with an air of freedom, yet of regard; to my Jeronymo, with the tenderness due to our friendship; and congratulated him on seeing him out of his chamber. His kind eyes glistened with pleasure; yet it was easy to read a mixture of pain in them; which grew stronger as the first emotions at seeing me enter gave way to reflection.

The Conte della Porretta seemed to measure me with his eye.

I addressed myself to Father Marescotti, and made my particular acknowledgments to him for the favour of his visit, and what had passed in it. He looked upon me with pleasure; probably with the more, as this was a farewell visit.

The two ladies whispered, and looked upon me, and seemed to bespeak each other's attention to what passed.

Signor Sebastiano placed himself next to Jeronymo, and often whispered him, and as often cast his eye upon me. He was partial to me, I believe, because my generous friend seemed pleased with what he said.

His brother, Signor Juliano, sat on the other hand of me. They are agreeable and polite young men.

A profound silence succeeded the general compliments.

I addressed myself to the marquis: Your lordship, and you, madam, turning to the marchioness, I hope will excuse me for having requested the favour of being once more admitted to your presence, and to that of three brothers, for whom I shall ever retain the most respectful affection. I could not think of leaving a city, where one of the first families in it has done me the highest honour, without taking such a leave as might show my gratitude.—Accept, my lords, bowing to each; accept, madam, more profoundly bowing to the marchioness, my respectful thanks for all your goodness to me. I shall, to the end of my life, number most of the days that I have passed at Bologna amongst its happiest, even were the remainder to be as happy as man ever knew.

The marquis said, We wish you, chevalier, very happy; happier than—he sighed, and was silent.

His lady only bowed. Her face spoke distress. Her voice was lost in sighs, though she struggled to suppress them.

Chevalier, said the bishop, with an air of solemnity, you have given us many happy hours; for them we thank you.

Jeronymo, for himself, will say more: he is the most grateful of men. We thank you also for what you have done for him.

I cannot, said Jeronymo, express suitably my gratitude: my prayers, my vows, should follow you whithersoever you go, best of friends, and best of men!

The general, with an air and a smile that might have been dispensed with, oddly said, High pleasure and high pain are very near neighbours: they are often guilty of excesses, and then are apt to mistake each other's house. I am one of those who think our whole house obliged to the chevalier for the seasonable assistance he gave to our Jeronymo. But——

Dear general, said Lady Juliana, bear with an interruption. The intent of this meeting is amicable. The chevalier is a man of honour. Things may have fallen out unhappily; yet nobody to blame.

As to blame, or otherwise, said the Conte della Porretta, that is not now to be talked of; else, I *know* where it lies: in short, among ourselves. The chevalier acted greatly by Signor Jeronymo: we were all obliged to him: but to let such a man as *this* have free admission to our daughter—she ought to have had no eyes.

Pray, my lord, pray, brother, said the marquis, are we not enough sufferers?

The chevalier, said the general, cannot but be gratified by so high a compliment; and smiled indignantly.

My lord, replied I to the general, you know very little of the man before you, if you don't believe him to be the most afflicted man present.

Impossible! said the marquis, with a sigh.

The marchioness arose from her seat, motioning to go; and turning round to the two ladies, and the count, I have resigned my will to the will of you all, my dearest friends! and shall be permitted to withdraw. This testimony, however, before I go, I cannot but bear: wherever the fault lay, it lay not with the chevalier. He has, from the first to the last, acted with the nicest honour. He is entitled to our respect. The unhappiness lies nowhere but in the difference of religion.

Well, and that now is absolutely out of the question, said the general: it is indeed, chevalier.

I hope, my lord, from a descendant of a family so illustrious, to find an equal exemption from wounding words and wounding looks; and that, sir, as well from your generosity, as from your *justice*.

My looks give you offence, chevalier! Do they?

I attended to the marchioness. She came towards me. I arose and respectfully took her hand.—Chevalier, said she, I could not withdraw without bearing the testimony I have borne to your merits. I wish you happy.—God protect you, whithersoever you go. Adieu.

She wept. I bowed on her hand with profound respect. She retired with precipitation. It was with difficulty that I suppressed the rising tear. I took my seat.

I made no answer to the general's last question, though it was spoken in such a way (I saw by their eyes) as took every other person's notice.

Lady Sforza, when her sister was retired, hinted that the last interview between the young lady and me was an unadvised permission, though intended for the best.

I then took upon me to defend that step. Lady Clementina, said I, had declared that if she were allowed to speak her whole mind to me, she should be easy. I had for some time given myself up to absolute despair. The marchioness intended not *favour* to me in allowing of the interview: it was the most affecting one to me I had ever known. But let me say, that far from having bad effects on the young lady's mind, it had good ones. I hardly knew how to talk upon a subject so very interesting to *every one* present, but not more so to *any one* than to myself. I thought of avoiding it; and have been led into it, but did not lead. And since it is before us, let me recommend, as the most effectual way to restore every one to peace and happiness, *gentle treatment*. The most generous, the meekest, the most dutiful of human minds, requires not harsh treatment.

How do *you* know, sir, said the general, and looked at Jeronymo, the methods now taken——

And *are* they then harsh, my lord? said I.

He was offended.

I had heard, proceeded I, that a change of measures was resolved on. I knew that the treatment before had been all gentle, condescending, indulgent. I received but yesterday letters from my father, signifying his intention of speedily recalling me to my native country. I shall set out very soon for Paris, where I hope to meet with his more direct commands for this long desired end. What may be my destiny I know not; but I shall carry with me a heart burdened with the woes of this family, and distressed for the beloved daughter of it. But let me bespeak you all, for your own sakes (mine is out of the question: I presume not upon any hope of my own account), that you will treat this angelic-minded lady with tenderness. I pretend to say that I know that harsh or severe methods will not do.

The general arose from his seat, and with a countenance of fervour, next to fierceness—Let me tell you, Grandison, said he——

I arose from mine, and going to Lady Sforza, who sat next him, he stopt, supposing me going to him, and seemed surprised, and attentive to my motions; but disregarding him, I addressed myself to that lady. You, madam, are the aunt of Lady Clementina: the tender, the indulgent mother is absent, and has declared that she resigns her will to the will of her friends present—allow me to supplicate that former measures may not be changed with her. Great dawnings of returning reason did I discover in our last interview. Her delicacy (never was there a more delicate mind) wanted but to be satisfied. It *was* satisfied, and she began to be easy. Were her mind but once composed, the sense she has of her duty, and what she owes to her religion, would restore her to your wishes: but if she should be treated harshly (though I am sure, if she *should,* it would be with the best intention), Clementina will be lost.

The general sat down. They all looked upon one another.

The two ladies dried their eyes. The starting tear *would* accompany my fervour. And then stepping to Jeronymo, who was extremely affected; My dear Jeronymo, said I, my friend, my beloved friend, cherish in your noble heart the memory of your Grandison: would to God I could attend you to England! We have baths there of sovereign efficacy. The balm of a friendly and grateful heart would promote the cure. I have urged it before. Consider of it.

My Grandison, my dear Grandison, my friend, my preserver! You are not going!——

I *am,* my Jeronymo; and embraced him. Love me in absence, as I shall you.

Chevalier, said the bishop, you don't go? We hope for your company at a small collation.—We must not part with you yet.

I cannot, my lord, accept the favour. Although I had given myself up to despair of obtaining the happiness to which I once aspired; yet I was not willing to quit a city that this family had made dear to me, with the precipitation of a man conscious of misbehaviour. I thank you for the permission I had to attend you all in full assembly. May God prosper *you,* my lord; and may you be invested with the first honours of that Church which must be adorned by so worthy a heart! It will be *my* glory, when I am in my native place, or *wherever* I am, to remember that I was once thought not unworthy of a rank in a family so respectable. Let me, my lord, be entitled to your kind remembrance.

He pulled out his handkerchief. My lord, said he, to his father; my lord, to the general; Grandison must not go!—and sat down with emotion.

Lady Sforza wept: Laurana seemed moved: the two young lords, Sebastiano and Juliano, were greatly affected.

I then addressed myself to the marquis, who sat undetermined, as to speech: My venerable lord, forgive me, that my address was not first paid here: my heart overflows with gratitude for your goodness in permitting me to throw myself at your feet, before I took a last farewell of a city favoured with your residence. Best of fathers, of friends, of men, let me entreat the continuance of your paternal indulgence to the child nearest, and *deserving* to be nearest, to your heart. She is all *you* and her *mother*. Restore her to yourself, and to her, by your indulgence: that alone, and a blessing on your prayers, *can* restore her. Adieu, my good lord: repeated thanks for all your hospitable goodness to a man that will ever retain a grateful sense of your favour.

You will not yet go, was all he said—he seemed in agitation. He could not say more.

I then, turning to the count his brother, who sat next him, said, I have not the honour to be fully known to your lordship: some prejudices, from differences in opinion, may have been conceived: but if you ever hear anything of the man before you *unworthy* of his name, and of the favour once designed him; then, my lord, blame, as well as wonder at, the condescension of your noble brother and sister in my favour.

Who, I! Who, I! said that lord, in some hurry—I think very well of you. I never saw a man in my life that I liked so well!

Your lordship does me honour. I say this the rather, as I may, on this solemn occasion, taking leave of such honourable friends, charge my future life with resolutions to behave worthy of the favour I have met with in this family.

I passed from him to the general—Forgive, my lord, said I, the seeming formality of my behaviour in this parting scene: it is a very solemn one to me. You have expressed yourself *of* me, and *to* me, my lord, with more passion (forgive me, I mean not to offend you) than perhaps you will approve in yourself when I am far removed from Italy. For have you not a noble mind? And are you not a son of the Marquis della Porretta? Permit me to observe that passion will make a man exalt himself, and degrade another; and the just medium will be then forgot. I am afraid I have been thought more lightly of than I ought to be, either in justice, or for the honour of a person who is dear to every one present. My country was once mentioned with disdain. Think not my vanity so much concerned in what I am going to say, as my honour: I am proud to be thought an Englishman: yet I think as highly of every worthy man of every nation under the sun, as I do of the worthy men of my own. I am not of a contemptible race in my own country. My father lives in it with the magnificence of a prince. He loves his son; yet I presume to add that that son deems his good name his riches; his integrity his grandeur. Princes, though they are entitled by their rank to respect, are princes only to him as they act.

A few words more, my lord.

I have been of the *hearing,* not of the *speaking* side of the question, in the two last conferences I had the honour to hold with your lordship. Once you unkindly mentioned the word *triumph.* The word at the time went to my heart. When I can subdue the natural warmth of my temper, then, and then only, I have a triumph. I should not have remembered this, had I not now, my lord, on this solemn occasion, been received by you with an indignant eye. I respect your lordship *too much* not to take notice of this angry reception. My silence upon it perhaps would look like subscribing before this illustrious company to the justice of your contempt: yet I mean no *other* notice than this; and *this,* to demonstrate that I was not, in my *own* opinion at least, absolutely unworthy of the favour I met with from the father, the mother, the brothers, you so justly honour, and which I wished to stand in with *you.*

And now, my lord, allow me the honour of your hand; and as I have given you no cause for displeasure, say that you will remember me with kindness, as I shall honour you and your whole family to the last day of my life.

The general heard me out; but it was with great emotion. He accepted not my hand; he returned not any answer: the bishop arose, and, taking him aside, endeavoured to calm him.

I addressed myself to the two young lords, and said that if ever their curiosity led them to visit England, where I hoped to be in a few months, I should be extremely glad of cultivating their esteem and favour, by the best offices I could do them.

They received my civility with politeness.

I addressed myself next to Lady Laurana—May you, madam, the friend, the intimate, the chosen companion of Lady Clementina, never know the hundredth part of the woe that fills the breast of the man before you, for the calamity that has befallen your admirable cousin, and, because of that, a whole excellent family. Let me recommend to you that tender and soothing treatment to *her,* which her tender heart would show to *you,* in any calamity that should befall you. I am not a bad man, madam, though of a different communion from yours. Think but half so charitably of me, as I do of every one of your religion who lives up to his professions, and I shall be happy in your favourable thoughts when you hear me spoken of.

It is easy to imagine, Dr. Bartlett, that I addressed myself in this manner to this lady, whom I had never before seen, that she might not think the harder of her cousin's prepossessions in favour of a Protestant.

I recommended myself to the favour of Father Marescotti. He assured me of his esteem in very warm terms.

And just as I was again applying to my Jeronymo, the general came to me: You cannot think, sir, said he, nor did you *design* it, I suppose, that I should be pleased with your address to me. I have only this question to ask, When do you quit Bologna?

Let me ask your lordship, said I, when do you return to Naples?

Why that question, sir? haughtily.

I will answer you frankly. Your lordship, at the first of my acquaintance with you, invited me to Naples. I promised to pay my respects to you there. If you think of being there in a week, I will attend you at your own palace in that city; and there, my lord, I hope, no cause to the contrary having arisen from me, to be received by you with the same kindness and favour that you showed when you gave me the invitation. I think to leave Bologna to-morrow.

O brother! said the bishop, are you not *now* overcome?

And are you in earnest? said the general.

I am, my lord; I have many valuable friends, at different courts and cities in Italy, to take leave of. I never intend to see it again. I would look upon your lordship as one of those friends: but you seem still displeased with me. You accepted not my offered hand before: once more I tender it. A man of spirit cannot be offended at a man of spirit, without lessening himself. I call upon your dignity, my lord.

He held out his hand, just as I was withdrawing mine. I have pride, you know, Dr. Bartlett; and I was conscious of a superiority in *this instance:* I took his hand, however, at his offer; yet pitied him that his motion was made at all, as it wanted that grace which generally accompanies all he does and says.

The bishop embraced me.—Your moderation, thus exerted, said he, must ever make you triumph. O Grandison! you are a prince of the Almighty's creation!

The noble Jeronymo dried his eyes and held out his arms to embrace me.

The general said, I shall certainly be at Naples in a week. I am too much affected by the woes of my family, to behave as perhaps I ought on this occasion. Indeed, Grandison, it is difficult for sufferers to act with spirit and temper at the same time.

It *is*, my lord: I have found it so. My hopes raised, as once they were, now sunk, and absolute despair having taken place of them—would to God I had never returned to Italy!—But I reproach not anybody.

Yet, said Jeronymo, you have some reason—to be sent for as you were——

He was going on—Pray, brother, said the general—and turning to me, I may expect you, sir, at Naples?

You may, my lord. But one favour I have to beg of you meantime. It is, that you will not treat harshly *your* dear Clementina. Would to Heaven I might have had the honour to say, *my* Clementina! And permit me to make one other request on my own account: and that is, that you will tell her that I took my leave of your whole family, by their kind permission; and that, at my departure, I wished her, from my soul, all the happiness that the best and tenderest of her friends can wish her! I make this request to you, my lord, rather than to Signor Jeronymo, because the tenderness which he has for me might induce him to mention me to her in a manner which might, at this time, affect her too sensibly for her peace.

Be pleased, my dear Signor Jeronymo, to make my devotion known to the marchioness. Would to Heaven—But adieu! and once more adieu, my Jeronymo! I shall hear from you when I get to Naples, if not before.—God restore your sister, and heal you!

I bowed to the marquis, to the ladies, to the general, to the bishop, particularly; to the rest in general; and was obliged, in order to conceal my emotion, to hurry out at the door. The servants had planted themselves in a row; not for selfish motives, as in England: they bowed to the ground, and blessed me, as I went through them. I had ready a purse of ducats. One hand and another declined it: I dropt it in their sight. God be with you, my honest friends! said I; and departed.—O Dr. Bartlett, with a heart how much distressed!

And now, my good Miss Byron, have I not reason, from the deep concern which you take in the woes of Lady Clementina, to regret the task you have put me upon? And do you, my good Lord and Lady L——, and Miss Grandison, now wonder that your brother has not been forward to give you the particulars of this melancholy tale? Yet, you all say I must proceed.

See, Lucy, the greatness of this man's behaviour! What a presumption was it in your Harriet ever to aspire to call such a one hers!

LETTER III.

Miss Byron to Miss Selby.

THIS Lady Olivia, Lucy, what can *she* pretend to—but I will not puzzle myself about her—yet *she* pretend to give disturbance to such a man! You will find her mentioned in Dr. Bartlett's next letter; or she would not have been named by *me*.

Dr. Bartlett's eleventh letter.

MR. GRANDISON, on his return to his lodgings, found there, in disguise, Lady Olivia. He wanted not any new disturbance. But I will not mix the stories.

The next morning he received a letter from Signor Jeronymo. The following is a translation of it:—

MY DEAREST GRANDISON!—How do you? ever amiable friend! What triumphs did your behaviour of last night obtain for you! Not a soul here but admires you!

Even Laurana declared that, were you a Catholic, it would be a *merit* to love you. Yet she reluctantly praised you, and once said, what, but *splendid sins,* are the *virtues* of a *heretic?*

Our two cousins, with the good-nature of youth, lamented that you could not be ours in the way you wish. My father wept like a child when you were gone, and seemed to enjoy the praises given you by every one. The Count said he never saw a nobler behaviour in man. Your free, your manly, your polite air and address, and your calmness and intrepidity, were applauded by every one.

What joy did this give to your Jeronymo! I thought I wanted neither crutches, helps, nor wheeled chair; and several times forgot that I ailed anything.

I begin to love Father Marescotti. He was with the foremost in praising you.

The general owned that he once was resolved to quarrel with you. But will he, do you think, Jeronymo, said he, make me a visit at Naples?

You may depend upon it he will, answered I——
I will be there to receive him, replied he.

They admired you particularly for your address to my sister, by the general, rather than by me. And Lady Sforza said it was a thousand pities that you and Clementina could not be one. They applauded, all of them, what they had not, any of them, the power to imitate, that largeness of heart which makes you think so well, and speak so tenderly, of those of communions different from your own. So much steadiness in your own religion, yet so much prudence in a man so young, they said, was astonishing! No wonder that your character ran so high in every court you had visited.

My mother came in soon after you had left us. She was equally surprised and grieved to find you gone. She thought she was sure of your staying supper; and not satisfied with the slight leave she had taken, she had been strengthening her mind to pass an hour in your company, in order to take a more solemn one.

My father asked her after her daughter.

Poor soul! said she, she has heard that the chevalier was to be here to take leave of us.

By whom? by whom? said my father.

I cannot tell: but the poor creature is half raving to be admitted among us. She has dressed herself in one of her best suits; and I found her sitting in a kind of form, expecting to be called down. Indeed, Lady Sforza, the method we are in does not do.

So the chevalier said, replied that lady. Well, let us change it with all my heart. It is no pleasure to treat the dear girl harshly.—O sister, this is a most extraordinary man!

That moment in bolted Camilla—Lady Clementina is just at the door. I could not prevail upon her——

We all looked upon one another.

Three soft taps at the door, and a hem, let us know she was there.

Let her come in, dear girl, let her come in, said the Count: the chevalier is not here.

Laurana arose and ran to the door, and led her in by the hand.

Dear creature, how wild she looked!—Tears ran down my cheeks: I had not seen her for two days before. Oh, how earnestly did she look round her! withdrawing her hand from her cousin, who would have led her to a chair, and standing quite still.

Come and sit by me, my sweet love! said her weeping mother.—She stept towards her.

Sit down, my dear girl.

No: you beat me, remember.

Who beat you, my dear?—Sure nobody would beat my child!—Who beat you, Clementina?

I don't know—still looking round her, as wanting somebody.

Again her mother courted her to sit down.

No, madam, you don't love me.

Indeed, my dear, I do.

So you say.

Her father held out his open arms to her. Tears ran down his cheeks. He could not speak.—Ah, my father! said she, stepping towards him.

He caught her in his arms—Don't, don't, sir, faintly struggling, with averted face—You love me not—you refused to see your child, when she wanted to claim your protection!—I was used cruelly.

By whom, my dear? by whom?

By everybody. I complained to one, and to another; but all were in a tone: and so I thought I would be contented. My mamma, too!—But it is no matter. I saw it was to be so; and I did not care.

By my soul, said I, this is not the way with her, Lady Sforza. The chevalier is in the right. You see how sensible she is of harsh treatment.

Well, well, said the general, let us change our measures.

Still the dear girl looked out earnestly, as for somebody.

She loosed herself from the arms of her sorrowing father.

Let us in silence, said the Count, observe her motions.

She went to him on tip-toe, and looking in his face over his shoulder, as he sat with his back towards her, passed him; then to the general; then to Signor Sebastiano; and to every one round, till she came to me; looking at each over his shoulder in the same manner: then folding her fingers, her hands open, and her arms hanging down to their full extent, she held up her face meditating, with such a significant woe, that I thought my heart would have burst.—Not a soul in the company had a dry eye.

Lady Sforza arose, took her two hands, the fingers still clasped; and would have spoken to her, but could not; and hastily retired to her seat.

Tears at last began to trickle down her cheeks, as she stood fixedly looking up. She started, looked about her, and hastening to her mother threw her arms about her neck; and hiding her face in her bosom, broke out into a flood of tears, mingled with sobs that penetrated every heart.

The first words she said were, Love me, my mamma! Love your child! your poor child! your Clementina! Then raising her head, and again laying it in her mother's bosom—If ever you loved me, love me now, my mamma!—I have need of your love!

My father was forced to withdraw. He was led out by his two sons.

Your poor Jeronymo was unable to help himself.

He wanted as much comfort as his father. What were the wounds of his body, at that time, to those of his mind!

My two brothers returned. This dear girl, said the bishop, will break all our hearts.

Her tears had seemed to relieve her. She held up her head. My mother's bosom seemed wet with her child's tears and her own. Still she looked round her.

Suppose, said I, somebody were to name the man she seems to look for? It may divert this wildness.

Did she come down, said Laurana to Camilla, with the expectation of seeing him?

She did.

Let *me,* said the bishop, speak to her. He arose, and taking her hand, walked with her about the room. You look pretty, my dear Clementina! Your ornaments are charmingly fancied. What made you dress yourself so prettily?

She looked earnestly at him, in silence. He repeated his question.—I speak, said she, all my heart; and then I suffer for it. Everybody is against me.

You shall not suffer for it: everybody is for you.

I confessed to Mrs. Beaumont; I confessed to you, brother: but what did I get by it?—Let go my hand. I don't love you, I believe.

I am sorry for it. I love you, Clementina, as I love my own soul!

Yet you never chide your own soul!

He turned his face from her to us. She must not be treated harshly, said he. He soothed her in a truly brotherly manner.

Tell me, added he to his soothings, did you expect anybody here, that you find not?

Did I? Yes, I did.—Camilla, come hither.—Let go my hand, brother.

He did. She took Camilla under the arm—Don't you know, Camilla, said she, what you heard said of somebody's threatening somebody?—Don't let anybody hear us; drawing her to one end of the room.—I want to take a walk with you into the garden, Camilla.

It is dark night, madam.

No matter. If you are afraid, I will go by myself.

Seem to humour her in talk, Camilla, said the Count; but don't go out of the room with her.

Be pleased to tell me, madam, what we are to walk in the garden for?

Why, Camilla, I had a horrid dream last night; and I cannot be easy till I go into the garden.

What, madam, was your dream?

In the orange grove I thought I stumbled over the body of a dead man!

And who was it, madam?

Don't you know who was threatened? And was not somebody here to-night? And was not somebody to sup here? And *is* he here?

The general then went to her. My dearest Clementina! my beloved sister! set your heart at rest. Somebody is safe: shall be safe.

She took first one of his hands, then the other; and looking in the palms of them, They are not bloody, said she.—What have you done with him, then? Where is he?

Where is who?

You know whom I ask after; but you want something against me.

Then stepping quick up to me: My Jeronymo!—Did I see *you* before? and stroked my cheek. Now, tell me, Jeronymo—Don't come near me, Camilla. Pray, sir, to the general, do you sit down. She leaned her arm upon my shoulder: I don't hurt you, Jeronymo, do I?

No, my dearest Clementina!

That's my best brother—Cruel assassins!—But the brave man came just in time to save you.—But do you know what is become of him?

He is safe, my dear. He could not stay.

Did anybody affront him?

No, my love.

Are you sure nobody did?—*Very* sure? Father Marescotti, said she, turning to him (who wept from the time she entered), you don't love him: but you are a good man, and will tell me truth. Where is he? Did nobody affront him?

No, madam.

Because, said she, he never did anything but good to any one.

Father Marescotti, said I, admires him as much as anybody.

Admire him! Father Marescotti admire him!—But he does not *love* him. And I never heard *him* say one word against Father Marescotti in my life.—Well, but, Jeronymo, what made him go away, then? Was he not to stay to supper?

He was desired to stay; but would not.

Jeronymo, let me whisper you—did he tell you that I wrote him a letter?

I guessed you did, whispered I.

You are a strange guesser: but you can't guess how I sent it to him—But hush, Jeronymo—Well, but, Jeronymo, did he say nothing of me, when he went away?

He left his compliments for you with the general.

With the general! The general won't tell me!

Yes, he will.—Brother, pray tell my sister what the chevalier said to you at parting.

He repeated exactly what you had desired him to say to her.

Why would they not let me see him? said she. Am I never to see him more?

I hope you will, replied the bishop.

If, resumed she, we could have done anything that might have looked like a return to his goodness to us (and to you, my Jeronymo, in particular), I believe I should have been easy.—And so you say he is gone?—And gone for ever! lifting up her hand from her wrist, as it lay over my shoulder. Poor chevalier!—But hush, hush, pray hush, Jeronymo.

She went from me to her aunt and cousin Laurana. Love me again, madam, said she, to the former. You loved me once.

I never loved you better than now, my dear.

Did *you*, Laurana, see the chevalier Grandison?

I did.

And did he go away safe, and unhurt?

Indeed he did.

A man who had preserved the life of our dear Jeronymo, said she, to have been hurt by us, would have been dreadful, you know. I wanted to say a few words to him. I was astonished to find him not here: and then my dream came into my head. It was a sad dream, indeed!—But, cousin, be good to me: pray do. You did not use to be cruel. You used to say you loved me. I am in calamity, my dear. I know I am miserable: at times I know I am: and then I am grieved at my heart, and think how happy every one is, but me: but then, again, I ail nothing, and am well. But do love me, Laurana: I am in calamity, my dear. I would love you, if you were in calamity: indeed I would.—Ah, Laurana! what is become of all your fine promises? But then everybody loved me, and I was happy!—Yet you tell me it is all for my good. Naughty Laurana, to wound my heart by your crossness, and then say it is for my good!—Do you think I should have served you so?

Laurana blushed and wept. Her aunt promised her, that everybody would love her, and comfort her, and not be angry with her, if she would make her heart easy.

I am very particular, my dear Grandison. I know you love I should be so. From this minuteness you will judge of the workings of her mind. They are resolved to take your advice (it was very seasonable), and treat her with indulgence. The Count is earnest to have it so.

CAMILLA has just left me. She says that her young lady had a tolerable night. The thinks it owing, in a great measure, to her being indulged in asking the servants, who saw you depart, how you looked; and being satisfied that you went away unhurt, and unaffronted.

Adieu, my dearest, my best friend. Let me hear from you as often as you can.

I JUST now understand from Camilla, that the dear girl has made an earnest request to my father, mother, and aunt; and been refused. She came back from them deeply afflicted; and, as Camilla fears, is going into one of her gloomy fits again. I hope to write again, if you depart not from Bologna before to-morrow: but I must, for my own sake, write shorter letters. Yet how can I? Since however melancholy the subject, when I am writing to you, I am conversing with you. My dear Grandison, once more adieu.

O LUCY, my dear! Whence come all the tears this melancholy story has cost me? I cannot dwell upon the scenes!—Begone all those wishes that would interfere with the interest of that sweet distressed saint at Bologna!

How impolitic, Lucy, was it in them, not to gratify her impatience to see him! She would, most probably, have been quieted in her mind, if she had been obliged by one other interview.

What a delicacy, my dear! what a generosity, is there in her love!

Sir Charles, in Lord L——'s study, said to me, that his compassion was engaged, but his honour was free: and so it seems to be: but a generosity, in return for her generosity, must bind such a mind as his.

LETTER IV.

Miss Byron to Miss Selby.

IN the Doctor's next letter, enclosed, you will find mention made of Sir Charles's Literary Journal. I fancy, my dear, it must be a charming thing. I wish we could have before us every line he wrote while he was in Italy. Once the presumptuous Harriet had hopes that she might have been entitled—but no more of these hopes—it can't be helped, Lucy.

Dr. Bartlett's twelfth letter.

MR. GRANDISON proceeds thus:

The next morning I employed myself in visiting and taking leave of several worthy members of the university, with whom I had passed many very agreeable and improving hours, during my residence in this noble city. In my Literary Journal you have an account of those worthy persons, and of some of our conversations. I paid my duty to the cardinal legate, and the gonfaloniere, and to three of his counsellors, by whom, you know, I had been likewise greatly honoured. My mind was not free enough to *enjoy* their conversation: such a weight upon my heart, how could it? But the debt of gratitude and civility was not to be left unpaid.

On my return to my lodgings, which was not till the evening, I found the general had been there to inquire after me.

I sent one of my servants to the palace of Porretta, with my compliments to the general, to the bishop, and Jeronymo; and with particular inquiries after the health of the ladies and the marquis; but had only a general answer, that they were much as I left them.

The two young lords, Sebastiano and Juliano, made me a visit of ceremony. They talked of visiting England in a year or two. I assured them of my best services, and urged them to go thither. I asked them after the healths of the marquis, the marchioness, and their beloved cousin Clementina. Signor Sebastiano shook his head: Very, *very* indifferent were his words. We parted with great civilities.

I will now turn my thoughts to Florence, and to the affairs there that have lain upon me, from the death of my good friend Mr. Jervois, and from my wardship. I told you, in their course, the steps I took in those affairs; and how happy I had been in some parts of management. There I hope soon to see you, my dear Dr. Bartlett, from the Levant, to whose care I can so safely consign my precious trust, while I go to Paris and attend the wished-for call of my father to my native country, from which I have been for so many years an exile.

There, also, I hope to have some opportunities of conversing with my good Mrs. Beaumont; resolving to make another effort to get so valuable a person to restore herself to my beloved England.

Thus, my dear Dr. Bartlett, do I endeavour to console myself, in order to lighten that load of grief which I labour under on the distresses of the dear Clementina. If I can leave her happy, I shall be sooner so, than I could have been in the same circumstances, had I, from the first of my acquaintance with the family (to the breach of all the laws of hospitality), indulged a passion for her.

Yet is the unhappy Olivia a damp upon my endeavours after consolation. When she made her unseasonable visit to me at Bologna, she refused to return to Florence without me, till I assured her that as my affairs would soon call me thither, I would visit her at her own palace, as often as those affairs would permit. Her pretence for coming to Bologna was to induce me to place Emily with her, till I had settled everything for my carrying the child to England; but I was obliged to be peremptory in my denial, though she had wrought so with Emily, as to induce her to be an earnest petitioner to me to permit her to live with Lady Olivia, whose equipages, and the glare in which she lives, had dazzled the eyes of the young lady.

I WAS impatient to hear again from Jeronymo; and just as I was setting out for Florence, in despair of that favour, it being the second day after my farewell visit, I had the following letter from him:—

I HAVE not been well, my dear Grandison! I am afraid the wound in my shoulder must be laid open again. God give me patience! But my life is a burden to me.

We are driving here at a strange rate. They promised to keep measures with the dear creature; but she has heard that you are leaving Bologna, and raves to see you.

Poor soul! She endeavoured to prevail upon her father, mother, aunt, to permit her to see you but for *five* minutes: that was the petition which was denied her, as I mentioned in my last.

Camilla was afraid she would go into a gloomy fit upon it, as I told you—She did; but it lasted not long: for she made an effort, soon after, to go out of the house by way of the garden. The gardener refused his key, and brought Camilla to her, whom she had, by an innocent piece of art, but just before sent to bring her something from her toilette.

The general went with Camilla to her. They found her just setting a ladder against the wall. She heard them, and screamed, and leaving the ladder, ran, to avoid them, till she came in sight of the great cascade; into which, had she not by a cross alley been intercepted by the general, it is feared she would have thrown herself.

This has terrified us all: she begs but for one interview; one parting interview; and she promises to make herself easy:

but it is not thought advisable. Yet Father Marescotti himself thought it best to indulge her. Had my mother been earnest, I believe it had been granted: but she is so much concerned at the blame she met with on permitting the last interview, that she will not contend, though she has let them know that she did not oppose the request.

The unhappy girl ran into my chamber this morning— Jeronymo; he will be *gone!* said she: I *know* he will. All I want, is but to see him! To wish him happy! And to know if he will remember me when he is gone, as I shall him!— Have *you* no interest, Jeronymo? Cannot I *once* see him? Not *once?*

The bishop, before I could answer, came in quest of her, followed by Laurana, from whom she had forcibly disengaged herself, to come to me.

Let me have but one parting interview, my lord, said she, looking to him, and clinging about my neck. He will be gone: gone for ever. Is there so much in being allowed to say, Farewell, and be happy, Grandison! and excuse all the trouble I have given you?—What has my brother's preserver done, what have I done, that I must not see him, nor he me, for one quarter of an hour only?

Indeed, my lord, said I, she should be complied with. Indeed she should.

My *father* thinks otherwise, said the bishop: the *Count* thinks otherwise: *I* think otherwise. Were the chevalier a common man, she might. But she dwells upon what passed in the last interview, and his behaviour to her. *That,* it is plain, did her harm.

The next may drive the thoughts of that out of her head, returned I.

Dear Jeronymo, replied he, a little peevishly, you will always think differently from everybody else! Mrs. Beaumont comes to-morrow.

What do I care for Mrs. Beaumont? said she.—I don't love her: she tells everything I say.

Come, my dear love! said Laurana, you afflict your brother Jeronymo. Let us go up to your own chamber.

I afflict everybody, and everybody afflicts me; and you are all cruel. Why, he will be *gone,* I tell you! That makes me so impatient: and I have something to say to him. My father won't see me: my mother renounces me. I have been looking for her, and she hides herself from me!—and I am a prisoner, and watched, and used ill!

Here comes my mother! said Laurana. You now *must* go up to your chamber, cousin Clementina.

So she does, said she: now I must go indeed! Ah, Jeronymo! Now there is no saying nay.—But it is hard! *very* hard!—And she burst into tears. I won't speak, though, said she, to my aunt. Remember, I will be silent, madam!—Then whispering me; My aunt, brother, is not the aunt she used to be to me!—But hush, I don't complain, you know!

By this I saw that Lady Sforza was severe with her.

She addressed herself to her aunt: You are not my mamma, are you, madam?

No, child.

No, child, indeed! I know that *too* well. But my brother Giacomo is as cruel to me as anybody. But, hush, Jeronymo!—Don't you betray me!—Now my aunt is come, I must go!—I wish I could run away from you all!

She was yesterday detected writing a letter to you. My mother was shown what she had written, and wept over it. My aunt took it out of my sister's bosom, where she had thrust it, on her coming in. This she resented highly.

When she was led into her own chamber, she refused to speak; but in great hurry went to her closet, and taking down her Bible, turned over one leaf and another very quick. Lady Sforza had a book in her hand, and sat over against the closet-door to observe her motions. She came to a place—*Pretty!* said she.

The bishop had formerly given her a smattering of Latin.—She took pen and ink, and wrote. You'll see, chevalier, the very great purity of her thoughts, by what she omitted, and what she chose, from the Canticles. *Velur unguentum diffunditur nomen tuum, &c.*

[In the English translation, thus: *Thy name is as ointment poured forth; therefore do the virgins love thee. Draw me; we will run after thee: the upright love thee.*

Look not upon me because I am black, because the sun hath looked upon me. My mother's children were angry with me: they made me the keeper of the vineyards, but mine own vineyard have I not kept.

Tell me, O thou whom my soul loveth! where thou feedest, where thou makest thy flock to rest at noon; for why should I be as one that turneth aside by the flocks of thy companions?]

She laid down her pen, and was thoughtful; her elbow resting on the escritoir she wrote upon, her hand supporting her head.

May I look over you, my dear? said her aunt, stepping to her; and taking up the paper, read it, and took it out of the closet with her, unopposed; her gentle bosom only heaving sighs.

I will write no more, so minutely, on this affecting subject, my Grandison.

They are all of opinion that she will be easy when she knows that you have actually left Bologna; and they strengthen their opinion by these words of her, above recited: 'Why, he will 'be gone, I tell you; and this makes me so impatient.'—At least, they are resolved to try the experiment. And so, my dear Grandison! you must be permitted to leave us.

God be your director and comforter, as well as ours! prays your ever affectionate JERONYMO.

Mr. Grandison having no hopes of being allowed to see the unhappy lady, set out with an afflicted heart for Florence. He gave orders there, and at Leghorn, that the clerks and agents of his late friend Mr. Jervois should prepare everything for his inspection against his return from Naples; and then he set out for that city, to attend the general.

He had other friends to whom he had endeared himself at Sienna, Ancona, and particularly at Rome, as he had also some at Naples; of whom he intended to take leave before he set out for Paris: and therefore went to attend the general with the greater pleasure.

Within the appointed time he arrived in Naples.

The general received me, said Mr. Grandison, with greater tokens of politeness than affection. You are the happiest man in the world, chevalier, said he, after the first compliments, in escaping dangers by braving them. I do assure you, that I had great difficulties to deny myself the favour of paying you a visit *in my own way* at Bologna. I had indeed resolved to do it, till you proposed this visit to me here.

I should have been very sorry, replied I, to have seen a brother of Lady Clementina in *any* way that should not have made me consider him as her brother. But before I say another word, let me ask after her health. How does the most excellent of women?

You have not heard, then?

I have not, my lord: but it is not for want of solicitude: I have sent three several messengers: but can hear nothing to my satisfaction.

Nor can you hear anything from me that will give you any.

I am grieved at my soul, that I cannot. How, my lord, do the marquis and marchioness?

Don't ask. They are extremely unhappy.

I hear that my dear friend, Signor Jeronymo, has undergone——

A dreadful operation, interrupted the general.—He has. Poor Jeronymo! He *could not* write to you. God preserve my brother! But, chevalier, you did not save half a life, though we thank you for that, when you restored him to our arms.

I had no reason to boast, my lord, of the accident. I never made a merit of it. It was a *mere* accident, and cost me nothing. The service was greatly over-rated.

Would to God, chevalier, it had been rendered by any other man in the world!

As it has proved, I am sure, my lord, I have reason to join in the wish.

He showed me his pictures, statues, and cabinet of curiosities, while dinner was preparing; but rather for the ostentation of his magnificence and taste, than to do me pleasure. I even observed an increasing coldness in his behaviour; and his eye was too often cast upon me with a fierceness that showed resentment; and not with the hospitable frankness that became him to a visitor and guest, who had undertaken a journey of above two hundred miles, principally to attend him, and to show him the confidence he had in his honour. This, as it was more to his discredit than mine, I pitied him for. But what most of all disturbed me, was, that I could not obtain from him any particular intelligence relating to the health of one person, whose distresses lay heavy upon my heart.

There were several persons of distinction at dinner; the discourse could therefore be only general. He paid me great respect at his table; but it was a solemn one. I was the more uneasy at it, as I apprehended that the situation of the Bologna family was more unhappy than when I left that city.

He retired with me into his garden. You stay with me at least the week out, chevalier?

No, my lord: I have affairs of a deceased friend at Florence and at Leghorn to settle. To-morrow, as early as I can, I shall set out for Rome, in my way to Tuscany.

I am surprised, chevalier! You take something amiss in my behaviour.

I cannot say that your lordship's countenance (I am a very free speaker) has that benignity in it, that complacency, which I have had the pleasure to see in it.

By G—! chevalier, I could have loved you better than any man in the world, next to the men of my own family; but I own I see you not here with so much love as admiration.

The word *admiration*, my lord, may require explanation. You may admire at my confidence: but I thank you for the manly freedom of your acknowledgment in general.

By *admiration* I mean all that may do you honour. Your bravery in coming hither, particularly; and your greatness of mind on your taking leave of us all. But did you not then mean to insult me?

I meant to observe to you then, as I now do in your own palace, that you had not treated me as my heart told me I deserved to be treated: but when I thought your warmth was rising to the uneasiness of your assembled friends, instead of answering your question about my stay at Bologna, as you seemed to mean it, I invited myself to an attendance upon you here, at Naples, in such a manner as surely could not be construed an insult.

I own, Grandison, you disconcerted me. I had intended to save you that journey.

Was that your lordship's meaning, when, in my absence, you called at my lodgings the day after the farewell visit?

Not absolutely: I was uneasy with myself. I intended to talk with you. What that talk might have produced, I know not: but had I invited you out, if I had found you at home, would you have answered my demands?

According as you had put them.

Will you answer me now, if I attend you as far as Rome, on your return to Florence?

If they are demands fit to be answered.

Do you expect I will make any that are *not* fit to be answered?

My lord, I will explain myself. You had conceived causeless prejudices against me: you seemed inclined to impute to me a misfortune that was not, could not be, greater to you than it was to me. I knew my own innocence, I knew that I was rather an injured man, in having hopes given me, in which I was disappointed, not by my own fault. Whom shall an innocent and an injured man fear?—Had I feared, my fear might have been my destruction. For was I not in the midst of your friends? A foreigner? If I *would* have avoided you, *could* I, had you been determined to seek me?— I would choose to meet even an enemy as a man of honour, rather than to avoid him as a malefactor. In my country, the law supposes flight a confession of guilt. Had you made demands upon me that I had not chosen to answer, I would have expostulated with you. I could, perhaps, have done so as calmly as I now speak. If you would not have been expostulated with, I would have stood upon my defence: but for the world I would not have hurt a brother of Clementina and Jeronymo, a son of the marquis and marchioness of Porretta, could I have avoided it. Had your passion given me any advantage over you, and I had obtained your sword (a pistol, had the choice been left to me, I had refused, for both our sakes), I would have presented both swords to you, and bared my breast. It was before penetrated by the distresses of the dear Clementina, and of all your family—perhaps I should only have said, 'If your lordship thinks I have injured you, 'take your revenge.'

And now that I am at Naples, let me say that if you are determined, contrary to all my hopes, to accompany me to Rome, or elsewhere, on my return, with an unfriendly purpose; such, and no other, shall be my behaviour to you, if the power be given me to show it. I will rely on my own innocence, and hope by generosity to overcome a *generous* man. Let the guilty secure themselves by violence and murder.

Superlative pride! angrily said he, and stood still, measuring me with his eye: and could you hope for such an advantage?

While I, my lord, was calm, and determined only upon self-defence; while you were passionate, and perhaps rash, as aggressors generally are, I did not doubt it: but could I have avoided drawing, and preserved your good opinion, I would not have drawn. Your lordship cannot but know my principles.

Grandison, I *do* know them; and also the general report in your favour for skill and courage. Do you think I would have heard with patience of the once proposed alliance, had not your character—and then he was pleased to say many things in my favour, from the report of persons who had weight with him; some of whom he named.

But still, Grandison, said he, this poor girl!—She could not have been so deeply affected, had not some lover-like arts——

Let me, my lord, interrupt you—I cannot bear an imputation of this kind. *Had* such arts been used, the lady could *not* have been so much affected. Cannot you think of your noble sister, as a daughter of the two houses from which you sprang? Cannot you see her, as by Mrs. Beaumont's means we now so lately have been able to see her, struggling nobly with her own heart [Why am I put upon this tender subject?], because of her duty and her religion; and resolved to die rather than encourage a wish that was not warranted by both? —I cannot, my lord, urge this subject: but there never was a passion so nobly contended with. There never was a man more disinterested, and so circumstanced. Remember only my voluntary departure from Bologna, against persuasion; and the great behaviour of your sister on that occasion; great, as it came out to be, when Mrs. Beaumont brought her to acknowledge what would have been my glory to have known, could it have been encouraged; but is now made my heaviest concern.

Indeed, Grandison, she ever was a noble girl! We are too apt, perhaps, to govern ourselves by events, without looking into causes: but the access you had to her; such a man! and who became known to us from circumstances so much in his favour, both as a man of principle and bravery——

This, my lord, interrupted I, is still judging from events. You have seen Mrs. Beaumont's letter. Surely you cannot have a nobler monument of magnanimity in woman! And to that I refer for a proof of my own integrity.

I *have* that letter: Jeronymo gave it me, at my taking leave of him; and with these words: ' Grandison will certainly 'visit you at Naples. I am afraid of your warmth. His spirit 'is well known. All my dependance is upon his principles. 'He will not draw but in his own defence. Cherish the noble 'visitor. Surely, brother, I may depend upon your hospitable 'temper. Read over again this letter, before you see him.'— I have not yet read it, proceeded the general; but I will, and that, if you will allow me, now.

He took it out of his pocket, walked from me, and read it; and then came to me, and took my hand—I am half ashamed of myself, my dear Grandison! I own I wanted magnanimity.

All the distresses of our family, on this **unhappy girl's** account, were before my eyes, and I received you, I behaved to you, as the author of them. I was *contriving* to be dissatisfied with you: forgive me, and command my best services. I will let our Jeronymo know how greatly you subdued me before I had recourse to the letter; but that I have since read that part of it which accounts for my sister's passion, and wish I had read it with equal attention before. I acquit *you:* I am proud of my *sister.* Yet I observe from this very letter, that Jeronymo's gratitude has contributed to the evil we deplore. But—let us not say one word more of the unhappy girl: it is painful to me to talk of her.

Not ask a question, my lord?——

Don't, Grandison, don't—Jeronymo and Clementina are my soul's woe—But they are not worse than might be apprehended. You go to court with me to-morrow: I will present you to the king.

I have had that honour formerly. I must depart to-morrow morning early. I have already taken leave of several of my friends here: I have some to make my compliments to at Rome, which I reserved for my return.

You stay with me to-night?—I intend it, my lord.

Well, we will return to company. I must make my excuses to my friends. Your departure to-morrow must be one. They all admire you. They are acquainted with your character. They will join with me to engage you, if possible, to stay longer.—We returned to the company.

LETTER V.

Miss Byron to Miss Selby.

RECEIVE now, my dear, the doctor's thirteenth letter, and the last he intends to favour us with, till he entertains us with the histories of Mrs. Beaumont and Lady Olivia.

Dr. Bartlett's thirteenth letter.

Mr. Grandison set out next morning. The general's behaviour to him at his departure was much more open and free than it was at receiving him.

Mr. Grandison, on his return to Florence, entered into the affairs of his late friend Mr. Jervois, with the spirit, and yet with the temper for which he is noted when he engages in any business. He put everything in a happy train in fewer days than it would have cost some other persons months; for he was present himself on every occasion, and in every business where his presence would accelerate it: yet he had embarrassments from Olivia.

He found, before he set out for Naples, that Mrs. Beaumont, at the earnest request of the marchioness, was gone to Bologna. At his return, not hearing anything from Signor Jeronymo, he wrote to Mrs. Beaumont, requesting her to inform him of the state of things in that family, as far as she thought proper; and, particularly, of the health of that dear friend, on whose silence to three letters he had written he had the most melancholy apprehensions. He let that lady know that he should set out in a very few days for Paris, if he had no probability of being of service to the family she favoured with her company.

To this letter Mrs. Beaumont returned the following answer:—

Sir,—I have the favour of yours. We are very miserable here. The servants are forbidden to answer any inquiries, but generally; and that not truly.

Your friend, Signor Jeronymo, has gone through a severe operation. He has been given over; but hopes are now entertained, not of his absolute recovery, but that he will be no worse than he was before the necessity for the operation arose. Poor man! He forgot not, however, his sister and you when he was out of the power of the opiates that were administered to him.

On my coming hither, I found Lady Clementina in a deplorable way: sometimes raving, sometimes gloomy; and in bonds.—Twice had she given them apprehensions of fate attempts: they therefore confined her hands.

They have been excessively wrong in their management of her: now soothing, now severe; observing no method.

She was extremely earnest to see you before you left Bologna. On her knees repeatedly she besought this favour, and promised to be easy if they would comply; but they imagined that their compliance would aggravate the symptoms.

I very freely blamed them for not complying at the time when she was so desirous of seeing you. I told them that soothing her would probably *then* have done good.

When they knew you were actually gone from Bologna, they told her so. Camilla shocked me with the description of her rage and despair on the communication. This was followed by fits of silence and deepest melancholy.

They had hopes, on my arrival, that my company would have been of service to her: but for two days together she regarded me not, nor anything I could say to her. On the third of my arrival, finding her confinement extremely uneasy to her, I prevailed, but with great difficulty, to have her restored to the use of her hands; and to be allowed to walk with me in the garden. They had hinted to me their apprehensions about a piece of water.

Her woman being near us, if there had been occasion for assistance, I insensibly led that way. She sat down on a seat over against the great cascade; but she made no motion that gave me apprehensions. From this time she has been fonder of me than before. The day I obtained this liberty for her, she often clasped her arms about me, and laid her face in my bosom; and I could plainly see it was in gratitude for restoring to her the use of her arms: but she cared not to speak.

Indeed she generally affects deep silence: yet, at times, I see her very soul is fretted. She moves to one place; is tired of that; shifts to another, and another, all round the room.

I am grieved at my heart for her: I never knew a more excellent young creature.

She is very fervent in her devotions, and as constant in

them as she used to be; every good habit she preserves; yet at other times rambles much.

She is often for writing letters to you; but when what she writes is privately taken from her, she makes no inquiry about it, but takes a new sheet and begins again.

Sometimes she draws; but her subjects are generally angels and saints. She often meditates in a map of the British dominions, and now and then wishes she were in England.

Lady Juliana de Sforza is earnest to have her with her at Urbino, or at Milan, where she has also a noble palace; but I hope it will not be granted. That lady professes to love her; but she cannot be persuaded out of her notion of harsh methods; which will never do with Clementina.

I shall not be able to stay long with her. The discomposure of so excellent a young creature affects me deeply. Could I do her either good or pleasure, I should be willing to deny myself the society of my dear friends at Florence: but I am persuaded, and have hinted as much, that one interview with you would do more to settle her mind than all the methods they have taken.

I hope, sir, to see you before I leave Italy. It must be at Florence, not at Bologna, I believe. It is generous of you to propose the latter.

I have now been here a week, without hope. The doctors they have consulted are all for severe methods and low diet. The first, I think, is in compliment to some of the family. She is so loath to take nourishment, and when she does, is so very abstemious, that the regimen is hardly necessary. She never, or but very seldom, used to drink anything but water.

She took it into her poor head several times this day, and perhaps it will hold, to sit in particular places, to put on attentive looks, as if she were listening to somebody. She sometimes smiled and seemed pleased; looked up, as if to somebody, and spoke English. I have no doubt, though I was not present when she assumed these airs and talked English, but her disordered imagination brought before her her tutor instructing her in that tongue.

You desired me, sir, to be very particular. I have been so,

but at the expense of my eyes: and I shall not wonder if your humane heart should be affected by my sad tale.

God preserve you, and prosper you in whatsoever you undertake! HORTENSIA BEAUMONT.

Mrs. Beaumont stayed at Bologna twelve days, and then left the unhappy young lady.

At taking leave, she asked her what commands she had for her?—Love me, said she, and pity me; that is one. Another is (whispering her), you will see the chevalier perhaps, though I must not.—Tell him that his poor friend Clementina is sometimes very unhappy!—Tell him that she shall rejoice to sit next him in heaven!—Tell him that I say he cannot go thither, good man as he is, while he shuts his eyes to the truth.—Tell him that I shall take it very kindly of him, if he will not think of marrying till he acquaints me with it; and can give me assurance that the lady will love him as well as somebody else would have done.—O Mrs. Beaumont! should the Chevalier Grandison marry a woman unworthy of him, what a disgrace would that be to me!

Mr. Grandison by this time had prepared everything for his journey to Paris. The friend he honoured with his love, was arrived from the Levant and the Archipelago. Thither, at his patron's request, he had accompanied Mr. Beauchamp, the amiable friend of both; and at parting engaged to continue by letter what had been the subject of their daily conversations, and transmit to him as many particulars as he could obtain of Mr. Grandison's sentiments and behaviour on every occasion; Mr. Beauchamp proposing him as a pattern to himself, that he might be worthy of the credential letters he had furnished him with to every one whom he had thought deserving of his own acquaintance, when he was in the parts which Mr. Beauchamp intended to visit.

To the care of the person so much honoured by his confidence, Mr. Grandison left his agreeable ward, Miss Jervois; requesting the assistance of Mrs. Beaumont, who kindly promised her inspection: and with the goodness for which she is so eminently noted, performed her promise in his absence.

He then made an offer to the bishop to visit Bologna once more; but that not being accepted, he set out for Paris.

It was not long before his father's death called him to England; and when he had been there a few weeks, he sent for his ward and his friend.

But, my good Miss Byron, you will say that I have not yet fully answered your last inquiry relating to the present situation of the unhappy Clementina.

I will briefly inform you of it.

When it was known, for certain, that Mr. Grandison had actually left Italy, the family at Bologna began to wish that they had permitted the interview so much desired by the poor lady: and when they afterwards understood that he was sent for to England to take possession of his paternal estate, that farther distance (the notion likewise of the seas between them appearing formidable) added to their regrets.

The poor lady was kept in travelling motion to quiet her mind: for still an interview with Mr. Grandison having never been granted, it was her first wish.

They carried her to Urbino, to Rome, to Naples; then back to Florence, then to Milan, to Turin.

Whether they made her hope that it was to meet with Mr. Grandison, I know not; but it is certain she herself expected to see him at the end of every journey; and while she was moving was easier and more composed; perhaps in that hope.

The marchioness was sometimes of the party. The air and exercise were thought proper for *her* health, as well as for that of her daughter. Her cousin Laurana was always with her in these excursions, and sometimes Lady Sforza; and their escort was generally Signors Sebastiano and Juliano.

But within these four months past, these journeyings have been discontinued. The young lady accuses them of deluding her with vain hopes. She is impatient, and has made two attempts to escape from them.

She is, for this reason, closely confined and watched.

They put her once into a nunnery, at the motion of Lady Sforza, as for a trial only. She was not uneasy in it: but this being done unknown to the general, when he was apprised of it, he, for reasons I cannot comprehend, was displeased, and had her taken out directly.

Her head runs more than ever upon seeing her tutor, her friend, her chevalier, once more. They have certainly been to blame, if they have let her travel with such hopes; because they have thereby kept up her ardour for an interview. Could she but once more see him, she says, and let him know the cruelty she has been treated with, she should be satisfied. *He* would pity her, she is sure, though nobody else will.

The bishop has written to beg that Sir Charles would pay them one more visit at Bologna.

I will refer to my patron himself the communicating to you, ladies, his resolution on this subject. I had but a moment's sight of the letters which so greatly affected him.

It is but *within* these few days past that this new request has been made to him in a *direct* manner. The question was before put, If such a request *should* be made, would he comply? And once Camilla wrote, as having heard Sir Charles's presence wished for.

Meantime the poor lady is hastening, they are afraid, into a consumptive malady. The Count of Belvedere, however, still adores her. The disorder in her mind being imputed chiefly to religious melancholy, and some of her particular flights not being generally known, he, who is a pious man himself, pities her; and declares that he would run all risks of her recovery, would the family give her to him: and yet he knows that she would choose to be the wife of the Chevalier Grandison, rather than that of any other man, were the article of religion to be got over; and generously applauds her for preferring her faith to her love.

Signor Jeronymo is in a very bad way. Sir Charles often writes to him, and with an affection worthy of the merits of that dear friend. He was to undergo another severe operation on the next day after the letters came from Bologna; the success of which was very doubtful.

How nobly does Sir Charles appear to support himself under such heavy afflictions! For those of his friends were ever his. But his heart bleeds in secret for them. A feeling heart is a blessing that no one, who has it, would be without; and it is a moral security of innocence; since the heart that is able to partake of the distress of another, cannot wilfully give it.

I think, my good Miss Byron, that I have now, as far as I am at present able, obeyed all your commands that concern the unhappy Clementina, and her family. I will defer, if you please, those which relate to Olivia and Mrs. Beaumont (ladies of very different characters from each other), having several letters to write.

Permit me, my good ladies, and my lord, after contributing so much to afflict your worthy hearts, to refer you, for relief under all the distresses of life, whether they affect ourselves or others, to those motives that can alone give support to a rational mind. This mortal scene, however perplexing, is a very short one; and the hour is hastening when all the intricacies of human affairs shall be cleared up; and all the sorrows that have had their foundation in virtue be changed into the highest joy: when all worthy minds shall be united in the same interests, the same happiness.

Allow me to be, my good Miss Byron, and you, my Lord and Lady L——, and Miss Grandison, your most faithful and obedient servant, AMBROSE BARTLETT.

Excellent Dr. Bartlett!—How worthy of himself is this advice! But think you not, my Lucy, that the doctor has in it a particular view to your poor Harriet? A generous one, meaning consolation and instruction to her? I will endeavour to profit by it. Let me have your prayers, my dear friends, that I may be enabled to succeed in my humble endeavours.

It will be no wonder to us now, that Sir Charles was not solicitous to make known a situation so embarrassing to himself, and so much involved in clouds and uncertainty. But whatever may be the event of this affair, you, Lucy, and all my friends, will hardly ever know me by any other name than that of HARRIET BYRON.

LETTER VI.

Miss Harriet Byron to Miss Lucy Selby.

Friday, March 31.

You now, my dear friends, have before you this affecting story, as far as Dr. Bartlett can give it. My cousins express a good deal of concern for your Harriet: so does Miss Grandison: so does my Lord and Lady L——: and the more, as I seem to carry off the matter with assumed bravery. This their kind concern for me, looks, however, as if they thought me a hypocrite; and I suppose, therefore, that I act my part very awkwardly.

But, my dear, as this case is one of those few in which a woman *can* show a bravery of spirit, I think an endeavour after it is laudable; and the rather, as in my conduct I aim at giving a tacit example to Miss Jervois.

The doctor has whispered to me that Lady Olivia is actually on her way to England; and that the intelligence Sir Charles received of her intention, was one of the things that disturbed him, as the news of his beloved Signor Jeronymo's dangerous condition was another.

Lady Anne S——, it seems, has not yet given up her hopes of Sir Charles. The two sisters, who once favoured her above all the women they knew, have not been able to bring themselves to acquaint a lady of her rank and merit, that there can be no hopes; and they are still more loath to say that their brother thinks himself under some obligations to a foreign lady. Yet you know that this was always what we were afraid of: but who, now, will say *afraid,* that knows the merit of Clementina?

I wish, methinks, that this man were proud, vain, arrogant, and a boaster. How easy then might one throw off one's shackles!

Lord G—— is very diligent in his court to Miss Grandison. His father and aunt are to visit her this afternoon.

She behaves whimsically to my lord: yet I cannot think that she *greatly* dislikes him.

The Earl of D—— and the Countess Dowager are both in town. The countess made a visit to my cousin Reeves last Tuesday: she spoke of me very kindly: she says my lord has heard so much of me, that he is very desirous of seeing me: but she was pleased to say that, since my heart was not disengaged, she should be afraid of the consequences of his visit to himself.

My grandmamma, though she was so kindly fond of me, would not suffer me to live with her; because she thought that her contemplative temper might influence mine, and make me grave, at a time of life, when she is always saying that cheerfulness is most becoming: she would therefore turn over her girl to the best of aunts. But now, I fancy, she will allow me to be more than two days in a week her attendant. My uncle Selby would be glad to spare me. I shall not be able to bear a jest: and then what shall I be good for?

I have made a fine hand of coming to town, he says: and so I have: but if my heart is not quite so easy as it was, it is, I hope, a better, at least not a *worse* heart than I brought up with me. Could I only have admired this man, my excursion would not have been unhappy. But this gratitude, this *entangling*, with all its painful consequences—but let me say, with my grandmamma, the man is Sir Charles Grandison! The very man by whose virtues a Clementina was attracted. Upon my word, my dear, unhappy as she is, I rank her with the first of women.

I have not had a great deal of Sir Charles Grandison's company; but yet more, I am afraid, than I shall ever have again. Very true.—O heart! the most wayward of hearts, sigh if thou wilt!

You have seen how seldom he was with us when we were absolutely in his reach, and when he, as we thought, was in ours. But such a man cannot, ought not to be engrossed by one family. Bless me, Lucy! when he comes into public life (for has not his country a superior claim to him beyond every private one?), what moment can he have at liberty? Let me enumerate some of his present engagements that we know of.

The Danby family must have some further portion of his time.

The executorship in the disposal of the 3000*l.* in charity, in France as well as in England, will take up a good deal more.

My Lord W—— may be said to be under his tutelage, as to the future happiness of his life.

Miss Jervois's affairs, and the care he has for her person, engage much of his attention.

He is his own steward.

He is making alterations at Grandison Hall; and has a large genteel neighbourhood there, who long to have him reside among them; and he himself is fond of that seat.

His estate in Ireland is in a prosperous way, from the works he set on foot there, when he was on the spot; and he talks, as Dr. Bartlett has hinted to us, of making another visit to it.

His sister's match with Lord G—— is one of his cares.

He has services to perform for his friend Beauchamp, with his father and mother-in-law, for the facilitating his coming over.

The apprehended visit of Olivia gives him disturbance.

And the Bologna family in its various branches, and more especially Signor Jeronymo's dangerous state of health, and Signora Clementina's disordered mind—O Lucy!—what leisure has this man to be in love!—Yet how can I say so, when he is in love already? And with Clementina. —And don't you think that when he goes to France on the executorship account, he will make a visit to Bologna?— Ah, my dear! to be sure he will.

After he has left England, therefore, which I suppose he will quickly do, and when I am in Northamptonshire, what opportunities will your Harriet have to see him, except she can obtain, as a favour, the power of obliging his Emily, in her request to be with her? Then, Lucy, he may, on his return to England, once a year or so, on his visiting his ward, see, and thank for her care and love of his Emily, his half-estranged Harriet! Perhaps Lady *Clementina Grandison* will be with him! God restore her! Surely I shall be capable, if she be Lady Grandison, of rejoicing in her recovery!——

Fie upon it!—Why this involuntary tear? You would see it by the large blot it has made, if I did not mention it.

Excellent man!—Dr. Bartlett has just been telling me of a morning visit he received, before he went out of town, from the two sons of Mrs. Oldham.

One of them is about seven years old; the other about five; very fine children. He embraced them, the doctor says, with as much tenderness as if they were children of his own mother. He inquired into their inclinations, behaviour, and diversions; and engaged equally their love and reverence.

He told them that if they were good, he would love them; and said he had a dear friend whom he reverenced as his father, a man with white curling locks, he told the children, that they might know him at first sight, who would now and then, as he happened to be in town, make inquiries after their good behaviour, and reward them, as they gave him cause. Accordingly he had desired Dr. Bartlett to give them occasionally his countenance; as also to let their mother know that he should be glad of a visit from her and her three children, on his return to town.

The doctor had been to see her when he came to me. He found all three with her. The two younger, impressed by the venerable description Sir Charles had given of him, of their own accord, the younger, by the elder's example, fell down on their knees before him, and begged his blessing.

Mr. Oldham is about eighteen years of age; a well-inclined, well-educated youth. He was full of acknowledgments of the favour done him in this invitation.

The grateful mother could not contain herself. Blessings without number she invoked on her benefactor, for his goodness in taking such kind notice of her two sons, as he had done; and said he had been, ever since his gracious behaviour to her in Essex, the first and last in her prayers to heaven. But the invitation to herself, she declared, was too great an honour for her to accept of: she should not be able to stand in his presence. Alas! sir, said she, can the severest, truest penitence recall the guilty past?

The doctor said that Sir Charles Grandison ever made it a rule with him to raise the dejected and humble spirit. Your birth and education, madam, entitle you to a place in the first company: and where there are two lights in which the behaviour of any person may be set, though there has been unhappiness, he always remembers the most favourable, and forgets the other. I would advise you, madam (as he has invited you), by all means to come. He speaks with pleasure of your humility and good sense.

The doctor told me that Sir Charles had made inquiries after the marriage of Major O'Hara with Mrs. Jervois, and had satisfied himself that they were actually man and wife. Methinks I am glad, for Miss Jervois's sake, that her mother has changed her name. They lived not happily together since their last enterprise: for the man, who had long been a sufferer from poverty, was in fear of losing one half, at least, of his wife's annuity by what passed on that occasion; and accused her of putting him upon the misbehaviour he was guilty of; which had brought upon him, he said, the resentments of a man admired by all the world.

The attorney who visited Sir Charles from these people, at their request waited on him again, in their names, with hopes that they should not suffer in their annuity, and expressing their concern for having offended him.

Mrs. O'Hara also requested it as a favour to see her daughter.

Sir Charles commissioned the attorney, who is a man of repute, to tell them that if Mrs. O'Hara would come to St. James's Square next Wednesday, about five o'clock, Miss Jervois should be introduced to her; and she should be welcome to bring with her her husband and Captain Salmonet, that they might be convinced he bore no ill-will to either of them.

Adieu, till by and by. Miss Grandison is come, in one of her usual hurries, to oblige me to be present at the visit to be made her this afternoon by the Earl of G—— and Lady Gertrude, his sister, a maiden lady advanced in years, who is exceedingly fond of her nephew, and intends to make him heir of her large fortune.

Friday Night.

THE earl is an agreeable man: Lady Gertrude is a *very* agreeable woman. They saw Miss Grandison with the young lord's eyes; and were better pleased with her, as I told her afterwards, than *I* should have been, or than *they* would, had they known her as well as I do. She doubted not, she answered me, but I should find fault with her; and yet she was as good as for her life she could be.

Such an archness in every motion! Such a turn of the eye to me on my Lord G——'s assiduities! Such a fear in him of her correcting glance! Such a half-timid, half-free parade, when he had done anything that he intended to be obliging, and now and then an aiming at raillery, as if he were not *very* much afraid of her, and dared to speak his mind even to *her!* On her part, on those occasions, such an air, as if she had a learner before her; and was ready to rap his knuckles, had nobody been present to mediate for him; that though I could not but love her for her very archness, yet in my mind I could, for their sakes, but more for her own, have severely chidden her.

She is a charming woman; and everything she says and does becomes her. But I am so much afraid of what may be the case when the lover is changed into the husband, that I wish to myself now and then, when I see her so lively, that she would remember that there was once such a man as Captain Anderson. But she makes it a rule, she says, to remember nothing that will vex her.

Is not my memory (said she once) given me for my benefit, and shall I make it my torment? No, Harriet, I will leave that to be done by you wise ones, and see what good you will get by it.

Why *this,* Charlotte, replied I, the wise ones may have a *chance* to get by it—They will, very probably, by remembering past mistakes, avoid many inconveniences into which forgetfulness will run you lively ones.

Well, well, returned she, we are not all of us born to equal honour. Some of us are to be set up for warnings, some for examples: and the first are generally of greater use to the world than the other.

Now, Charlotte, said I, do you destroy the force of your own argument. Can the person who is singled out for the warning be near so happy as she that is set up for the example?

You are right, as far as I know, Harriet: but I obey the present impulse, and try to find an excuse afterwards for what that puts me upon: and all the difference is this, as to the reward I have a *joy;* you a *comfort:* but comfort is a poor word; and I can't bear it.

So Biddy, in 'The Tender Husband,' would have said, Charlotte. But, poor as the word is with you and her, give me *comfort* rather than joy, if they *must* be separated. But I see not but that a woman of my Charlotte's happy turn may have *both.*

She tapped my cheek—Take that, Harriet, for making a Biddy of me. I believe, if you have not *joy,* you have *comfort,* in your severity.

My heart as well as my cheeks glowed at the praises the earl and the lady both joined in (with a fervour that was creditable to their own hearts) of Sir Charles Grandison, while they told us what this man and that woman, of quality or consideration, said of him. Who would not be good? What is life without reputation? Do we not wish to be remembered with honour after death? And what a share of it has this excellent man in this life!—May nothing, for the honour-sake of human nature, to which he is so great an ornament, ever happen to tarnish it!

They were extremely obliging to *me*. I could not but be pleased at standing well in their opinion: but believe me, my dear, I did not enjoy their praises of *me* as I did those they gave *him*. Indeed I had the presumption, from the approbation given to what they said of him by my own heart, to imagine myself a sharer in them, though not in his merits. O Lucy! *ought* there not to have been a relation between us, since what I have said, from what I found in myself on hearing him praised, is a demonstration of a regard for him superior to the love of self?

Adieu, my Lucy. I know I have all your prayers.

Adieu, my dear!

LETTER VII.

Miss Byron.—In continuation.

Saturday, April 1.

DR. BARTLETT is one of the kindest as well as best of men. I believe he loves me as if I were his own child, but good men must be affectionate men. He received but this morning a letter from Sir Charles, and hastened to communicate some of its contents to me, though I could pretend to no other motive but curiosity for wishing to be acquainted with the proceedings of his patron.

Sir Charles dined, as he had intended, with Sir Hargrave and his friends. He complains, in his letter, of a riotous day: yet I think, adds he, it has led me into some useful reflections. It is not indeed agreeable to be the spectator of riot; but how easy to shun being a partaker in it! How easy to avoid the too freely circling glass, if a man is known to have established a rule to himself, from which he will not depart; and if it be not refused sullenly, but mirth and good humour the more studiously kept up by the person; who would else indeed be looked upon as a spy on unguarded folly! I heartily pitied a young man who, I daresay, has a good heart, but from false shame durst not assert the *freedom* to which every Englishman would claim a right in almost every other instance! He had once put by the glass, and excused himself on account of his health; but on being laughed at for a *sober dog,* as they phrased it, and asked if his *spouse* had not lectured him before he came out, he gave way to the wretched raillery: nor could I interfere at such a noisy moment with effect: they had laughed him out of his caution before I could be heard; and I left him there, at nine o'clock, trying with Bagenhall which should drink the deepest.

I wish my good Dr. Bartlett, you would throw together some serious considerations on this subject. You could touch it delicately; and such a discourse would not be un-useful to some of our neighbours even at Grandison Hall. What is it not that, in this single article, men sacrifice to false shame and false glory! Reason, health, fortune, personal elegance, the peace and order of their families; and all the comfort and honour of their after years. How peevish, how wretched, is the decline of a man worn out with intemperance! In a cool hour, resolutions might be formed that should stand the attack of a boisterous jest.

I obtained leave from Dr. Bartlett to transcribe this part of the letter. I thought my uncle would be pleased with it.

It was near ten at night before Sir Charles got to Lord W———'s, though but three miles from Sir Hargrave's. My lord rejoiced to see him; and after first compliments asked him if he had thought of what he had undertaken for him. Sir Charles told him that he was the more desirous of seeing him in his way to the Hall, because he wanted to know if his lordship held his mind as to marriage. He assured him he did, and would sign and seal to whatever he should stipulate for him.

I wished for a copy of this part of Sir Charles's letter, for the sake of my aunt, whose delicacy would, I thought, be charmed with it. He has been so good as to say he would transcribe it for me. I will enclose it, Lucy; and you will read it here:

"I cannot, my lord, said Sir Charles, engage that the lady will comply with the proposal I shall take the liberty to make to her mother and her. She is not more than three or four and thirty: she is handsome: she has a fine understanding: she is brought up an economist: she is a woman of good family: she has not, however, though born to happier prospects, a fortune worthy of your lordship's acceptance. Whatever that is, you will perhaps choose to give it to her family.

With all my heart and soul, nephew: but do you say she is handsome? Do you say she is of family? And has she so many good qualities?—Ah, nephew! she won't have me, I doubt.—And is she not too young, Sir Charles, to think of such a poor decrepit soul as I am?

All I can say to this, my lord, is, that the proposals on your part must be the more generous——

I will leave all those matters to you, kinsman——

This, my lord, I will take upon me to answer for, that she is a woman of principle; she will not give your lordship her hand, if she thinks she cannot make you a wife worthy of your utmost kindness: and now, my lord, I will tell you who she is, that you may make what other inquiries you think proper.

And then I named her to him and gave him pretty near the account of the family, and the circumstances and affairs of it, that I shall by and by give you: though you are not quite a stranger to the unhappy case.

My lord was in raptures: He knew something, he said, of the lady's father, and enough of the family, by hearsay, to confirm all I had said of them; and besought me to do my utmost to bring the affair to a speedy conclusion.

Sir Thomas Mansfield was a very good man, and much respected in his neighbourhood. He was once possessed of a large estate; but his father left him involved in a lawsuit to support his title to more than one half of it.

After it had been depending several years, it was at last, to the deep regret of all who knew him, by the chicanery of the lawyers of the opposite side, and the remissness of his

own, carried against him; and his expenses having been
very great in supporting for years his possession, he found
himself reduced, from an estate of near three thousand
pounds a year, to little more than five hundred. He had
six children: four sons and two daughters. His eldest son
died of grief in two months after the loss of the cause. The
second, now the eldest, is a melancholy man. The third is
a cornet of horse. The fourth is unprovided for; but all
three are men of worthy minds, and deserve better fortune.

The daughters are remarkable for their piety, patience,
good economy, and prudence. They are the most dutiful
of children, and most affectionate of sisters. They were
for three years the support of their father's spirits, and have
always been the consolation of their mother. They lost
their father about four years ago: and it is even edifying to
observe how elegantly they support the family reputation in
their fine old mansion-house, by the prudent management
of their little income; for the mother leaves every house-
hold care to them; and they make it a rule to conclude
the year with discharging every demand that can be made
upon them, and to commence the new year absolutely clear
of the world, and with some cash in hand; yet were brought
up in affluence, and to the expectation of handsome fortunes; for besides that they could have no thought of losing
their cause, they had very great and reasonable prospects from
Mr. Calvert, an uncle by their mother's side; who was rich
in money, and had besides an estate in land of 1500*l.* a
year. He always declared that for the sake of his sister's
children he would continue a single man; and kept his
word till he was upwards of seventy; when, being very in-
firm in health, and defective even to dotage in his understanding, Bolton, his steward, who had always stood in the
way of his inclination to have his eldest niece for his companion and manager, at last contrived to get him married
to a young creature under twenty, one of the servants in the
house; who brought him a child at seven months; and was
with child again at the old man's death, which happened in
eighteen months after his marriage: and then a will was

provided, in which he gave all he had to his wife and her children born, and to be born, within a year after his demise. This steward and woman now live together as man and wife.

A worthy clergyman, who hoped it might be in my power to procure them redress, either in the one case or in the other, gave me the above particulars; and, upon inquiry, finding everything to be as represented, I made myself acquainted with the widow lady and her sons: and it was impossible to see them at their own house and not respect the daughters for their amiable qualities.

I desired them, when I was last down, to put into my hands their titles, deeds, and papers; which they have done; and they have been laid before counsel, who give a very hopeful account of them.

Being fully authorised by my lord, I took leave of him over-night, and set out early in the morning directly for Mansfield House. I arrived there soon after their breakfast was over, and was received by Lady Mansfield, her sons (who happened to be all at home), and her two daughters, with politeness.

After some general conversation, I took Lady Mansfield aside; and making an apology for my freedom, asked her if Miss Mansfield were, to her knowledge, engaged in her affections?

She answered she was *sure* she was not: Ah, sir! said she, a man of your observation must know that the daughters of a decayed family of some note in the world do not easily get husbands. Men of great fortunes look higher: men of small must look out for wives to enlarge them; and men of genteel businesses are afraid of young women better born than portioned. Everybody knows not that my girls can bend to their condition; and they must be contented to live single all their lives; and so they will choose to do, rather than not marry creditably, and with some prospect.

I then opened my mind fully to her. She was agreeably surprised: But who, sir, said she, would expect such a proposal from the next heir to Lord W——?

I made known to her how much in earnest I was in this proposal, as well for my lord's sake as for the young lady's. I will take care, madam, said I, that Miss Mansfield, if she will consent to make Lord W—— happy, shall have very handsome settlements, and such an allowance of pinmoney as shall enable her to gratify every moderate, every reasonable wish of her heart.

Was it possible, she asked, for such an affair to be brought about? Would my lord—there she stopt.

I said I would be answerable for him: and desired her to break the matter to her daughter directly.

I left Lady Mansfield and joined the brothers, who were with their two sisters; and soon after Miss Mansfield was sent for by her mother.

After they had been a little while together, my Lady Mansfield sent to speak with me. They were both silent when I came in. The mother was at a loss what to say: the daughter was still in greater confusion.

I addressed myself to the mother. You have, I perceive, madam, acquainted Miss Mansfield with the proposal I made to you. I am fully authorised to make it. Propitious be your silence!—There never was, proceeded I, a treaty of marriage set on foot, which had not its conveniencies and inconveniencies. My lord is greatly afflicted with the gout: there is too great a disparity in years. These are the inconveniencies wnich are to be considered of for the lady.

On the other hand, if Miss Mansfield can give in to the proposal, she will be received by my lord as a blessing; as one whose acceptance of him will lay him under an obligation to her. If this proposal could not have been made with dignity and honour to the lady, it had not come from me.

The conveniencies to yourselves will more properly fall under the consideration of yourselves and family. One thing only I will suggest, that an alliance with so rich a man as Lord W——, will make perhaps some people tremble, who now think themselves secure.

But, madam (to the still silent daughter), let not a regard

for me bias you: your family may be sure of my best services, whether my proposal be received or rejected.

My lord (I must deal sincerely with you) has lived a life of error. He thinks so himself. I am earnest to have him see the difference, and to have an opportunity to rejoice with him upon it.

I stopt; but both being still silent, the mother looking on the daughter, the daughter glancing now and then her conscious eye on the mother, If, madam, said I, you *can* give your hand to Lord W——, I will take care that settlements shall exceed your expectation. What I have observed, as well as heard, of Miss Mansfield's temper and goodness, is the principal motive of my application to her, in preference to all the women I know.

But permit me to say that were your affections engaged to the lowest honest man on earth, I would not wish for your favour to Lord W——. And, further, if, madam, you think you should have but the shadow of a hope to induce your compliance, that my lord's death would be more agreeable to you than his life, then would I not, for your morality's sake, wish you to engage. In a word, I address myself to you, Miss Mansfield, as to a woman of honour and conscience: if your conscience bids you *doubt,* reject the proposal; and this not only for my lord's sake, but for your own.

Consider, if, without too great a force upon your inclinations, you can behave with that condescension and indulgence to a man who has hastened advanced age upon himself, which I have thought from your temper I might hope.

I have said a great deal, because you, ladies, were silent; and because explicitness in every case becomes the proposer. Give me leave to retire for a few moments.

I withdrew, accordingly, to the brothers and sister. I did not think I ought to mention to *them* the proposal I had made: it might perhaps have engaged them all in its favour, as it was of such evident advantage to the whole family; and that might have imposed a difficulty on the lady, that neither for her own sake, nor my lord's, it would have been just to lay upon her.

Lady Mansfield came out to me and said, I presume, sir, as we are a family which misfortune as well as love has closely bound together, you will allow it to be mentioned——

To the whole family, Madam!—By all means. I wanted only first to know whether Miss Mansfield's affections were disengaged: and now you shall give me leave to attend Miss Mansfield. I am party for my Lord W——: Miss Mansfield is a party: your debates will be the more free in our absence. If I find her averse, believe me, madam, I will not endeavour to persuade her. On the contrary, if she declare against accepting the proposal, I will be her advocate, though every one else should vote in its favour.

The brothers and sisters looked upon one another: I left the mother to propose it to them; and stept into the inner parlour to Miss Mansfield.

She was sitting with her back to the door, in a meditating posture. She started at my entrance.

I talked of indifferent subjects, in order to divert her from the important one that had taken up her whole attention.

It would have been a degree of oppression to her to have entered with her upon a subject of so much consequence to her while we were alone; and when her not having given a negative was to be taken as a modest affirmative.

Lady Mansfield soon joined us.—My dear daughter, said she, we are all unanimous. We are agreed to leave everything to Sir Charles Grandison: and we hope *you* will.

She was silent. I will only ask you, madam, said I to her, if you have any wish to take time to consider of the matter? Do you think you shall be easier in your mind if you take time?—She was silent.

I will not at this time, my good Miss Mansfield, urge you further. I will make my report to Lord W——, and you shall be sure of his joyful approbation of the steps I have taken, before your final consent shall be asked for. But that I may not be employed in a doubtful cause, let me be commissioned to tell my lord that you are disengaged; and that you wholly resign yourself to your mother's advice.

She bowed her head.

And that *you,* madam, to Lady Mansfield, are not averse to enter into treaty upon this important subject.

Averse, sir! said the mother, bowing, and gratefully smiling.

I will write the particulars of our conversation to Lord W——, and my opinion of settlements, and advise him (if I am not forbid) to make a visit at Mansfield House. [I stopt: they were both silent.] If possible, I will attend my lord in his first visit. I hope, madam, to Miss Mansfield, you will not dislike him; I am sure he will be charmed with you: he is far from being disagreeable in his person: his temper is not bad. *Your* goodness will make *him* good. I daresay that he will engage your gratitude; and I defy a good mind to separate love from gratitude.

We returned to the company. I had all their blessings pronounced at once, as from one mouth. The melancholy brother was enlivened: who knows but the consequence of this alliance may illuminate his mind? I could see by the pleasure they all had, in beholding him capable of joy on the occasion, that they *hoped* it would. The unhappy situation of the family affairs, as it broke the heart of the eldest brother, fixed a gloom on the temper of this gentleman.

I was prevailed upon to dine with them. In the conversation we had at and after dinner, their minds opened, and their characters rose upon me. Lord W—— will be charmed with Miss Mansfield. I am delighted to think that my mother's brother will be happy, in the latter part of his life, with a wife of so much prudence and goodness as I am sure this lady will make him. On one instance of her very obliging behaviour to me, I whispered her sister, Pray, Miss Fanny, tell Miss Mansfield, but not till I am gone, that she knows not the inconveniences she is bringing upon herself. I may perhaps hereafter have the boldness to look for the same favour from my aunt, that I meet with from Miss Mansfield.

If my sister, returned she, should ever misbehave to her benefactor, I will deny my relation to her.

You will soon have another letter from me, with an account of the success of my visit to Sir Harry Beauchamp and his lady. *We* must have our Beauchamp among us, my dear friend: I should rather say, *you* must among *you;* for I shall not be long in England. He will supply to you, my dear Dr. Bartlett, the absence (it will not, I hope, be a long one) of your   CHARLES GRANDISON."

SIR CHARLES, I remember, as the doctor read, mentions getting leave for his Beauchamp to come over, who, he says, will supply his absence to *him*—but, ah, Lucy! Who, let me have the boldness to ask, shall supply it to your *Harriet?* —Time, my dear, will do *nothing* for me, except I could hear something very much amiss of this man.

I have a great suspicion that the first part of the letter enclosed related to me. The doctor looked *so* earnestly at me when he skipt two sides of it; and, as I thought, with so much compassion!—To be sure, it was about me.

What would I give to know as much of his mind as Dr. Bartlett knows! If I thought he pitied the poor Harriet—I should scorn myself. I am, I *will* be, above his pity, Lucy. In this believe your   HARRIET BYRON.

LETTER VIII.

Miss Byron.—In continuation.

Sunday Night, April 2.

DR. BARTLETT has received from Sir Charles an account of what passed last Friday between him and Sir Harry and Lady Beauchamp. By the doctor's allowance, I enclose it to you.

In this letter, Lucy, you will see him in a new light; and as a man whom there is no resisting when he resolves to carry a point. But it absolutely convinces me of what indeed I before suspected, that he has not a high opinion of our sex in general: and this I will put down as a blot in his character. He treats us, in Lady Beauchamp, as perverse, humorsome babies; loving power, yet not knowing how to use it. See him so delicate in his behaviour and address to Miss Mansfield, and carry in your thoughts his gaiety and adroit management to Lady Beauchamp, as in this letter, and you will hardly think him the same man. Could he be anything to me, I should be more than half afraid of him: yet *this* may be said in his behalf;—He but accommodates himself to the persons he has to deal with:—He can be a man of gay wit, when he pleases to *descend,* as indeed his sister Charlotte has often found, as she has given occasion for the exercise of that talent in him:—yet, that virtue for its *own sake,* is his choice; since, had he been a free liver, he would have been a dangerous man.

But I will not anticipate too much: read it here, if you please.

LETTER IX.

Sir Charles Grandison to Dr. Bartlett.
[Enclosed in the preceding.]

Grandison Hall, Friday Night, March 31.

I ARRIVED at Sir Harry Beauchamp's about twelve this day. He and his lady expected me from the letter which I wrote and showed you before I left the town; in which, you know, I acquainted Sir Harry with his son's earnest desire to throw himself at his feet, and to pay his duty to his mother, in England; and engaged to call myself, either this day or to-morrow, for an answer.

Sir Harry received me with great civility, and even affection. Lady Beauchamp, said he, will be with us in a moment. I am afraid you will not meet with all the civility from her on the errand you are come upon, that a man of Sir Charles Grandison's character deserves to meet with from all the world. We have been unhappy together ever since we had your letter. I long to see my son: your friendship for him establishes him in my heart. But—and then he cursed the apron-string tenure by which, he said, he held his peace.

You will allow me, Sir Harry, said I, to address myself in my own way to my lady. You give me pleasure in letting me know that the difficulty is not with you. You have indeed, sir, one of the most prudent young men in the world for your son. His heart is in your hand: you may form it as you please.

She is coming! she is coming! interupted he. We are all in pieces: we were in the midst of a feud when you arrived. If she is not civil to you——

In swam the lady; her complexion raised; displeasure in her looks to me, and indignation in her air to Sir Harry; as if they had not had their contention out, and she was ready to renew it.

With as obliging an air as I could assume, I paid my compliments to her. She received them with great stiffness; swelling at Sir Harry: who sidled to the door, in a moody and sullen manner, and then slipt out.

You are Sir Charles Grandison, I suppose, sir, said she; I never saw you before: I have heard much talk of you.—But, pray, sir, are good men *always* officious men? Cannot they perform the obligations of friendship without discomposing families?

You see me *now,* madam, in an evil moment, if you are displeased with me: but I am not used to the displeasure of ladies; I do my utmost not to deserve it; and let me tell you, madam, that I will not suffer *you* to be displeased with me.

I took her half-reluctant hand and led her to a chair, and seated myself in another near her.

I see, sir, you have your arts.

She took the fire-screen that hung by the side of the chimney and held it before her face, now glancing at me, now turning away her eye, as if resolved to be displeased.

You come upon a hateful errand, sir: I have been unhappy ever since your officious letter came.

I am sorry for it, madam. While you are warm with the remembrance of a past misunderstanding, I will not offer to reason with you: but let me, madam, see less discomposure in your looks. I want to take my impressions of you from more placid features: I am a painter, madam: I love to draw ladies' pictures. Will you have this pass for a first sitting?

She knew not what to do with her anger: she was loath to part with it.

You are impertinent, Sir Charles—excuse me—you are impertinent.

I do excuse you, Lady Beauchamp; and the rather, as I am sure you do not think me so. Your freedom is a mark of your favour; and I thank you for it.

You treat me as a child, sir——

I treat all angry people as children: I love to humour them. Indeed, Lady Beauchamp, you must not be angry with me. *Can* I be mistaken? Don't I see in your aspect the woman of sense and reason?—I never blame a lady for her humorsomeness, so much as, in my mind, I blame her mother.

Sir! said she. I smiled. She bit her lip to avoid returning a smile.

Her character, my dear friend, is not, you know, that of an ill-tempered woman, though haughty, and a lover of power.

I have heard much of you, Sir Charles Grandison: but I am quite mistaken in you: I expected to see a grave, formal young man, his prim mouth set in plaits: but you are a joker; and a free man; a *very* free man, I do assure you.

I would be *thought* decently free, madam; but not *impertinent*. I see with pleasure a returning smile. Oh that ladies knew how much smiles become their features!—Very few causes can justify a woman's anger—your sex, madam, was given to delight, not to torment us.

Torment you, sir!—Pray, has Sir Harry——

Sir Harry cannot look pleased when his lady is *dis*-pleased: I saw that you were, madam, the moment I beheld you. I hope I am not an unwelcome visitor to Sir Harry for one hour (I intend to stay no longer), that he received me with so disturbed a countenance, and has now withdrawn himself, as if to avoid me.

To tell you the truth, Sir Harry and I have had a dispute: but he always speaks of Sir Charles Grandison with pleasure.

Is he not offended with me, madam, for the contents of the letter——

No, sir, and I suppose you hardly think he is—But *I* am——

Dear madam, let me beg your interest in favour of the contents of it.

She took fire—rose up——

I besought her patience—Why should you wish to keep abroad a young man who is a credit to his family, and who *ought* to be, if he is *not,* the joy of his father! Let him owe to your generosity, madam, that recall which he solicits: it will become your character: he cannot be always kept abroad: be it your own generous work——

What, sir—pray, sir—with an angry brow——

You must not be angry with me, madam—(I took her hand)—you can't be angry in earnest——

Sir Charles Grandison—you are—she withdrew her hand; *you are,* repeated she—and seemed ready to call names——

I *am* the Grandison you call me; and I honour the maternal character. You must permit me to honour *you,* madam.

I *wonder,* sir——

I will not be denied. The world reports misunderstandings between you and Mr. Beauchamp. That busy world that will be meddling knows your power and his dependence. You must not let it charge you with an ill use of that power: if you do, *you* will have its blame, when you might have its praise: *he* will have its pity.

What, sir, do you think your fine letters and smooth words will avail in favour of a young fellow who has treated me with disrespect?

You are misinformed, madam.—I am willing to have a

greater dependence upon your justice, upon your goodnature, than upon anything I can urge either by letter or speech. Don't let it be said that you are not to be prevailed on— A woman not to be prevailed on to join in an act of justice, of kindness; for the honour of the sex, let it not be said.

Honour of the sex, sir!—Fine talking!—Don't I know that were I to consent to his coming over, the first thing would be to have his annuity augmented out of my fortune? He and his father would be in a party against me. Am I not already a sufferer through him in his father's love?— You don't know, sir, what has passed between Sir Harry and me within this half-hour—but don't talk to me: I won't hear of it: the young man hates me: I hate him; and ever will.

She made a motion to go.

With a respectful air, I told her she must not leave me. My motive deserved not, I said, that both she and Sir Harry should leave me in displeasure.

You know but too well, resumed she, how acceptable your officiousness (I must call it so) is to Sir Harry.

And *does* Sir Harry, madam, favour his son's suit? You rejoice me: let not Mr. Beauchamp know that he does; and do *you,* my dear Lady Beauchamp, take the whole merit of it to yourself. How will he revere you for your goodness to him! And what an obligation, if, as you say, Sir Harry is inclined to favour him, will you, by your generous first motion, lay upon Sir Harry!

Obligation upon Sir Harry! Yes, Sir Charles Grandison, I have laid too many obligations already upon him for his gratitude.

Lay this one more. You own you have had a misunderstanding this morning; Sir Harry is withdrawn, I suppose, with his heart full; let me, I beseech you, make up the misunderstanding. I have been happy in this way— Thus we will order it—We will desire him to walk in. I will beg *your* interest with him in favour of the contents of the letter I sent. His compliance will follow as an act of obligingness to you. The grace of the action will be yours. I will be answerable for Mr. Beauchamp's gratitude.—Dear madam, hesitate not. The young gentleman must come over one day: let the favour of its being an early one be owing entirely to you.

You are a strange man, sir: I don't like you at all: you will persuade me out of my reason.

Let us, madam, as Mr. Beauchamp and I are already the dearest of friends, begin a *family* understanding. Let St. James's Square, and Berkley Square, when you come to town, be a next-door neighbourhood. Give me the consideration of being the bondsman for the duty of Mr. Beauchamp to you, as well as to his father.

She was silent: but looked vexed and irresolute.

My sisters, madam, are amiable women. You will be pleased with them. Lord L—— is a man worthy of Sir Harry's acquaintance. We shall want nothing, if you would think so, but Mr. Beauchamp's presence among us.

What! I suppose you design your maiden sister for the *young fellow*—but if you do, sir, you must ask me for—there she stopt.

Indeed, I do not. He is not at present disposed to marry. He never will without his father's approbation, and let me say —*yours*. My sister is addressed to by Lord G——, and I hope will soon be married to him.

And do you say so, Sir Charles Grandison?—Why then you are a more disinterested man that I thought you in this application to Sir Harry. I had no doubt but the *young fellow* was to be brought over to marry Miss Grandison; and that he was to be made worthy of her at my expense.

She enjoyed, as it seemed, by her manner of pronouncing the words *young fellow,* that designed contempt which was a tacit confession of the consequence he once was of to her.

I do assure you, madam, that I know not his heart, if he has at present any thoughts of marriage.

She seemed pleased at this assurance.

I repeated my wishes that she would take to herself the merit of allowing Mr. Beauchamp to return to his native country: and that she would let me see her hand in Sir Harry's before I left them.

And pray, sir, as to his place of residence, *were* he to come: do you think he shall live under the same roof with me?

You shall govern that point, madam, as you approve, or disapprove of his behaviour to you.

His behaviour to me, sir?—One house cannot, shall not, hold him and me.

I think, madam, that *you* should direct in this article. I hope, after a little while, so to order my affairs as constantly to reside in England. I should think myself very happy, if I could prevail upon Mr. Beauchamp to live with *me*.

But I must see him, I suppose?

Not, madam, unless you shall think it right, for the sake of the world's opinion, that you should.

I can't consent——

You *can,* madam! You *do!*—I cannot allow Lady Beauchamp to be one of those women who, having insisted upon a wrong point, can be convinced, yet not know how to recede with a grace.—Be so kind to *yourself,* as to let Sir Harry know that you think it right for Mr. Beauchamp to return; but that it must be upon your own conditions: then, madam, make those conditions generous ones; and how will Sir Harry adore you! How will Mr. Beauchamp revere you! How shall I esteem you!

What a strange impertinent have I before me!

I love to be called names by a lady. If undeservedly, she lays herself by them under obligation to me, which she cannot be generous, if she resolves not to repay. Shall I endeavour to find out Sir Harry? Or will you, madam?

Was you ever, Sir Charles Grandison, denied by any woman to whom you sued for favour?

I think, madam, I hardly ever was: but it was because I never sued for a favour that it was not for a lady's honour to grant. This is the case now; and this makes me determine that I will not be denied the grant of my present request. Come, come, madam! How can a woman of your ladyship's good sense (taking her hand and leading her to the door) seem to want to be persuaded to do a thing she knows in her heart to be right! Let us find Sir Harry.

Strange man!—Unhand me!—*He* has used me unkindly—
Overcome him then by your generosity. But, dear Lady Beauchamp, taking both her hands and smiling confidently in her face [I could, my dear Dr. Bartlett, do so to Lady Beauchamp], will you make me believe that a woman of your spirit (you have a charming spirit, Lady Beauchamp) did not give Sir Harry as much reason to complain as he gave you?—I am sure by his disturbed countenance——

Now, Sir Charles Grandison, you are downright affronting. Unhand me!

This misunderstanding is owing to my officious letter. I should have waited on you in person. I should from the first have put it in your power to do a graceful and obliging thing. I ask your pardon. I am not *used* to make differences between man and wife.

I touched first one hand, then the other, of the perverse baby with my lips—Now am I forgiven: now is my friend Beauchamp permitted to return to his native country: now are Sir Harry and his lady reconciled—come, come, madam, it must be so.—What foolish things are the quarrels of married people!—They must come to an agreement again; and the sooner the better; before hard blows are struck that will leave marks—Let us, dear madam, find out Sir Harry——

And then, with an air of vivacity, that women, whether in courtship or out of it, dislike not, I was leading her once more to the door, and, as I intended, *to* Sir Harry, wherever he could be found.

Hold, hold, sir! resisting; but with features far more placid than she had suffered to be before visible—If I *must* be compelled—You are a strange man, Sir Charles Grandison—if I must be compelled to see Sir Harry—but you are a strange man—and she rang the bell.

Lady Beauchamp, Dr. Bartlett, is one of those who would be more ready to forgive an innocent freedom, than to be gratified by a profound respect; otherwise I had not treated her with so little ceremony. Such women are formidable only to those who are afraid of their anger, or who make it a serious thing.

But when the servant appeared, she not knowing how to condescend, I said, Go to your master, sir, and tell him that your lady requests the favour——

Requests the favour! repeated she; but in a low voice: which was no bad sign.

The servant went with a message worded with more civility than perhaps he was used to carry to his master from his lady.

Now, dear Lady Beauchamp, for your own sake; for Sir Harry's sake; make happy; and be happy: are there not, dear madam, unhappinesses enow in life, that we must willfully add to them?

Sir Harry came in sight. He stalked towards us with a parade like that of a young officer wanting to look martial at the head of his company.

Could I have seen him before he entered, my work would have been easier. But his hostile air disposed my lady to renew hostilities.

She turned her face aside, then her person; and the cloudy indignation with which she entered at first, again overspread her features. Ought wrath, Dr. Bartlett, to be so ready to attend a female will?—Surely, thought I, my lady's present airs, after what has passed between her and me, can be only owing to the fear of making a precedent, and being thought too easily persuaded.

Sir Harry, said I, addressing myself to him, I have obtained Lady Beauchamp's pardon for the officious letter——

Pardon, Sir Charles Grandison! You are a good man, and it was kindly intended——

He was going on: anger from his eyes flashed upon his cheek bones, and made them shine. My lady's eyes struck fire at Sir Harry, and showed that she was not *afraid* of him.

Better *intended* than done, interrupted I, since my lady tells me that it was the occasion of a misunderstanding—But, sir, all will be right: my lady assures me that you are not disinclined to comply with the contents; and she has the goodness——

Sir Harry cleared up at once—May I hope Madam—And offered to take her hand. She withdrew it with an air.

Stothard del.

Pray, Sir Charles, interrupted the lady——
To give me hopes that she——
Pray, Sir Charles——
Will use her interest to confirm you in your favourable sentiments——

Sir Harry cleared up at once—May I hope, madam—And offered to take her hand.

She withdrew it with an air. O Dr. Bartlett! I must have been thought an unpolite husband, had she been my wife!

I took her hand. Excuse this freedom, Sir Harry—For Heaven's sake, madam (whispering), do what I know you *will* do, with a grace—Shall there be a misunderstanding, and the husband court a refused hand?—I then forced her half unwilling hand into his, with an air that I intended should have both freedom and respect in it.

What a man have we got here, Sir Harry? This cannot be the modest man that you have praised to me—I thought a good man must of necessity be bashful, if not sheepish; and here your visitor is the boldest man in England.

The righteous, Lady Beauchamp, said Sir Harry, with an aspect but half-conceding, *is bold as a lion.*

And *must* I be compelled thus, and by such a man, to forgive you, Sir Harry?—Indeed you were very unkind.

And you, Lady Beauchamp, were very cruel.

I did not think, sir, when I laid my fortune at your feet——

O Lady Beauchamp! You said cutting things! *Very* cutting things!

And did not you, Sir Harry, say it should be so?—So *very* peremptorily!

Not, madam, till you *as* peremptorily——

A little recrimination, thought I, there must be, to keep each in countenance on their past folly.

Ah! Sir Charles—You may rejoice that you are not married, said Sir Harry.

Dear Sir Harry, said I, we must bear with ladies. They are *meek* good creatures—They——

Meek! Sir Charles, repeated Sir Harry, with a half-angry

smile, and shrugging, as if his shoulder had been hurt with his wife's meekness—I say, *meek!*

Now, Sir Charles Grandison, said my lady, with an air of threatening——

I was desirous either of turning the lady's displeasure into a jest, or of diverting it from the first object, in order to make her play with it, till she had lost it.

Women are of gentle natures, pursued I; and being accustomed to be humoured, opposition sits not easy upon them. Are they not kind to us, Sir Harry, when they allow of our superiority, by expecting us to bear with their pretty perversenesses?

O Sir Charles Grandison! said my lady; both her hands lifted up.

Let us be contented, proceeded I, with such their kind acknowledgments; and in pity to them, and in compliment to ourselves, bear with their foibles.—See, madam, I ever was an advocate for the ladies.

Sir Charles, I have no patience with you——

What can a poor woman do, continued I, when opposed? She can only be a little violent in *words,* and when she has said as much as she chooses to say, be perhaps a little sullen. For my part, were I so happy as to call a woman mine, and she *happened* to be in the wrong, I would endeavour to be in the right, and trust to her good sense to recover her temper: arguments only beget arguments.—Those reconciliations are the most durable, in which the lady makes the first advances.

What doctrine is this, Sir Charles! You are not the man I took you for.—I believe, in my conscience, that you are not near so good a man as the world reports you.

What, madam! because I pretend to know a little of the sex? Surely, Lady Beauchamp, a man of common penetration may see to the bottom of a woman's heart. A cunning woman cannot hide it: a good woman will not. You are not, madam, such mysteries, as some of us think you. Whenever you know your *own* minds, we need not be long doubtful: that is all the difficulty: and I will vindicate you, as to that——

As how, pray, sir?

Women, madam, were designed to be *dependent,* as well as *gentle* creatures; and, of consequence, when left to their own wills, they know not what to resolve upon.

I was hoping, Sir Charles, just now, that you would stay to dinner: but if you talk at this rate, I believe I shall be ready to wish you out of the house.

Sir Harry looked as if he were half willing to be diverted at what passed between his lady and me. It was better for *me* to say what he could not but subscribe to by his feeling than for him to say it. Though reproof seldom amends a determinate spirit, such a one as this lady's; yet a man who suffers by it, cannot but have some joy when he hears his sentiments spoken by a by-stander. This freedom of mine seemed to save the married pair a good deal of recrimination.

You remind me, madam, that I must be gone; rising, and looking at my watch.

You must not leave us, Sir Charles, said Sir Harry.

I beg excuse, Sir Harry—yours, also, madam, smiling—Lady Beauchamp must not twice wish me out of the house.

I will *not* excuse you, sir, replied she—if you have a desire to see the matter completed—she stopt—You must stay to dinner, be *that* as it will.

' Be that is it will,' madam!—You shall not recede.

Recede! I have not yet complied——

Oh these women! they are so used to courtship, that they know not how to do right things without it—and, pardon me, madam, not always with it.

Bold man—have I consented——

Have you not, madam, given a *lady's* consent? *That,* we men expect not to be very explicit, very gracious—it is from such *non-*negative consents, that we men make silence answer all we wish.

I leave Sir Charles Grandison to manage this point, said Sir Harry. In my conscience, I think the common observation just: a stander-by sees more of the game than he that plays.

It ever will be so, Sir Harry—But I will tell you, my lady and I have as good as agreed the matter——

I have agreed to nothing, Sir Harry——

Hush, madam—I am doing you credit.—Lady Beauchamp speaks *aside* sometimes, Sir Harry: you are not to hear anything she says that you don't like.

Then I am afraid I must stop my ears for eight hours out of twelve.

That was *aside,* Lady Beauchamp—you are not to hear that.

To sit like a fool and hear myself abused—a pretty figure I make! Sir Charles Grandison, let me tell you, that you are the first man that ever treated me like a fool.

Excuse, madam, a little innocent raillery—I met you both with a discomposure on your countenances. I was the occasion of it by the letter I sent to Sir Harry. I will not *leave* you discomposed. I think you a woman of sense; and my request is of such a nature, that the granting of it will confirm to me that you are so—but you *have* granted it——

I have *not.*

That's charmingly said—my lady will not undervalue the compliment she is inclined to make you, Sir Harry. The moment *you* ask for her compliance, she will not refuse to your affection what she makes a difficulty to grant to the entreaty of an almost stranger.

Let it, let it be so! Lady Beauchamp, said Sir Harry: and he clasped his arms about her as she sat——

There never was such a man as this Sir Charles Grandison in the world!—It is a contrivance between you, Sir Harry—

Dear Lady Beauchamp, resumed I, depreciate not your compliment to Sir Harry. There wanted not contrivance, I dare to hope (if there *did,* it had it not), to induce Lady Beauchamp to do a right, a kind, an obliging thing.

Let me, my dearest Lady Beauchamp, said Sir Harry—Let me request——

At *your* request, Sir Harry—But not at Sir Charles's.

This is noble, said I. I thank you, madam, for the absent youth. Both husband and son will think themselves favoured by you: and the more, as I am sure that you will, by the cheerful welcome which you will give the young man, show that it is a sincere compliment that you have made to Sir Harry.

This man has a strange way of flattering one into acts of—of—what shall I call them?—But, Sir Harry, Mr. Beauchamp must not, I believe, live with us——

Sir Harry hesitated.

I was afraid of opening the wound. I have a request to make to you both, said I. It is this: that Mr. Beauchamp may be permitted to live with me; and attend you, madam, and his father, as a visitor, at your own command. My sister, I believe, will be very soon married to Lord G——.

That is to be certainly so? interrupted the lady.

It is, madam.

But what shall we say, my dear, resumed Sir Harry—don't fly out again—as to the provision for my son?—Two hundred a year—what is two hundred a year——

Why then let it be three, answered she.

I have a handsome and improvable estate, said I. I have no demands but those of reason upon me. I would not offer a plea for his coming to England (and I am sure he would not have come if I had) without his father's consent: in which, madam, he hoped for yours. You shall not, sir, allow him either the two or three hundred a year. See him with love, with indulgence (he will deserve both); and think not of anything else for my Beauchamp.

There is no bearing this, my dear, said Sir Harry; leaning upon his lady's shoulder, as he sat, tears in his eyes—My son is already, as I have heard, greatly obliged to this his true friend—Do you, do you, madam, answer for me, and for yourself.

She was overcome: yet pride had its share with generosity. You *are*, said she, the Grandison I have heard of: but I will not be under obligations to you—not *pecuniary* ones, however. No, Sir Harry! Recall your son: I will trust to your love: do for him what you please: let him be independent on this *insolent* man [she said this with a smile, that made it obliging]; and if we are to be visitors, friends, neighbours, let it be on an equal foot, and let him have nothing to reproach us with.

I was agreeably surprised at this emanation (shall I call

it?) of goodness: she is really not a bad woman, but a perverse one: in short, one of those whose passions, when rightly touched, are liable to sudden and surprising turns.

Generous, charming Lady Beauchamp! said I: now *are* you the woman whom I have so often heard praised for many good qualities: now will the portrait be a just one!

Sir Harry was in raptures; but had liked to have spoiled all, by making me a compliment on the force of example.

Be this, said I, the result—Mr. Beauchamp comes over. He will be pleased with whatever you do: at your feet, madam, he shall acknowledge your favour: my home shall be his, if you permit it: on *me,* he shall *confer* obligations: from *you* he shall receive them. If any considerations of family prudence (there *are* such, and very just ones) restrain you from allowing him, at present, what your generosity would wish to do——

Lady Beauchamp's colour was heightened: She interrupted me—We are not, Sir Charles, so scanty in our fortune——

Well, my dear Lady Beauchamp, be all that as you please: not one retrospect of the past——

Yes, Sir Charles, but there shall: his allowance has been lessened for some years; not from considerations of *family prudence*—but—well, 'tis all at an end, proceeded she—When the young man returns, you, Sir Harry, for my sake, and for the sake of this strange, unaccountable creature, shall pay him the whole arrear.

Now, my dear Lady Beauchamp, said I, lifting her hand to my lips, permit me to give you joy. All doubts and misgivings so triumphantly got over, so solid a foundation laid for family harmony—What was the moment of your nuptials to this? Sir Harry, I congratulate you: you may be, and I believe you have been, as happy as most men; but now you will be still happier.

Indeed, Sir Harry, said she, you provoked me in the morning: I should not else——

Sir Harry owned himself to blame; and thus the lady's pride was set down softly.

She desired Sir Harry to write, before the day concluded,

the invitation of return to Mr. Beauchamp; and to do her all the credit in it that she might claim from the last part of the conversation; but not to mention anything of the first.

She afterwards abated a little of this right spirit by saying, I think, Sir Harry, you need not mention anything of the *arrears,* as I may call them—but only the future 600*l.* a year. One would surprise him a little, you know, and be twice thanked——

Surprises of such a nature as this, my dear Dr. Bartlett; *pecuniary* surprises!—I don't love them—they are double taxes upon the gratitude of a worthy heart. Is it not enough for a generous mind to labour under a sense of obligation? —Pride, vainglory, must be the motive of such narrow-minded benefactors: a truly beneficent spirit cannot take delight in beholding the quivering lip indicating the palpitating heart; in seeing the downcast countenance, the uplifted hands, and working muscles of a fellow-creature, who, but for unfortunate accidents, would perhaps himself have had the *will,* with the *power,* of showing a more graceful benevolence!

I was so much afraid of hearing *further* abatements of Lady Beauchamp's goodness; so willing to depart with favourable impressions of her for her own sake; and at the same time so desirous to reach the Hall that night; that I got myself excused, though with difficulty, staying to dine; and accepting of a dish of chocolate, I parted with Sir Harry and my lady, both in equal good humour with themselves and me.

Could you have thought, my dear friend, that I should have succeeded so very happily as I have done, in this affair, and at one meeting?

I think that the father and step-mother should have the full merit with our Beauchamp of a turn so unexpected. Let him not, therefore, ever see this letter, that he may take his impression of the favour done him from that which Sir Harry will write to him.

My cousin Grandison, whom I hoped to find here, left the Hall on Tuesday last, though he knew of my intention to be down. I am sorry for it. Poor Everard! He has been a great while pretty good. I am afraid he will get among his old acquaintance; and then we shall not hear of him for some months perhaps. If you see him in town, try to engage him till I return. I should be glad of his company to Paris, if his going with me will keep him out of harm's way, as it is called.

Saturday, April 1.

I HAVE had compliments sent me by many of my neighbours, who had hoped I was come to reside among them. They professed themselves disappointed on my acquainting them that I must go up early on Monday morning. I have invited myself to their Saturday assembly at the Bowling-green house.

Our reverend friend Mr. Dobson has been so good as to leave with me the sermon he is to preach to-morrow on the opening of the church: it is a very good discourse: I have only exceptions to three or four compliments he makes to the patron in as many different places of it: I doubt not but he will have the goodness to omit them.

I have already looked into all that has been done in the church, and all that is doing in the house and gardens. When both have had the direction and inspection of my dear Dr. Bartlett, need I say that nothing could have been better?

HALDEN is just arrived from my lord, with a letter which has enabled me to write to Lady Mansfield his lordship's high approbation of all our proceedings; and that he intends some one early day in next week to pay to her and Miss Mansfield his personal compliments.

He has left to me the article of settlements; declaring that his regard for *my* future interest is all that he wishes may be attended to.

I have therefore written, as from himself, that he proposes a jointure of 1200*l.* a year, penny-rents, and 400 guineas a year for her private purse; and that his lordship desires that Miss Mansfield will make a present to her sister of whatever she may be entitled to in her own right. Something was mentioned to me at Mansfield House of a thousand pounds left to her by a godmother.

Halden being very desirous to see his future lady, I shall, at his request, send the letter I have written to Lady Mansfield by him early in the morning; with a line recommending him to the notice of that lady as Lord W——'s principal steward.

Adieu, my dear Dr. Bartlett: I have joy in the joy of all these good people. If Providence graciously makes me instrumental to it, I look upon myself *but* as its *instrument*. I hope ostentation has no share in what draws on me more thanks and praises than I love to hear.

Lord W—— has a right to be made happy by his next relation, if his next relation *can* make him so. Is he not my mother's brother? Would not her enlarged soul have rejoiced on the occasion, and blessed her son for an instance of duty to her, paid by his disinterested regard for her brother? Who, my dear Dr. Bartlett, is so happy, yet who, in some cases, so unhappy, as your

CHARLES GRANDISON.

LETTER X.

Miss Byron to Miss Selby.

Monday, April 3.

THE Countess of D——, and the earl, her son, have but just left us. The countess sent last night, to let my cousin Reeves know of their intended morning visit, and they came together. As the visit was made to my cousin, I did not think myself obliged to be in waiting for them below, I was therefore in my closet, comforting myself with my own *agreeable* reflections. They were there a quarter of an hour before I was sent to.

Their talk was of me. I am used to recite my own praises, you know; and what signifies making a parade of apologies for continuing the use? I don't value myself so much as I once did on people's favourable opinions. If I had a heart in my own keeping, I should be glad it was thought a good one; that's all. Yet, though it has littlenesses in it that I knew nothing of formerly, I hope it is not a bad one.

My Lord D——, by the whole turn of the partial conversation, was led to expect a very extraordinary young woman. The lady declared that she would have her talk out, and hear all my two cousins were inclined to say of me, before I was sent up to, as I was not below when they came.

I was therefore to be seen only as a subject of curiosity. My lord had declared, it seems, that he would not be denied an introduction to me by his mother. But there were no thoughts of making any application to a girl whose heart was acknowledged not to be her own. My lord's honour would not allow of such an intention. Nor ought it.

His impatience, however, hastened the message to me. The countess met me half way, and embraced me: My lovely girl, how do you do?—My lord, said she, turning to the earl, I need not say—This is Miss Byron.

He bowed low, and made me a polite compliment; but it had sense in it, though high, and above my merits. Girls, writing of themselves on these occasions, must be disclaimers, you know: But, my dear uncle, what care I *now* for compliments? The man from whose mouth only they could be acceptable, is not at liberty to make me any.

The countess engaged me in an easy general conversation; part of which turned upon Lord and Lady L——, Miss Grandison, and Miss Jervois; and how I had passed my time at Colnebrook, in this wintry season, when there were so many diversions in town. But, said she, you had a man with you who is the general admiration wherever he goes.

Is there no making an acquaintance, said my lord, with Sir Charles Grandison? What I hear said of him, every time he is mentioned in company, is enough to fire a young man with emulation. I should be happy, did I deserve to be thought as a second or third man to Sir Charles Grandison.

I daresay, returned I, your lordship's acquaintance would be highly acceptable to him. He is easy of access. Men of rank, if men of merit, must be of kindred, and recognise one another the moment they meet. But Sir Charles will soon leave England.

The fool sighed: it was, you may believe involuntarily. I felt myself blush, and was the more silly for that.

The countess took my hand—One word with you, my dear —and led me out into the next room, and sitting down, made me sit on the same settee with her.

Oh that I could call you daughter! began she at once; and, turning half round to me, put one arm about me, with the other hand taking one of mine, and earnestly looking in my downcast face.

I was silent. Ah, Lucy! had Lady D—— been the mother of Sir Charles Grandison, with what pleasure could I have listened to her!

You said, my dear, that Sir Charles Grandison will soon leave England:—and then you sighed—Will you be quite open-hearted—May I ask you a question in hope that you will?

I was silent: yet the word Yes was on my lips.

You have caused it to be told me that your affections are engaged. This has been a cruel blow upon us. My lord, nevertheless, has heard so much of you [he is really a good young man, my dear], that (against my advice, I own) he would have me introduce him into your company. I see by his looks that he could admire you above all women. *He never was in love:* I should be sorry if he were disappointed in his first love. I hope his *promised* prudence will be his guard, if there be no prospect of his succeeding with you— she paused—I was still silent——

It will be a mark of your frankness of heart, my dear, if when you take my full meaning, you prevent me speaking more than I need.—I would not oppress you, my sweet love. —Such a delicacy, and such a frankness mingled, have I never seen in a young woman.—But tell me, my dear, has Sir Charles Grandison made his addresses to you?

It was a grievous question for me to answer—But *why* was it so, my Lucy, when all the hopes I ever had, proceeded from my own presumption, confirmed (that's true, of late!) by his sister's partiality in my favour; and when his unhappy Clementina has such a preferable claim?

What says Miss Byron?

She says, madam, that she reveres Lady D——, and will answer any questions that she puts to her, however affecting —Sir Charles Grandison has not.

Once I thought, proceeded she, that I never would make a second motion, were the woman a princess, who had confessed a prior love, or even liking; but the man is Sir Charles Grandison, whom all women must esteem: and the woman is Miss Byron, whom all men must love. Let me ask you, my dear—Have you any expectation that the first of men (I will call him so) and the loveliest and most amiable-minded of women, can come together?—You sighed, you know, when you mentioned that Sir Charles was soon to leave England; and you own that he has not made addresses to you—Don't be uneasy, my love!—We women, in these tender cases, see into each other's hearts from small openings—Look upon me as your mother—What say you, love?

Your ladyship compliments me with delicacy and frankness—It is too hard a question, if I have any of the first, to answer without blushes. A young woman to be supposed to have an esteem for a man, who has made no declaration, and whose behaviour to her is such only as shows a politeness to which he is accustomed, and only the same kind of tenderness, as he shows to his sisters;—and whom sometimes he *calls* sister—as if—Ah, madam! how can one answer?

You *have* answered, my dear, and with that delicacy and frankness too, which make a principal part of your character. If my son (and he shall not be encouraged in his hopes, if he sees you not, mind, as well as person, with his mother's eyes) should not be able to check himself by the apprehensions he has had reason for, of being but a second man in the favour of the object of his wishes [*We,* my dear, have our delicacies]; could you not allow him a second place in your favour, that might, in time, as he should merit, and as you should subdue your prepossessions, give him a first?—Hush

—my dear, for one moment—Your honour, your piety, are my just dependence, and will be his.—And now speak: it is to *me*, my dear: speak your whole heart: let not any apprehended difficulty—I am a woman as well as you. And prepared to indulge——

Your *goodness,* madam, and nothing else, interrupted I, gives me difficulty.—My Lord D—— seems to me to be a man of merit, and not disagreeable in his person and manners. What he said of Sir Charles Grandison, and of his emulation being fired by his example, gave him additional merit with me. He must have a good mind. I wish him acquainted with Sir Charles, for his own sake, and for the sake of the world, which might be benefited by his large power so happily directed!—But as to myself, I should forfeit the character of frankness of heart, which your ladyship's goodness ascribes to me, if I did not declare that although I cannot, and, I think, *ought not* to entertain a hope with regard to Sir Charles Grandison, since there is a lady who deserved him by severe sufferings before I knew him; yet is my heart so wholly attached, that I cannot think it just to give the least encouragement to any other proposal.

You are an excellent young woman; but, my dear, if Sir Charles Grandison is engaged—your mind will, it *must* change. Few women marry their first loves. Your heart——

O madam! it is *already* a wedded heart: it is wedded to his merits; his merits will be *always* the object of my esteem: I can never think of any *other* as I *ought* to think of the man to whom I give my hand.

Like merits, my dear, as *person* is not the principal motive, may produce like attachments. My Lord D—— will be, in your hands, another Sir Charles Grandison.

How good you are, my dear Lady D——! But allow me to repeat, as the strongest expression I can use, because I mean it to carry all the force that can be given it, that my heart is already a wedded heart.

You have spoken with great force: God bless you, my dear, as I love you! The matter shall take its course. If my lord should happen to be a single man some time hence (and, I can tell you, that your excellences will make our choice difficult); and if your mind, from any accident, or from persuasion of friends, should then have received alteration: you may still be happy in each other. I will therefore only thank you for that openness of heart which must set free the heart of my son.—Had you had the least lurking inclination to coquetry, and could have taken pride in conquests, he might have been an undone man.—We will return to the company.—But spare him, my dear: you must not talk much: he will love you, if you do, too fervently for his own peace. Try to be a little awkward—I am afraid for him: indeed I am. Oh that you had never seen Sir Charles Grandison!

I could not answer one word. She took my hand; and led me in to the company.

Had I been silent when my lord directed his discourse to me, or answered only No, or Yes, the countess would have thought me very vain; and that I ascribed to myself the consequence she so generously gave me with respect to my lord. I therefore behaved and answered unaffectedly; but avoided such a promptness of speech as would have looked like making pretensions to knowledge and opinion, though some of my lord's questions were apparently designed to engage me into freedom of discourse. The countess observed me narrowly. She whispered to me that she *did;* and made me a very high compliment on my behaviour. How much, Lucy, do I love and reverence her!

My lord was spoken too slightly of by Miss Grandison, in a former conversation. He is really a fine gentleman. Any woman, who is not engaged in her affections, may think herself very happy with him. His conversation was easy and polite, and he said nothing that was low or trifling. Indeed, Lucy, I think Mr. Greville and Mr. Fenwick are as greatly inferior to Lord D——, as Lord D—— is to Sir Charles Grandison.

At parting, he requested of me to be allowed to repeat his visits.

My lord, said the countess, before I could answer, you must **not** expect a mere stiff maiden answer from Miss Byron:

she is above all vulgar forms. She and her cousins have too much politeness, and I will venture to say, discernment, not to be glad of your acquaintance *as* an acquaintance—but, for the rest, you must look to your heart.

I shall be afraid, said he, turning to the countess, to ask your ladyship for an explanation. Miss Byron, I hope, sir, addressing himself to Mr. Reeves, will not refuse me her company when I pay you my compliments. Then turning to me; I hope, madam, I shall not be punished for admiring you.

My Lord D——, replied I, will be entitled to every civility. I had said more, had he not snatched my hand a little too eagerly and kissed it.

And thus much for the visit of the Countess of D—— and the earl.

Did I tell you in my former letter that Emily is with me half her time? She is a most engaging young creature. Her manners are so pure! Her heart is so sincere and open!—O Lucy! you would dearly love her. I wish I may be asked to carry her down with me. Yet she adores her guardian: but her reverence for him will not allow of the innocent familiarity in thinking of him, that—I don't know what I would say. But to love with an ardour, that would be dangerous to one's peace, one must have more tenderness than reverence for the object: don't you think so, Lucy?

Miss Grandison made me one of her flying visits, as she calls them, soon after the countess and my lord went away.

Mr. and Mrs. Reeves told her all that had been said before them by the earl and countess, as well before I went down to them as after. They could not tell what had passed between that lady and me when she took me aside. I had not had time to tell *them*. They referred to me for that: but besides that I was not in spirits, and cared not to say much, I was not willing to be thought, by my refusal of so great an offer, to seem to fasten myself upon her brother.

She pitied (who but must?) Lady Clementina. She pitied her brother also: and seeing me dejected, she clasped her arms about me and wetted my cheek with a sisterly tear.

Is it not strange, Lucy, that Sir Charles's father should keep him so long abroad? These free-living men! of what absurdities are they not guilty! What misfortunes to others do they occasion? One might, with the excellent Clementina, ask, What had Mr. Grandison to do in Italy? Or why, if he must go abroad, did he stay so long.

Travelling! Young men travelling! I cannot, my dear, but think it a very nonsensical thing! What can they see but the ruins of the gay, once busy world, of which they have read?

To see a parcel of giddy boys under the direction of tutors or governors hunting after—what?—Nothing; or, at best but ruins of ruins: for the imagination, aided by reflection, must be left, after all, to make out the greater glories which the grave-digger Time has buried too deep for discovery.

And when this *grand tour* is completed, the travelled youth returns: and what is his boast? Why, to be able to tell, perhaps his *better* taught friend who has never been out of his native country, that he has seen in ruins what the other has a juster idea of from reading; and of which it is more than probable he can give a much better account than the traveller.

And are these, petulant Harriet (methinks, Lucy, you demand), all the benefits that you will suppose Sir CHARLES GRANDISON has reaped from his travelling?

Why, no. But then, in turn, I ask, Is every traveller a Sir Charles Grandison?—And does not even *he* confess to Dr. Bartlett that he wished he had never seen Italy? And may not the poor Clementina, and all her family, for *her* sake, wish he never had?

If an opportunity offers, I don't know but I may ask Sir Charles, whether, in his conscience, he thinks that, taking in every consideration relating to time, expense, risks of life, health, morals, this part of the fashionable education of youth of condition is such an indispensable one as some seem to suppose it? If Sir Charles Grandison give it not in favour of travelling, I believe it will be concluded that six parts out of eight of the little masters who are sent abroad for improvement, might as well be kept at home; if, especially, they would be *orderly,* and let their fathers and mothers know what to do with them.

Oh, my uncle! I am afraid of you: but spare the poor girl: she acknowledges her petulance, her presumption. The occasion you know, and will pity her for it. Neither petulance nor presumption, however, shall make her declare as her sentiments what really are not so in her unprejudiced hours; and she hopes to have her heart always open to conviction.

For the present, adieu, my Lucy.

P.S. Dr. Bartlett tells me that Mr. Beauchamp is at Calais, waiting the pleasure of his father; and that Sir Harry has sent express for him, as at his lady's motion.

LETTER XI.

Miss Byron.—In continuation.

Tuesday, April 4.

SIR CHARLES GRANDISON came to town last night. He was so polite as to send to inquire after my health; and to let Mr. Reeves know that he would do himself the honour, as he called it, of breakfasting with *him* this morning. Very ceremonious, either for his own sake or for mine—perhaps for both.

So I am in expectation of seeing, within this half hour, the noble Clementina's future—ah, Lucy!

The compliment, you see, is to Mr. Reeves. Shall I stay above and see if he will ask for *me?* He owes me something for the emotion he gave me in Lord L——'s library. Very little of him since have I seen.

'Honour forbids me,' said he, then: 'Yet honour bids 'me—But I cannot be ungenerous, selfish.'—These words are still in my ear.—What could he mean by them?—

Honour forbids me—What! to explain himself? He had been telling me a tender tale: he had *ended* it. What did honour forbid him to do?—*Yet honour bids me!* Why then did he not follow the dictates of honour?

But *I cannot be unjust:*—To Clementina he means. Who *wished* him to be so?—*Unjust!* I hope not. It is a diminution to your glory, Sir Charles Grandison, to have the word *unjust,* in this way of speaking, in your thoughts! As if a good man had lain under a temptation to be *unjust;* and had but then recollected himself.

'*I cannot be ungenerous.*' To the noble lady, I suppose? He *must* take compassion on her. And did he think himself under an obligation to my forwardness to make this declaration to me, as to one who *wished* him to be *ungenerous* to such a lady for my sake?—I cannot bear the thought of this. Is it not as if he had said, 'Fond Harriet, I see 'what you expect from me—but I must have compassion '*for,* I cannot be ungenerous *to,* Clementina?'—But what a poor word is *compassion!* Noble Clementina, I grieve for you, though the man be indeed a generous man!—Oh defend me, my better genius, from wanting the compassion even of a Sir Charles Grandison!

But what means me by the word *selfish!* He *cannot be selfish!*—I comprehend not the meaning of this word—Clementina has a very high fortune—Harriet but a very middling one. He cannot be *unjust, ungenerous* to Clementina—nor yet *selfish*—This word confounds me, from a man that says nothing at random!

Well, but breakfast time is come, while I am busy in self-debatings. I will go down, that I may not seem to affect parade. I will endeavour to see with indifference him that we have all been admiring and studying for this last fortnight in such a variety of lights—The Christian: the hero: the friend:—Ah, Lucy! the lover of Clementina! the generous kinsman of Lord W——: the modest and delicate benefactor of the Mansfields: the free, gay raillier of Lady Beauchamp; and, in her, of all our sex's foibles!

But he is come! While I am prating to you with my pen,

he is come—why, Lucy, would you detain me?—Now must the fool go down in a kind of hurry. Yet stay till she is sent for.—And that is *now*.

LETTER XII.

Miss Byron.—In continuation.

O LUCY, I have such a conversation to relate to you!—But let me lead to it.

Sir Charles met me at the opening of the door. He was all himself—such an unaffected modesty and politeness; yet such an ease and freedom!

I thought, by his address, that he would have taken my hand; and both hands were *so emulatively* passive.—How does he manage it to be so free in a first address, yet so respectful that a princess could not blame him!

After breakfast, my cousins being sent for out to attend Sir John Allestree and his niece, Sir Charles and I were left alone: and then, with an air equally solemn and free, he addressed himself to me.

The last time I had the honour of being alone with my good Miss Byron, I told her a very tender tale. I was sure it would raise in such a heart as hers generous compassion for the noblest lady on the continent; and I presumed, as my difficulties were not owing either to rashness or indiscretion, that she would also pity the relater.

The story did indeed affect you; yet, for my own sake, as well as yours, I referred you to Dr. Bartlett for the particulars of some part of it, upon which I could not expatiate.

The doctor, madam, has let me know the particulars which he communicated to you. I remember with pain the pain I gave to your generous heart in Lord L——'s study. I am sure you must have suffered still more from the same compassionate goodness on the communications he made you. May I, madam, however, add a few particulars to the same subject, which he then could not give you? Now you have been let into so considerable a part of my story, I am desirous to acquaint you, and that rather than any woman in the world, with all that I know myself of this arduous affair.

He ceased speaking. I was in tremors. Sir, sir—the story, I must own, is a most affecting one. How much is the unhappy lady to be pitied! You will do me honour in acquainting me with further particulars of it.

Dr. Bartlett has told you, madam, that the bishop of Nocera, second brother to Lady Clementina, has very lately written to me, requesting that I will make one more visit to Bologna—I have the letter. You read Italian, madam. Shall I—or will you—He held it to me.

I took it. These, Lucy, are the contents.

'The bishop acquaints him with the very melancholy way 'they are in. The father and mother declining in their 'healths. Signor Jeronymo worse than when Sir Charles 'left them. His sister also declining in her health: yet 'earnest still to see him.

'He says that she is at present at Urbino; but is soon to 'go to Naples to the general's. He urges him to make them 'one visit more; yet owns that his family are not unanimous 'in the request: but that he and Father Marescotti, and the 'marchioness, are extremely earnest that this indulgence 'should be granted to the wishes of his sister.

'He offers to meet him, at his own appointment, and con-'duct him to Bologna; where, he tells him, his presence will 'rejoice every heart, and procure a unanimous consent to 'the interview so much desired: and says, that if this meas-'ure, which he is sorry he has so long withstood, answers 'not his hopes, he will advise the shutting up of their 'Clementina in a nunnery, or to consign her to private 'hands, where she shall be treated kindly, but as persons 'in her unhappy circumstances are accustomed to be treated.'

Sir Charles then showed me a letter from Signor Jeronymo; in which he acquaints him with the dangerous way he is in. He tells him, 'That his life is a burden to him.

'He wishes it was brought to its period. He does not think
' himself in skilful hands. He complains most of the wound
' which is in his hip joint; and which has hitherto baffled
' the art both of the Italian and French surgeons who have
' been consulted. He wishes, that himself and Sir Charles
' had been of one country, he says, since the greatest felicity
' he now has to wish for, is to yield up his life to the Giver
' of it, in the arms of his Grandison.'

He mentions not one word in this melancholy letter of his unhappy sister: which Sir Charles accounted for by supposing that she not being at Bologna, they kept from him, in his deplorable way, everything relating to her that was likely to disturb him.

He then read part of a letter written in English by the admired Mrs. Beaumont; some of the contents of which were, as you shall hear, extremely affecting.

' Mrs. Beaumont gives him in it an account of the situ-
' ation of the unhappy young lady; and excuses herself for
' not having done it before, in answer to his request, because
' of an indisposition under which he had for some time
' laboured, which had hindered her from making the neces-
' sary inquiries.

' She mentions that the lady had received no benefit from
' her journeyings from place to place; and from her voyage
' from Leghorn to Naples and back again; and blames her
' attendants, who, to quiet her, unknown to their principals,
' for some time kept her in expectation of seeing her chev-
' alier at the end of each; for her more prudent Camilla,
' she says, had been hindered by illness from attending
' her in several of the excursions.

' They had a second time, at her own request, put her
' into a nunnery. She at first was so sedate in it, as gave
' them hopes: but the novelty going off, and one of the
' sisters, to try her, having officiously asked her to go with
' her into the parlour, where she said she would be allowed
' to converse through the grate with a *certain* English gen-
' tleman, her impatience, on her disappointment, made her
' more ungovernable than they had ever known her; for she

'had been, for two hours before, meditating what she should
' say to him.

' For a week together, she was vehemently intent upon
' being allowed to visit England; and had engaged her
' cousins, Sebastiano and Juliano, to promise to escort her
' thither if she could obtain leave.

' Her mother brought her off this when nobody else could,
' only by entreating her, for *her* sake, never to think of it more.

' The marchioness then, encouraged by this instance of
' her obedience, took her under her own care: but the young
' lady going on from flight to flight; and the way she was
' in visibly affecting the health of her indulgent mother,
' a doctor was found who was absolutely of opinion that
' nothing but harsh methods would avail: and in this advice
' Lady Sforza, and her daughter Laurana, and the general,
' concurring, she was told that she must prepare to go to
' Milan. She was so earnest to be excused from going
' thither, and to be permitted to go to Florence to Mrs.
' Beaumont, that they gave way to her entreaties; and the
' marquis himself, accompanying her to Florence, prevailed
' on Mrs. Beaumont to take her under her care.

' With her she stayed three weeks: she was tolerably sedate
' in that space of time; but most so, when she was talking
' of England and the Chevalier Grandison, and his sisters,
' with whom she wished to be acquainted. She delighted
' to speak English, and to talk of the tenderness and good-
' ness of her tutor; and of what he said to her upon such
' and such a subject.

' At the three weeks' end the general made her a visit,
' in company of Lady Sforza; and her talk being all on
' this subject, they were both highly displeased; and hinted
' that she was too much indulged in it: and, unhappily,
' she repeating some tender passages that passed in the
' interview her mother had permitted her to hold with the
' chevalier, the general would have it that Mr. Grandison
' had designedly, from the first, sought to give himself con-
' sequence with her; and expressed himself, on the occasion,
' with great violence against him.

'He carried his displeasure to extremity, and obliged her 'to go away with his aunt and him that very day, to her 'great regret; and as much to the regret of Mrs. Beaumont, 'and of the ladies her friends; who tenderly loved the *in-* '*nocent visionary,* as sometimes they called her. And Mrs. 'Beaumont is sure that the gentle treatment she met with 'from them, would in time, though perhaps slowly, have 'greatly helped her.'

Mrs. Beaumont then gives an account of the harsh treatment the poor young lady met with.

Sir Charles Grandison would have stopt reading here, He said he could not read it to me, without such a change of voice as would add to my pain as well as to his own.

Tears often stole down my cheeks when I read the letters of the bishop and Signor Jeronymo, and as Sir Charles read a part of Mrs. Beaumont's letter: and I doubted not but what was to follow would make them flow. Yet I said, Be pleased, sir, to let *me* read on. I am not a stranger to distress. I can pity others, or I should not deserve pity myself.

He pointed to the place; and withdrew to the window.

Mrs. Beaumont says, 'That the poor mother was pre-'vailed upon to resign her child wholly to the management 'of Lady Sforza and her daughter Laurana, who took her 'with them to their palace in Milan.

'The tender parent, however, besought them to spare all 'unnecessary severity; which they promised: but Laurana 'objected to Camilla's attendance. She was thought too 'indulgent; and her servant Laura, as a more manageable 'person, was taken in her place.' And oh how cruelly, as you shall hear, did they treat her!

Father Marescotti, being obliged to visit a dying relation at Milan, was desired by the marchioness to inform himself of the way her beloved daughter was in, and of the methods taken with her, Lady Laurana having in her letters boasted of both. The good father acquainted Mrs. Beaumont with the following particulars:

'He was surprised to find a difficulty made of his seeing

'the lady: but insisting on it, he found her to be wholly
' spiritless, and in terror; afraid to speak, afraid to look,
' before her cousin Laurana; yet seeming to want to com-
' plain to him. He took notice of this to Laurana—O
' father! said she, we are in the right way, I assure you:
' when we had her first, her chevalier, and an interview
' with him, were ever in her mouth; but now she is in such
' order, that she never speaks a word of him. But what,
' asked the compassionate father, must she have suffered, to
' be brought to this?—Don't you, father, trouble yourself
' about that, replied the cruel Laurana: the doctors have
' given their opinion that some severity was necessary. It
' is all for her good.

' The poor lady expressed herself to him, with earnestness,
' after the veil; a subject on which it seems they indulged
' her; urging that the only way to secure her health of
' mind, if it could be restored, was to yield to her wishes.
' Lady Sforza said that it was not a point that she herself
' would press; but it was her opinion that her family sinned
' in opposing a divine dedication; and perhaps their daugh-
' ter's malady might be a judgment upon them for it.'

The father, in his letter to Mrs. Beaumont, ascribes to
' Lady Sforza self-interested motives for her conduct; to
' Laurana, envy, on account of Lady Clementina's superior
' qualities: but nobody, he says, till now, doubted Laurana's
' love of her.'

Father Marescotti then gives a shocking instance of the
barbarous Laurana's treatment of the noble sufferer—*All
for her good*—Wretch! how my heart rises against her!
Her servant Laura, under pretence of *confessing* to her
Bologna father, in tears, acquainted him with it. It was
perpetrated but the day before.

' When any severity was to be exercised upon the un-
' happy lady, Laura was always shut out of her apartment.
' Her lady had said something that she was to be chidden
' for. Lady Sforza, who was not altogether so severe as
' her daughter, was not at home. Laura listened in tears:
' she heard Laurana in great wrath with Lady Clementina,

'and threaten her—and her young lady break out to this
'effect—What have I done to you, Laurana, to be so used?
'—You are not the cousin Laurana you used to be! You
'know I am not able to help myself: why do you call me
'crazy and frantic, Laurana? [Vile upbraider, Lucy!] If
'the Almighty has laid His hand upon me, should I not be
'pitied?——

'It is all for your good! It is all for your good, Clemen-
'tina! You could not always have spoken so sensibly,
'cousin.

'Cruel Laurana! You loved me once!—I have no mother,
'as you have. My mother was a good mother: but she is
'gone! Or I am gone, I know not which.

'She threatened her then with the strait waistcoat, a
'punishment at which the unhappy lady was always greatly
'terrified. Laura heard her beg and pray; but Laurana
'coming out, she was forced to retire.

'The poor young lady apprehending her cruel cousin's
'return with the threatened waistcoat, and with the woman
'that used to be brought in when they were disposed to
'terrify her, went down and hid herself under a staircase,
'where she was soon discovered by her clothes, which she
'had not been careful to draw in after her.'

O Lucy! how I wept! How insupportable to me, said
Sir Charles, would have been my reflections, had my con-
science told me that I had been the wilful cause of the noble
Clementina's calamity!

After I had a little recovered, I read to myself the next
paragraph, which related 'that the cruel Laurana dragged
'the sweet sufferer by her gown, from her hiding-place,
'inveighing against her, threatening her: she, all patient,
'resigned, her hands crossed on her bosom, praying for
'mercy, not by speech, but by her eyes, which, however wept
'not: and causing her to be carried up to her chamber, there
'punished her with the strait waistcoat, as she had threat-
'ened.

'Father Marescotti was greatly affected with Laura's re-
'lation, as well as with what he had himself observed: but

'on his return to Bologna, dreading to acquaint her mother,
'for her own sake, with the treatment her Clementina met
'with, he only said he did not quite approve of it; and
'advised her not to oppose the young lady's being brought
'home, if the bishop and the general came into it: but he
'laid the whole matter before the bishop, who wrote to the
'general to join with him out of hand to release their sister
'from her present bondage: and the general meeting the
'bishop on a set day at Milan, for that purpose, the lady
'was accordingly released.

'A breach ensued upon it, with Lady Sforza and her
'daughter; who would have it Clementina was much better
'for their management. They had by terror broken her
'spirit, and her passiveness was reckoned upon as an indica-
'tion of amendment.

'The marchioness being much indisposed, the young lady,
'attended by her Camilla, was carried to Naples; where it
'is supposed she now is. Poor young lady, how has she
'been hurried about!—But who can think of her cousin
'Laurana without extreme indignation?

'Mrs. Beaumont writes that the bishop would fain have
'prevailed upon his brother the general to join with him
'in an invitation to Sir Charles Grandison to come over,
'as a last expedient, before they locked her up either in a
'nunnery, or in some private house: but the general would
'by no means come into it.

'He asked, What was proposed to be the end of Sir Charles's
'visit, were all that was wished from it to follow, in his
'sister's restored mind?—He never, he said, would give
'his consent that she should be the wife of an English Prot-
'estant.

'The bishop declared that he was far from wishing her to
'be so: but he was for leaving that to after-consideration.
'Could they but restore his sister to her reason, that reason,
'co-operating with her principles, might answer all their
'hopes.

'He might *try* his expedient, the general said, with all his
'heart: but he looked upon the Chevalier Grandison to be a

'man of art; and he was sure he must have entangled his
'sister by methods imperceptible to her and to them; but
'yet more efficacious to his ends than an open declaration.
'Had he not, he asked, found means to fascinate Olivia and
'as many women as he came into company with?—For his
'part, he loved not the chevalier. He had *forced* him, by
'his intrepidity, to be civil to him: but forced civility was
'but a temporary one. It was his way to judge of causes by
'the effects: and this he knew, that he had lost a sister who
'would have been a jewel in the crown of a prince; and
'would not be answerable for consequences, if he and Sir
'Charles Grandison were once more to meet, be it where it
'would.

'Father Marescotti, however, joining, as the bishop writes,
'with him and the marchioness, in a desire to try this
'expedient; and being sure that the marquis and Signor
'Jeronymo would not be averse to it, he took a resolution
'to write over to him, as has been related.'

This, Lucy, is the state of the unhappy case, as briefly and
as clearly as my memory will serve to give it. And what a
rememberer, if I may make a word, is the heart!—Not a
circumstance escapes it.

And now it remained for me to know of Sir Charles what
answer he had returned.

Was not my situation critical, my dear? Had Sir Charles
asked my opinion, *before* he had taken his resolutions, I
should have given it with my whole heart, that he should fly
to the comfort of the poor lady. But then he would have
shown a suspense unworthy of Clementina; and a compliment to me; which a good man, so circumstanced, ought not
to make.

My regard for him (yet what a poor affected word is
regard!) was, nevertheless, as strong as ever. Generosity,
or rather justice, to Clementina, and that so often, to you,
avowed regard to him, pulled my heart two ways. I thought
I wanted to consider with myself for a few moments, being
desirous to clear to my own heart the conduct that I was to
show on this trying occasion, as well of precipitation as of

affectation; and my cousin Reeves just then coming in for something she wanted, I took the opportunity to walk to the other end of the room; and while a short complimental discourse passed between them, 'Harriet Byron,' said I to myself, 'be not mean. Hast thou not the example of a 'Clementina before thee? Her religion and her love, com-'bating together, have overturned the noble creature's reason. 'Thou canst not be called to such a trial: but canst thou 'not show, that if thou *wert,* thou couldst have acted greatly, 'if not *so* greatly? Sir Charles Grandison is just: he *ought* 'to prefer to thee the excellent Clementina. Priority of 'claim, compassion for the noble sufferer, merits *so* su-'perior!—I love him for *his* merits: shall I not love merits, 'nearly as great, in one of my *own sex?* The struggle will 'cost thee something: but try to be above thyself. Banish to 'thy retirement, to thy pillow, thought I, be all the *girl.* 'Often have I contended for the dignity of my sex: let me 'now be an example to *myself,* and not unworthy in my 'own eyes (when I come to reflect) of a union, could it 'have been effected, with a man whom a Clementina looked 'up to with hope.'

My cousin being withdrawn, and Sir Charles, approaching me, I attempted to assume a dignity of aspect, without pride; and I spoke, while spirit was high in me, and to keep myself up to it—My heart bleeds, sir, for the distresses of your Clementina [yes, Lucy, said I, *your* Clementina]: beyond expression I admire the greatness of her behaviour, and most sincerely lament her distresses. What, that is in the power of man, cannot Sir Charles Grandison do? You have honoured me, sir, with the title of *sister;* in the tenderness of that relation, permit me to say, that I dread the effects of the general's petulance: I feel next for you the pain that it must give to your humane heart to be once more personally present to the woes of the inimitable Clementina: but I am sure you did not hesitate a moment about leaving all your friends here in England, and resolving to hasten over to *try,* at least, what can be done for the noble sufferer.

Had he praised me highly for this my address to him, it

would have looked, such was the situation on both sides, as if he had thought this disinterested behaviour in me, an extraordinary piece of magnanimity and self-denial; and, of consequence, as if he had supposed I had views upon him, which he wondered I could give up. His is the most delicate of human minds!

He led me to my seat, and taking his by me, still holding my passive hand—Ever since I have had the honour of Miss Byron's acquaintance, I have considered her as one of the most excellent of women. My heart demands alliance with hers, and hopes to be allowed its claim; though such are the delicacies of situation, that I scarcely dare trust to myself to speak upon the subject. From the first, I called Miss Byron my sister; but she is *more* to me than the dearest sister; and there is a more tender friendship that I aspire to hold with her, whatever may be the accidents on either side, to bar a further wish: and *this* I must hope, that she will not deny me, so long as it shall be consistent with her other attachments.

He paused. I made an effort to speak: but speech was denied me. My face, as I felt, glowed like the fire before me.

My heart, resumed he, is ever on my lips. It is tortured when I cannot speak all that is in it. Professions I am not accustomed to make. As I am not conscious of being unworthy of your friendship, I will *suppose* it; and further talk to you of my affairs and engagements, as that tender friendship may warrant.

Sir, you do me honour, was all I could say.

I had a letter from the faithful Camilla. I hold not a correspondence with her: but the treatment that her young lady met with, of which she had got some general intimations, and some words that the bishop said to her, which expressed his wishes that I would make them one more visit at Bologna, urged her to write, begging of me, for Heaven's sake, to go over. But unless one of the family had written to me, and by consent of others of it, what hope had I of a welcome, after I had been as often refused as I had requested while I was in Italy, to be admitted to the presence of the lady who was so desirous of one interview more?—Especially, as Mrs. Beaumont gave me no encouragement to go, but the contrary, from what she observed of the inclinations of the family.

Mrs. Beaumont is still of opinion, as in the conclusion of the letter before you, that I should not go, unless the general and the marquis join their requests to those of the marchioness, the bishop, and Father Marescotti. But I had no sooner perused the bishop's letter, than I wrote that I would most cheerfully comply with his wishes: but that I should be glad that I might not be under any obligation to go farther than Bologna; where I might have the happiness to attend my Jeronymo, as well as his sister.

I had a little twitch at my heart, Lucy. I was sorry for it: but my judgment was entirely with him.

And now, madam, you will wonder that you see not any preparations for my departure. All *is* prepared: I only wait for the company of one gentleman, who is settling his affairs with all expedition to go with me. He is an able, a skilful surgeon, who has had great practice abroad, and in the armies: and having acquired an easy fortune, is come to settle in his native country. My Jeronymo expresses himself dissatisfied with his surgeons. If Mr. Lowther can be of service to him, how happy shall I think myself! And if my presence can be a means to restore the noble Clementina—but how dare I hope it?—And yet I am persuaded that in her case, and with such a temper of mind (unused to hardship and opposition as she had been), the only way to recover her would have been by complying with her in everything that her heart or head was earnestly set upon: for what control was necessary to a young lady who never, even in the height of her malady, uttered a wish or thought that was contrary to her duty either to God or her parents; nor yet to the honour of her name; and allow me, madam, to say, to the *pride* of her sex?

I am under an obligation to go to Paris, proceeded he, from the will of my late friend, Mr. Danby. I shall stop there for a day or two only, in order to put things in a way for my last hand, on my return from Italy.

When I am in Italy, I shall perhaps be enabled to adjust two or three accounts that stand out, in relation to the affairs of my ward.

This day, at dinner, I shall see Mrs. Oldham and her sons; and in the afternoon, at tea, Mrs. O'Hara and her husband, and Captain Salmonet.

To-morrow, I hope for the honour of your company, madam, and Mr. and Mrs. Reeves's, at dinner; and be so good as to engage them for the rest of the day. You must not deny me; because I shall want your influence upon Charlotte, to make her fix Lord G——'s happy day, that I may be able to see their hands united before I set out; as my return will be uncertain——

Ah, Lucy! *more* twitches just then!——

Thursday next is the day set for the triple marriage of the Danbys. I have promised to give Miss Danby to Mr. Galliard, and to dine with them and their friends at Enfield.

If I can see my Lord W—— and Charlotte happy before I go, I shall be highly gratified.

It is another of my wishes to see my friend Beauchamp in England first, and to leave him in possession of his father's love, and of his mother-in-law's civility. Dr. Bartlett and he will be happy in each other. I shall correspond with the doctor. He greatly admires you, madam, and will communicate to you all you shall think worthy of your notice, relating to the proceedings of a man who will always think himself honoured by your inquiries after him.

Ah, Lucy! Sir Charles Grandison then sighed. He seemed to look more than he spoke. I will not promise for my heart if he treats me with more than the tenderness of friendship: if he gives me room to think that he wishes—but what can he wish? He *ought* to be, he *must* be, Clementina's: and I will endeavour to make myself happy, if I can maintain the second place in his friendship: and when he offers me this, shall I, Lucy, be so *little* as to be displeased with the man who cannot be to me all that I had once hoped he could be?—No!—He shall be the same glorious creature in my eyes; I will admire his goodness of heart and greatness of mind; and I will think him entitled to my utmost gratitude for the protection he gave me from a man of violence, and for the kindness he has already shown me. Is not friendship the basis of my love? And does he not tender me *that?*

Nevertheless, at the time, do what I could, I found a tear ready to start. My heart was very untoward, Lucy; and I was guilty of a little female turn. When I found the twinkling of my eyes would not disperse the too ready drop, and felt it stealing down my cheek, I wiped it off—The poor Emily, said I—*She* will be grieved at parting with you. Emily loves her guardian.

And I love my ward. I once had a thought, madam, of begging *your* protection of Emily: but as I have two sisters, I think she will be happy under their wings, and in the protection of my good Lord L——; and the rather, as I have no doubt of overcoming her unhappy mother, by making her husband's interest a guarantee for her tolerable, if not good, behaviour to her child.

I was glad to carry my thoughts out of myself, as I may say, and from my own concerns. We all, sir, said I, look upon Mr. Beauchamp as a future——

Husband for Emily, madam? interrupted he—it must not be at *my* motion. My friend shall be entitled to share with me my whole estate; but I will never seek to lead the choice of my WARD. Let Emily, some time hence, find out the husband she can be happy with; Beauchamp the wife he can love; Emily, if I can help it, shall not be the wife of any man's convenience. Beauchamp is nice, and I will be as nice for my WARD. And the more so, as I hope she herself wants not delicacy. There is a cruelty in persuasion, where the hearts rejects the person proposed, whether the urger be parent or guardian.

Lord bless me, thought I, what a man is this!

Do you expect Mr. Beauchamp soon, sir?

Every day, madam.

And is it possible, sir, that you can bring all these things to bear before you leave England, and go so soon?

I fear nothing but Charlotte's whimsies. Have you, madam, any reason to apprehend that she is averse to an alliance with Lord G——? His father and aunt are very importunate for an early celebration.

None at all, sir.

Then I shall depend much upon yours and Lord and Lady L——'s influence over her.

He besought my excuse for detaining my attention so long. Upon his motion to go, my two cousins came in. He took even a solemn leave of me, and a very respectful one of them.

I had kept up my spirits to their utmost stretch: I desired my cousins to excuse me for a few minutes: his departure from me was *too* solemn; and I hurried up to my closet, and after a few involuntary sobs, a flood of tears relieved me. I besought, on my knees, peace to the disturbed mind of the excellent Clementina, calmness and resignation to my own, and safety to Sir Charles. And then, drying my eyes at the glass, I went down stairs to my cousins; and on their inquiries (with looks of deep concern) after the occasion of my red eyes, I said, All is over! All is over! my dear cousins. I cannot blame him: he is all that is noble and good—I can say no more just now. The particulars you shall have from my pen.

I went upstairs to write: and except for one half hour at dinner, and another at tea, I stopt not until I had done.

And here, quite tired, uneasy, vexed with myself, yet hardly knowing why, I laid down my pen.—Take what I have written, my dear cousin Reeves: if you can read it, do; and then despatch it to my Lucy.

But on second thoughts I will show it to the two ladies and Lord L—— before it is sent away. They will be curious to know what passed in a conversation, where the critical circumstances both of us were in required a delicacy which I am not sure was so well observed on my side as on his.

I shall, I know, have their pity: but let nobody, who pities not the noble Clementina, show any for

HARRIET BYRON.

LETTER XIII.

Miss Byron.—In continuation.

Tuesday Night, April 4.

MISS GRANDISON came to me just as we had supped. She longed, she said, to see me; but was prevented coming before, and desired to know what had passed between her brother and me this morning. I gave her the letter which I had but a little while before concluded. He had owned, she said, that he had breakfasted with me; and spoke of me to her, and Lord and Lady L——, with an ardour that gave them pleasure. She put my letter into her bosom, I *may,* I hope, Harriet—if you please, madam, said I.

If you please, madam, repeated she; and with that *dolorous* accent too, my Harriet! My sister and I have been in tears this morning: Lord L—— had much ado to forbear. Sir Charles will soon leave us.

It can't be helped, Charlotte. Did you dine to-day in St. James's Square?

No, indeed!—My brother had a certain tribe with him, and the *woman* also. It is very difficult, I believe, Harriet, for good people to forbear doing sometimes *more* than goodness requires of them.

Could you not, Charlotte, have sat at table with them for one hour or two?

My brother did not ask me. He did not expect it. He gives everybody their choice, you know. He told me last night who were to dine with him to-day, and supposed I would choose to dine with Lady L——, or with *you,* he was so free as to say.

He did us an honour which you thought too great a one. But if he *had* asked you, Charlotte——

Then I should have bridled. Indeed, I asked him if he did not over-do it?

What was his answer?

Perhaps he might—But I, said he, may never see Mrs.

Oldham again. I want to inform myself of her future intentions, with a view (*over-do* it again, Charlotte!) to make her easy and happy for life. Her children *are* in the world. I want to give her a credit that will make her remembered by them, as they grow up, with duty. I hope I am superior to forms. She is conscious. I can pity her. She is a gentlewoman; and entitled to a place at any man's table to whom she never was a servant. She never was mine.

And what, Miss Grandison, could you say in answer? asked I.

What!—Why I put up my lip.

Ungracious girl!

I can't help it. That may become a man to do in such cases as this that would not a woman.

Sir Charles wants not *delicacy,* my dear, said I.

He must suppose that I should have sat swelling and been reserved: he was right not to ask me—So be quiet, Harriet —And yet perhaps you would be as tame to a husband's mistress as you seem favourable to a father's.

She then put on one of her arch looks——

The cases differ, Charlotte—But do you know what passed between the generous man and the mortified woman and her children: mortified as they *must* be by his goodness?

Yes, yes; I had curiosity enough to ask Dr. Bartlett about it all.

Pray, Charlotte——

Dr. Bartlett is favourable to everybody, sinners as well as saints.—He began with praising the modesty of her dress, the humility of her behaviour: he said that she trembled and looked down, till she was re-assured by Sir Charles. Such creatures have all their tricks, Harriet.

You, Charlotte, are not favourable to sinners, and hardly to saints. But pray proceed.

Why, he re-assured the woman, as I told you: and then proceeded to ask many questions of the elder Oldham—I pitied that young fellow—to have a mother in his eye, whose very tenderness to the young ones kept alive the sense of her guilt. And yet what would she have been, had she not been doubly tender to the innocents, who were born to shame from her fault? The young man acknowledged a military genius; and Sir Charles told him that he would, on his return from a journey he was going to take, consider whether he could not do him service in the way he chose. He gave him, it seems, a brief lecture on what he should aim to be, and what avoid, to qualify himself for a man of true honour; and spoke very handsomely of such gentlemen of the army as are real gentlemen. The young fellow, continued Miss Grandison, may look upon himself to be as good as provided for, since my brother never gives the most distant hope, that is not followed by absolute certainty, the first opportunity, not that *offers,* but which he can *make.*

He took great notice of the little boys. He dilated their hearts, and set them a prating; and was pleased with their prate. The doctor, who had never seen him before in the company of children, applauded him for his vivacity, and condescending talk to them. The tenderest father in the world, he said, could not have behaved more tenderly, or showed himself more delighted with his own children, than he did with those brats of Mrs. Oldham.

Ah, Charlotte! And is it out of doubt that you are the daughter of Lady Grandison, and sister of Sir Charles Grandison?—Well, but I believe you are—Some children take after the father, some after the mother!—Forgive me, my dear.

But I won't. I have a great mind to quarrel with you, Harriet.

Pray don't; because I could neither help, nor can be sorry for, what I have said. But pray proceed.

Why, he made presents to the children. I don't know what they were; nor could the doctor tell me. I suppose very handsome ones; for he has the spirit of a prince. He inquired very particularly after the circumstances of the mother; and was more kind to her than many people would be to their own mothers.—*He* can account for this, I suppose—though *I* cannot. The woman, it is true, is of a good family, and so forth: but that enhances her crime. Natural-children abound in the present age. Keeping is fashionable. Good men should not countenance such wretches.—But my brother and you are charitable creatures!—With all my heart, child. Virtue, however, has at least as much to say on one side of the question as on the other.

When the poor children are in the world, as your brother said—when the poor women are penitents, *true* penitents —your brother's treatment of Mrs. Giffard was different. He is in both instances an imitator of the Almighty; an humbler of the impenitent, and an encourager of those who repent.

Well, well: he is undoubtedly a good sort of young man; and, Harriet, you are a good sort of young woman. Where much is given, much is required: but I have not given me such a large quantity of charity as either of you may boast: and how can I help it? But, however, the woman went away blessing and praising him; and that, the doctor says, more with her eyes, than she was able to do in words. The elder youth departed in rapturous reverence: the children hung about *his* knees, on *theirs*. The doctor will have it, that it was without bidding—perhaps so—he raised them by turns to his arms, and kissed them. Why, Harriet, your eyes glisten, child. They would have run over, I suppose, had you been there! Is it that your heart is weakened with your present situation? I hope not. No, you are a good creature! And I see that the mention of a behaviour greatly generous, however slightly made, will have its force upon a heart so truly benevolent as yours. You *must* be Lady Grandison, my dear: *indeed* you must.—Well, but I must be gone. You dine with us to-morrow, my brother says.

He did ask me: and desired me to engage my cousins. But he repeated not the invitation when he went away.

He depends upon your coming: and so do we. He is to talk to me before you, it seems: I can't tell about what: but by his hurrying on everything, it is plain he is preparing to leave us.

He is, madam.

'He is, madam!' And with that dejected air, and mendicant voice—Speak up like a woman!—The sooner he sets out, if he *must* go, the sooner he will deturn. Come, come, Harriet, you *shall* be Lady Grandison still.—*Ah!* and that *sigh* too! These love-sick folks have a language that nobody else can talk to them in! and then she affectedly sighed—Is that right, Harriet?—She sighed again—No, it is not: I never knew what a sigh was, but when my father vexed my sister; and that was more for fear he should one day be as cruel to me, than for her sake. We can be very generous for others, Harriet, when we apprehend that one day we may want the same pity ourselves. Our best passions, my dear, have their mixtures of self-love.

You have drawn a picture of human nature, Charlotte, that I don't like.

It *is* a likeness for all that.

She arose, snatched my hand, hurried to the door—Be with us, Harriet, and cousin Reeves, and cousin Reeves, as soon as you can to-morrow. I want to talk to you, my dear (to me), of a hundred thousand things before dinner. Remember we dine early.

Away she fluttered.—Happy Miss Grandison! What charming spirits she has!

LETTER XIV.

Miss Byron.—In continuation.

Wednesday, April 5.

Miss Jervois came to me this morning by six; impatient, as she said, to communicate good news to me. I was in my closet writing. I could not sleep.

I have seen my mother, said she; and we are good friends. Was she ever unkind to me, madam?

Dear creature! said I, and clasped her to my bosom, you are a sweet girl! Oblige me with the particulars.

Let me, Lucy, give you, as near as I can recollect, the amiable young creature's words and actions on this occasion.

Sit down, my love, said I.—What! when I am talking of a reconciled mother! and to dear Miss Byron!—No, indeed.

She often held out one open hand, while the forefinger of the other, in full action, patted it; as at other times both were spread, with pretty wonder and delight: and thus she began—

Why, you must know, it was about six o'clock yesterday afternoon, that my mother and her husband, and Captain Salmonet, came. I was told of their visit but two hours before: and when the coach stopped, and I at the window saw them alight, I thought I should have fainted away. I would have given half I was worth in the world to have been a hundred miles off.

Dr. Bartlett was there, and received them. My guardian was unexpectedly engaged in answering a letter sent him by Lord W——, for which a gentleman waited: but they had not been there a quarter of an hour, when he entered and made apologies to them, in his usual gracious manner. Never, the doctor says, did anybody look so respectful as the major and the captain; and they would have made apologies to my guardian for their last behaviour to him, but he would not let them. And my mother, the doctor says, from the very first, behaved prettily.

The moment she asked for me, my guardian himself condescended to come up to me, and took my hand—Was not that very good of him?—My dear, said he, as he led me down stairs (and spoke *so* kindly), don't tremble so: am I not with you?—Your mother is very calm and composed: you must ask her blessing. I shall ease your tender heart of every pang. I shall hint to you what to do, and how to behave to the gentlemen, as occasions arise.

He had no sooner said the words, but the drawing-room door gave way to his hand, and I was in the room with him.

Down on my knees dropt I—as I now do to you: but I could not speak. Thus I did. [And she kissed my hand, and bowed her face upon it.] And my mother raised me—*You* must raise me, madam—Yes, just so—And she kissed me *too,* and wept on my neck; and called me pretty names; and encouraged me, and said she loved me as she loved her own *soul*—And I *was* encouraged.

My guardian then, with the air and manner of a gracious prince, took my hand and presented it first to the major, then to the captain: and they each kissed my hand, and spoke in my praise I can't tell how many fine things.

Major, said my guardian, when he presented me to him, you must excuse the dear child's weakness of spirits: she wishes you all happiness on your nuptials: she has let me know that she is very desirous to do you service, for her mother's sake.

The major swore by his soul, that I was an angel!—Captain Salmonet said that, by his salvation, I was a charming young lady!

My mother wept.—Oh, sir! said she to my guardian: and dropping down in a chair by the window, not a word more could she speak.

I ran to her and clasped my arms about her. She wept the more: I wiped her eyes with her own handkerchief: I told her, it went to my heart to see her cry: I begged she would spare me *this* grief.

She clasped her arms then about me, and kissed my cheek and my forehead. Oh, thought I, it is very good of you, my dear mother.

Then came my guardian to us, and he kindly took my mother's hand, and conducted her to the fireside; and he led me, and placed me by her, at the tea-table; and he made the major and the captain sit down by him: *so* much graciousness in his countenance. O madam! I shall be an idolater, I am afraid. And he said, Emily, my dear, you will make tea for us. My sister dined abroad, madam, to my mother. Yes, sir, I will, said I: and I was as lively as a bird.

But before the servants came in, Let me tell you, madam,

said he, what Miss Jervois has proposed to me.—They were in silent expectation.

She has desired that you, major, will accept from her, for your mutual use, of an additional 100*l.* a year; which I shall order to be paid you quarterly, during Mrs. O'Hara's life, not doubting but you will make her as happy as it is in your power to make her.

My mother bowed, coloured with gratitude, and looked obliged.

And she begs of you, madam, turning to my mother, that you will accept, as from the *major,* another 100*l.* a year for pin-money, which he, or which *you,* madam, will draw upon me for; also quarterly, if you choose not to *trouble him* to do it: for this 100*l.* a year must be appropriated to your sole and separate use, madam; and not be subject to your control, Major O'Hara.

Good God! sir! said the major—What a wretch was I, the last time I was here!—There is no bearing of this!

He got up, and went to the window: and the Captain said, Blessed Jesu! and something else, which I could not mind; for I was weeping like a baby.

What, sir! said my mother, 400*l.* a year! Do you mean so?—I do, madam—And, sir, to be so generously paid me my 100*l.* of it, as if I received it not from my child, but from my husband!—Good God! how you overpower me, sir! What shame, what remorse do you strike into my heart!

And my poor mother's tears ran down as fast as mine.

O madam! said the dear girl to me, clasping her arms about me, how your tender heart is touched!—It is well you were not there!

Dr. Bartlett came in to tea. My guardian would not permit Antony, who offered himself, to wait. Antony had been my own papa's servant, when my mother was not so good.

Nothing but blessings, nothing but looks and words of admiration and gratitude, passed all the tea-time. How their hearts rejoiced, I warrant!—Is it not a charming thing, madam, to make people's hearts glad?—To be sure it is!

How many hearts has my guardian rejoiced! You must bid him be cross to me, or I shall not know what to do with myself!—But then, if he were, I should only get by myself and cry, and be angry with myself, and think *he* could not be to blame.

Oh my love! my Emily! said I, take care of your gratitude: that drew in your true friend.

Well, but how can it be helped, madam? Can a right heart be ungrateful?—Dr. Bartlett says, There is no such thing as true happiness in this life: and is it not better to be unhappy from good men and women, than from bad?—Dear madam, why *you* have often made me unhappy, because of your goodness to me; and because I knew that I neither could deserve nor return it.

The dear prater went on—My guardian called me aside, when tea was over: My Emily, said he [I do love he should call me *his* Emily!—But all the world is *his* Emily, I think], let me see what you will do with these two notes; giving me two bank-notes of 25*l.* each.—Present pin-money and cash may be wanted. We will suppose that your mother has been married a quarter of a year. Her pin-money and the additional annuity may commence from the 25th of December last. Let me, Emily, when they go away, see the graceful manner in which you will dispose of the notes: and from Mr. O'Hara's behaviour upon it, we shall observe whether he is a man with whom your mother, if it be not her own fault (now *you* have made it their interest to be kind to each other), may live well: but let the motion be all your own.

How *good* this was! I could have kissed the hand that gave me the notes, if I thought it would not have looked too free.

I understand you, sir, said I.

And when they went away, pouring out their very hearts in grateful joy, I addressed myself to Mr. O'Hara. Sir, said I, it is proper that the payment of the additional annuity should have a commencement: let it be from Christmas last. Accept of the first payment from my own hands—and I gave him one 25*l.* note: and looking at my mother, with a look of duty, for fear he should mistake, and discredit himself in the eyes of the deepest discerner in the world, gave him the other.

He looked first upon one, then upon the other note, with surprise—And then bowing to the ground to me, and to my guardian, he stept to my mother and presented them both to her—You, madam, said he, must *speak:* I cannot as I ought. God send me with a whole heart out of this house! He hurried out; and when he was in the hall, wiped his eyes, and sobbed like a child, as one of the servants told my Anne.

My mother looked upon one note, as her husband had done, and upon the other; and lifting up her eyes, embraced me—And would have said something to my guardian; but he prevented her, by saying—Emily will be always dutiful to you, madam, and respectful to Mr. O'Hara: may you be happy together!

And he led her out—was ever such a condescension! He led her out to her husband, who, being a little recovered, was just about to give some money to the servant, who was retiring from the offer.—Nobody, said my guardian, graciously smiling, pays my servants but myself, Mr. O'Hara. They are good people, and *merit* my favour.

And he went to the very door with my mother. I could not. I ran back, crying for joy, into the drawing-room, when *they* went out of it. I could not bear myself. How could I, you know, madam?—Captain Salmonet all the time wiped his eyes, shrugged his shoulders, lifted up his hands, and cried out upon Jesu; and once or twice he crossed himself: but all the time my guardian looked and acted, as if those actions and praises were nothing to be proud of.

When he came in to me, I arose, and threw myself at his feet; but could only say, Thank you, sir, for your goodness to my mother. He raised me. He sat down by me: See, child (said he, and he took my hand: my heart was sensible of the favour, and throbbed with joy), what it is in the power of people of fortune to do. You have a great one. Now your mother is married, I have hopes of her. They will at least keep up appearances to each other, and to the world. They neither of them want sense. *You* have done an act of duty and benevolence both in one. The man who would grudge them this additional 200*l.* a year out of your fortune, to make your parent happy, shall not have my Emily—shall he?

Your Emily, your *happy* Emily, sir, has not, cannot have a heart that is worth notice, if it be not implicitly guided by you.—This I said, madam: and it is true.

And did he not, said I, clasp his Emily to his generous bosom when you said so?

No, Madam; that would have been too great an honour: but he called me, good child! and said, You shall never be put to pay me an *implicit* regard: your own reason (and he called me *child* again) shall always be the judge of my conduct to you, and direct your observances of my advice. Something like this he said; but in a better manner than I can say it

He calls me oftener *child,* madam, than anything else, when we are alone together; and is not quite so free, I think, at such times, in his behaviour to me (yet is *vastly* gracious, I don't know how), as when we are in company—Why is that? —I am sure I equally respect *him* at one time as at another —Do you think, madam, there is anything in the observation? Is there any *reason* for it? I *do* love to study him, and to find out the meaning of his very looks, as well as words. Sir Charles Grandison's heart is the book of heaven—May I *not* study it?

Study it, my love, while you have an opportunity. But he will soon leave us: he will soon leave England.

So I fear: and I will love and pity the poor Clementina, whose heart is so much wounded and oppressed. But my guardian shall be nobody's but yours. I have prayed night and day, the first thing, and the last thing, ever since I have heard of Lady Clementina, that you, and nobody but you, may be Lady Grandison: and I will continue my prayers.—But will you forgive me? I always conclude them with praying, that you will both consent to let the poor Emily live with you.

Sweet girl! The *poor* Emily, said she?—I embraced her and we mingled tears, both our hearts full, each for the other; and each perhaps for herself.

She hurried away. I resumed my pen—Run off what had passed almost as swift as thought. I quit it to prepare to attend my cousins to St. James's Square.

LETTER XV.

Miss Byron.—In continuation.

Wednesday Night, April 5.

MISS GRANDISON, as I told you, took with her my letter of yesterday. As soon as my cousins Reeves and I entered Sir Charles's house, the two sisters conducted us into the drawing-room adjoining to the dining-parlour, and congratulated me on the high compliment their brother had made me, though in preference to themselves, and his communicativeness and tender behaviour to me. Lord L—— joined us; and he, having read the letter, congratulated me also—On what, Lucy?—Why on the *possibility,* that if the unhappy Clementina should die; or if she should be buried for life in a nunnery; or if she should be otherwise disposed of; why then, that your Harriet may have room given her to hope for a *civil* husband in Sir Charles Grandison, and *half* a heart: is not this the sum of these humbling congratulations?

Sir Charles, when we came, was in his study with Mr. Lowther, the surgeon, whom he had engaged to go abroad with him: but he just came out to welcome us; and then returned. —He had also with him two physicians, eminent for their knowledge in disorders of the head, to whom he had before communicated the case of the unhappy Clementina; and who brought to him in writing their opinions of the manner in which she ought to be treated, according to the various symptoms of her disorder.

When he joined us, he told us this, and said very high things at the same time in praise of the English surgeons; and particularly of this gentleman: and added, that as nervous disorders were more frequent in England than in any country in the world, he was willing to hope that the English physicians were more skilful than those of any other country in the management of persons afflicted with such maladies: and as he was now invited over, he was determined to furnish himself with all the means he could think of that were likely to be useful in restoring and healing friends so dear to him.

Miss Grandison told him that we were all in some apprehensions, on his going to Italy, of that fierce and wrongheaded man the general. Miss Byron, said she, has told us that Mrs. Beaumont advises not your going over.

The young Marquis della Porretta, said he, is hasty; but he is a gallant man, and loves his sister. His grief on the unhappy situation they are in, demands allowances. It is natural in a heavy calamity to look out for ourselves for the occasion. I have not any apprehensions from him, or from anybody else. The call upon me is a proper one. The issue must be left where it ought to be left. If my visit will give comfort to any *one* of the family, I shall be rewarded: if to *more* than one, happy—and whatever be the event, shall be easier in myself than I could be, were I not to comply with the request of the bishop, were *he* only to have made it.

Lord L—— asked Sir Charles whether he had fixed the day of his setting out?

I have, said he, within this half hour. Mr. Lowther has told me that he shall be ready by the beginning of next week; and on Saturday se'nnight I hope to be at Dover on my way.

We looked upon one another. Miss Grandison told me afterwards that my colour went and came several times, and that she was afraid for me. My heart was *indeed* a little affected. I believe I must not think of taking leave of him when he sets out. Ah, Lucy! Nine days hence!—Yet, in less than nine days after that, I shall be embraced by the tenderest relations that ever creature had to boast of.

Sir Charles taking his sister aside, I want, said he, to say a few words to you, Charlotte. They were about half an hour together; and then returning, I am encouraged to think, said he, that Charlotte will give her hand to Lord G——. She is a woman of honour, and her heart must therefore go with it.—I have a request to make to her, before all you, our common friends—The Earl of G——, Lady Gertrude, Lord G——, all join in one suit: it is, that I may be allowed to give my sister to Lord G—— before I leave England.

I have told you, brother, that it is impossible, if you go away in nine or ten days' time.

Sir Charles particularly requested my influence. I could have no doubt, I said, but Miss Grandison would oblige her brother.

She vehemently opposed so early a day.

In a most affectionate manner, yet with an air of seriousness, he urged his request. He said, that it was very proper for him to make some disposition of his affairs before he went abroad. He should leave England with much more pleasure, if he saw his Charlotte the wife of a man so worthy as Lord G——: Lord G——, said he, adores you: You *intended* to be his: resolve to oblige your brother, who, though he cannot be happy himself, wishes to see you so.

O Sir Charles! said she, you ruin me by your solemnity, and by your goodness.

The subject is not a light one. I am greatly in earnest, Charlotte. I have many affairs on my hands. My heart is in this company: yet my engagements will permit me but few opportunities to enjoy it between this and Tuesday next. If you deny me now, I must acquiesce: if you have more than punctilio to plead, say you have; and I will not urge you further.

And so this is the last time of asking, sir?—A little archly—

Not the last time of my Lord G——'s, but of mine—But I will not allow you now to answer me lightly. If you can name a day before Tuesday, you will greatly oblige me. I will leave you to consider of it. And he withdrew.

Every one then urged her to oblige her brother. Lady L—— very particularly. She told her, that he was *entitled* to her compliance; and that he had spoken to *her* on this subject in a still more earnest manner. She should hardly be able to excuse her, she said, if the serious hint he had given about settling his affairs before he went abroad, had not weight with her. You know, Charlotte, continued she, that he can have no motive but your good; and you have told me that you intend to have Lord G——; and that you esteem his father, his aunt, and every one of his family, whom you have seen; and they are highly pleased with you. Settlements are already drawn: that my brother told you last night. Nothing is wanting but your day.

I wish he was in half the hurry to be married himself.

So he would be, I daresay, Charlotte, if marriage were as much in his power as it is in yours.

What a deuce, to be married to a man in a week's time, with whom I have quarrelled every day for a fortnight past!—Pride and petulance must go down by degrees, sister. A month, at least, is necessary, to bring my features to such a placidness with him, as to allow him to smile in my face.

Your brother has hinted, Charlotte, said I, that he loves you for your vivacity; and should still more, if you consulted *time* and *occasion*.

He has withdrawn, sister, said Lord L——, with a resolution, if you deny him, to urge you no further.

I *hate* his peremptoriness.

Has he not told you, Charlotte, said I, and that in a manner so serious as to affect everybody, that there is a kind of necessity for it?

I don't love this Clementina, Harriet: all this is owing to her.

Just then a rapping at the door signified visitors; and Emily ran in—Lord G——, the Earl, and Lady Gertrude, believe me!

Miss Grandison changed colour. A contrivance of my brother's!—Ah, Lord! Now shall I be beset!—I will be sullen, that I may not be saucy.

Sullen you can't be, Charlotte, said Lady L——: but *saucy* you can. Remember, however, my brother's earnestness, and spare Lord G—— before his father and aunt, or you will give me, and everybody, pain.

How can I? Our last quarrel is not made up: but advise him not to be either impertinent or secure.

Immediately entered Sir Charles, introducing the Earl and Lady Gertrude. After the first compliments, Pray, Sir Charles, said Miss Grandison, drawing him aside towards me, and whispering, Tell me truly: did not you know of this visit?

I *invited* them, Charlotte, whispered he. I meant not, however, to surprise you. If you comply, you will give me great pleasure: if you do not, I will not be *dis*-pleased with my sister.

What *can* I do? Either be less good to me, sir, or less hurrying.

You have sacrificed enough to female punctilio, Charlotte. Lord G—— has been a zealous courtier. You have no doubt of the ardour of his passion, nor of your own power. Leave the day to me. Let it be Tuesday next.

Good Heaven! I can't bear you, after such a—— and she gasped, as if for breath; and he turning from her to me, she went to Lady Gertrude, who, rising, took her hand, and withdrew with her into the next room.

They stayed out till they were told dinner was served: and when they returned, I thought I never saw Miss Grandison look so lovely. A charming flush had overspread her cheeks: a sweet consciousness in her eyes gave a *female* grace to her whole aspect, and softened, as I may say, the natural majesty of her fine features.

Lord G—— looked delighted, as if his heart were filled with happy presages. The Earl seemed no less pleased.

Miss Grandison was unusually thoughtful all dinner-time. She gave me great joy to see her so, in the hope, that when the lover becomes the husband, the over-lively mistress will be sunk in the obliging wife—And yet, now and then, as the joy in my lord's heart overflowed at his lips, I could observe *that* archness rising to her eye, that makes one both love and fear her.

After dinner, the Earl of G—— and Lady Gertrude desired a conference with Sir Charles and Lady L——. They were not long absent, when Sir Charles came in, and carried out Miss Grandison to them. Lord G——'s complexion varied often.

Sir Charles left them together and joined us. We were standing; and he singled me out—I hope, madam, said he, that Charlotte may be prevailed upon for Tuesday next: But I will not urge it further.

I thought he was framing himself to say something particular to me, when Lady L—— came in, and desired him and me to step to her sister, who had retired from the Earl and Lady Gertrude by consent.

Ah, my Harriet! said she, pity me, my dear!—Debasement is the child of pride!—Then turning to Sir Charles, I acknowledge myself overcome, said she, by your earnestness, as you are so soon to leave us, and by the importunities of the Earl of G——, Lady Gertrude, and my sister—Unprepared in mind, in clothes, I am resolved to oblige the best of brothers. Do you, sir, dispose of me as you think fit.

My sister consents, sir, said Lady L——, for next Tuesday.

Cheerfully, I hope. If Charlotte balances whether, if she took more time, she should have Lord G—— at all, let her take it. Lord L——, in my absence, will be to her all that I wish to be, when she shall determine.

I balanced *not*, sir: But I thought to have had a month's time, at least, to look about me; and having treated Lord G—— too flippantly, to give him by degrees some fairer prospects of happiness with me, than hitherto he has had.

Sir Charles embraced her. She was all his sister, he said. Let the alteration *now* begin. Lord G—— would rejoice in it, and consider all that had passed, as trials only of his love for her. The obliging wife would banish from his remembrance the petulant mistress. And now allow me, my dear sister, to present you to the Earl and Lady Gertrude.

He led her into them. Lady L—— took my hand, and led me in also.—Charlotte, my lord, yields to yours and Lady Gertrude's importunities. Next Tuesday will give the two families a near and tender relation to each other.

The earl saluted her in a very affectionate manner: so did

Lady Gertrude; who afterwards ran out for her nephew: and, leading him in, presented him to Miss Grandison.

She had just time to whisper me, as he approached her: Ah, Harriet! now comes the worst part of the show.—He kneeled on one knee, kissed her hand: but was too much overjoyed to speak; for Lady Gertrude had told him, as she led him in, that Tuesday was to be his happy day.

It is impossible, Lucy, but Sir Charles Grandison must carry every point he sets his heart upon. When he shall appear before the family of Porretta in Italy, *who* will be able to withstand him?—Is not his consequence doubled, *more* than doubled, since he was with them? The man whose *absence* they wished for, they now *invite* to come among them. They have tried every experiment to restore their Clementina. He has a noble estate now in possession. The fame of his goodness is gone out to distant countries. Oh, my dear! all opposition must fly before him. And if it be the will of Heaven to restore Clementina, all her friends must concur in giving her to him upon the terms he has proposed: and from which, having *himself* proposed them, Sir Charles Grandison cannot recede.

His heart, it is evident, is at Bologna. Well, and so it *ought* to be. And yet I could not forbear being sensibly touched by the following words, which I overheard him say to Lord L——, in answer to something my lord said to him:

'I am impatient to be abroad. Had I not waited for Mr. 'Lowther, the last letters I received from Italy should have 'been answered in person.'

But as honour, compassion, love, *friendship* (still nobler than love!) have demands upon him, let him obey the call. He has set me high in his esteem. Let me be worthy of his friendship. Pangs I shall occasionally feel; but who, that values one person above the rest of the world, does not?

Sir Charles, as we sat at tea, mentioned his cousin Grandison to Lord L——: It is strange, my lord, said he, that we hear nothing of our cousin Everard, since he was seen at White's. But whenever he *emerges,* Charlotte, if I am absent, receive him without reproaches: yet I should be glad that he could have rejoiced with us. Must I leave England, and not see him?

It has been, it seems, the way of this unhappy man, to shut himself up with some woman in private lodgings, for fear his cousin should find him out; and in two or three months, when he has been tired of his wicked companion, *emerge,* as Sir Charles called it, to notice, and then seek for his cousin's favour and company, and live for as many more months in a state of contrition. And Sir Charles, in his great charity, believes that, till some new temptation arises, he is in earnest in his penitence; and hopes, that in time he will see his errors.

O Lucy! What a poor, creeping, mean wretch is a libertine, when one looks *down* upon him, and *up* to such a glorious creature as Sir Charles Grandison!

Sir Charles was led to talk of his engagement for to-morrow, on the triple marriage in the Danby family. We all gave him joy of the happy success that had rewarded his beneficent spirit, with regard to that family. He gave us the characters of the three couples greatly to their advantage, and praised the families on both sides, which were to be so closely united on the morrow; not forgetting to mention kindly *honest* Mr. Silvester the attorney.

He told us, that he should set out on Friday early for Windsor, in order to attend Lord W—— in his first visit to Mansfield House. You, Lady L——, will have the trouble given you, said he, of causing to be new-set the jewels of the late Lady W——, for a present to the future bride. My lord shewed them to me (among a great number of other valuable trinkets of his late wife's) in my last return from the Hall. They are rich, and will do credit to his quality. You, my Lord L——, you my sisters, will be charmed with your new aunt, and her whole family. I have joy on the happiness in prospect that will gild the latter days of my mother's brother; and at the same time be a means of freeing from oppression an ancient and worthy family.

Tears were in every eye. There *now,* thought I, sits this princely man, rejoicing every one that sees him and hears him speak: But *where* will he be nine days hence? And *whose* this day twelvemonth?

He talked with particular pleasure of the expected arrival of his Beauchamp. He pleased himself, that he should leave behind him a man who would delight everybody, and supply to his friends *his* absence.—What a character did he give, and Dr. Bartlett confirm, of that amiable friend of his!

How did the Earl and Lady Gertrude dwell upon all he said! They prided themselves on the relation they were likely so soon to stand in to so valuable a man.

In your last letter, you tell me, Lucy, that Mr. Greville has the confidence to throw out menaces against this excellent man—Sorry wretch!—How my heart rises against him!—He— But no more of such an earth-born creature.

LETTER XVI.

Miss Byron.—In continuation.

Thursday Morning, April 6.

MISS GRANDISON, accompanied by Miss Jervois, has just left us. Lady L—— has undertaken, she says, to set all hands at work, to have things in tolerable order, early as the day is, for Tuesday next. Miss Grandison (would you believe it?) owns, that she wants *spirits* to order anything. What must be the solemnity of that circumstance, when near, that shall make Charlotte Grandison want spirits?

She withdrew with me to my apartment. She threw herself into a chair: 'Tis a folly to deny it, Harriet, but I am very low, and very silly: I don't like next Tuesday, by any means.

Is your objection only to the day, my dear?

I do not like the man.

Is there any man whom you like better?

I can't say that neither. But this brother of mine makes

me think contemptibly of all other men. I would compound for a man but half as good—Tender, kind, humane, polite, and even cheerful in affliction!—O Harriet! where is there such another man?

Nowhere.—But you don't by marriage lose; on the contrary, you further engage and secure the affection of this brother. You will have a good-natured worthy man for your husband, a man who loves you; and who will have your brother besides.

Do you think I can be happy with Lord G——?

I am sure you may, if it be not your own fault.

That's the thing: I may, perhaps, bear with the man; but I cannot honour him.

Then don't vow to honour him. Don't meet him at the altar.

Yet I must. But I believe I *think* too much: and consideration is no friend to wedlock.—Would to Heaven that the same hour that my hand and Lord G——'s were joined, yours and my brother's were also united!

Ah, Miss Grandison, if you love me, try to wean me; and not to encourage hopes of what never, never can be.

Dear creature! You will be greater than Clementina, and that is greater than the greatest, if you can conquer a passion which overturned her reason.

Do not, my Charlotte, make comparison in which the conscience of your Harriet tells her she must be a sufferer. There is no occasion for me to despise myself in order to hold myself inferior to Clementina.

Well, you are a noble creature!—But, the approaching Tuesday—I cannot *bear* to think of it.

Dear Charlotte!

And dear Harriet too!—But the officiousness, the assiduities of this trifling man, are disgustful to me.

You don't hate him?——

Hate him—true—I don't *hate* him—but I have been so much accustomed to treat him like a fool, that I can't help thinking him one. He should not have been so tame to such a spirit as mine. He should have been angry when I played upon him. I have got a knack of it, and shall never leave it off, that's certain.

Then I hope he *will* be angry with you. I hope that he *will* resent your ill treatment of him.

Too late, too late to begin, Harriet. I won't take it of him now. He has never let me see that his face can become two sorts of features. The poor man can look sorrowful; that I know full well: but I shall always laugh when he attempts to look angry.

You *know* better, Charlotte. You may give him so much cause for anger, that you may make it habitual to him, and then would be glad to see him pleased. Men have a hundred ways, that women have not, to divert themselves abroad, when they cannot be happy at home. This I have heard observed by——

By your grandmother, Harriet? Good old lady! In *her* reign it might be so; but you will find that women now have as many ways to divert themselves abroad as the men. Have you not observed this yourself in one of your letters to Lucy? Ah, my dear! we can every hour in the twenty-four be up with our monarchs, if they are undutiful.

But Charlotte Grandison will not, cannot——

Why, that's true, my dear—but I shall not *then* be a Grandison. Yet the man will have some security from my brother's goodness. He is not only good himself, but he makes every one related to him, either for fear or shame, good likewise. But I think that when one week or fortnight is happily over and my spirits are got up again from the depression into which this abominable hurry puts them, I could fall upon some inventions that would make every one laugh, except the person who might take it into his head that he may be a sufferer by them: and who can *laugh,* and be *angry,* in the same moment?

You should not marry, Charlotte, till this wicked vein of humour and raillery is stopt.

I hope it will hold me till fifty.

Don't say so, Charlotte—say rather that you hope it will hold you so long only as it may be thought innocent or inoffensive, by the man whom it will be your duty to oblige; and so long as it will bring no discredit to yourself.

Your servant, Goody Gravity!—But what *must* be, must. The man is bound to see it. It will be all his own seeking. He will sin with his eyes open. I think he has seen enough of me to take warning. All that I am concerned about, is for the next week or fortnight. He will be king all that time, —yet, perhaps, not *quite* all neither. And I shall be his sovereign ever after, or I am mistaken. What a deuce, shall a woman marry a man of talents not superior to her own, and forget to reward herself for her condescension?—But, high-ho!—There's a sigh, Harriet. Were I at home, I would either sing you a song, or play you a tune, in order to raise my own heart.

She besought me then, with great earnestness, to give her my company till the day arrived, and *on* the day. You see, said she, that my brother has engagements till Monday. Dear creature! support, comfort me—don't you see my heart beat through my stays?—If you love me, come to me to-morrow to breakfast; and leave me not for the whole time—are you not my sister, and the friend of my heart? I will give you a month for it, upon demand. Come, let us go down; I will ask the consent of both your cousins.

She did: and they, with their usual goodness to me, cheerfully complied.

Sir Charles set out this morning to attend the triple marriages; dressed charmingly, his sister says. I have made Miss Grandison promise to give me an account of such particulars, as, by the help of Saunders, and Sir Charles's own relation, she can pick up. All we single girls, I believe, are pretty attentive to such subjects as these; as what one day may be our own concern.

LETTER XVII.

Miss Grandison to Miss Byron.

Thursday Night.

UNREASONABLE, wicked, cruel Byron! To expect a poor creature, so near her execution, to write an account of other people's behaviour in the same tremendous circumstances! The matrimonial noose has hung over my head for some time past; and now it is actually fitted to my devoted neck.—Almost chocked, my dear!—This moment done hearing read, the firsts, seconds, thirds, fourths, to near a dozen of them—Lord be merciful to us!—And the villanous lawyer rearing up to me his spectacled nose, as if to see how I bore it! Lord G—— insulting me, as I thought, by his odious leers: Lady Gertrude simpering; little Emily ready to bless herself—how will the dear Harriet bear these abominable recitatives?—But I am now up stairs from them all, in order to recover my breath, and obey my Byron.

Well, but what am I now to say about the Danbys? Saunders has made his report; Sir Charles has told us some things: yet I will only give you heads: make out the rest.

In the first place, my brother went to Mrs. Harrington's: (Miss Danby's aunt:) *she* did everything but worship him. She had with her two young ladies, relations of her late husband, dainty damsels of the city, who had procured themselves to be invited, that they might see the man, whom they called, a wonder of generosity and goodness. Richard heard one of them say to the other, Ah, sister, this is a king of a man! What pity there are not many such! But, Harriet, if there were a hundred of them, we would not let one of them go into the city for a wife; would we, my dear?

Sir Charles praised Miss Danby. She was full of gratitude; and of humility, I suppose. Meek, modest, and humble, are qualities in which men are mighty fond in women. But matrimony, and a sense of obligation, are equally great humblers even of spirits prouder than that of Miss Danby; as you poor Charlotte can testify.

The young gentlemen, with the rest, were to meet Sir Charles, the bride, and these ladies, at St. Helen's, I think the church is called.

As if wedlock were an honour, the Danby girl, in respect to Sir Charles, was to be first yoked. He gave her away to the son Galliard. The father Galliard gave his daughter to Edward Danby: but first Mr. Hervey gave his niece to the elder.

One of the brides, I forgot which, fainted away; another half fainted—Saved by timely salts: the third, poor soul, wept heartily—as I suppose I shall do on Tuesday.

Never, surely, was there such a matrimony promoter as my brother. God give me soon my revenge upon him in the same way!

The procession afterwards was triumphant—Six coaches, four silly souls in each; and to Mr. Poussin's, at Enfield, they all drove. There they found another large company.

My brother was all cheerfulness; and both men and women seemed to contend for his notice: but they were much disappointed at finding he meant to leave them early in the evening.

One married lady, the wife of Sir —— somebody (I am very bad at remembering the names of city knights), was resolved, she said, since they could not have Sir Charles to open the ball, to have one dance before dinner with the handsomest man in England. The music was accordingly called in; and he made no scruple to oblige the company on a day so happy.

Do you know, Harriet, that Sir Charles is supposed to be one of the finest dancers in England? Remember, my dear, that on Tuesday—[Lord help me! I shall then be stupid, and remember nothing]—you take him out yourself: and then you will judge for yourself of his excellence in this science— May we not call dancing a science? If we judge by the *few,* who perform gracefully in it, I am sure we may; and a difficult one too.

Oh!—And remember, Harriet, that you get somebody to

call upon him to sing—*You* shall play—I believe I shall forget, in that only agreeable moment of the day (for you have a sweet finger, my love), that I am the principal fool in the play of the evening.

O Harriet!—How *can I,* in the circumstances I am in, write any more about the soft souls, and silly? Come to me by day-dawn, and leave me not till—I don't know when. Come, and take my part, my dear: I shall hate this man: he does nothing but hop, skip, and dance about me, grin, and make mouths; and everybody upholds him in it.

Must this (I hope not!) be the last time that I write myself to you   CHARLOTTE GRANDISON.

LETTER XVIII.

Miss Byron to Miss Selby.

St. James's Square, Friday Morning, April 7.

SIR CHARLES GRANDISON set out early this morning for Lord W——'s, in his way to Lady Mansfield's. I am here with this whimsical Charlotte.

Lady L——, Miss Jervois, myself, and every female of the family, or who do business for both sisters out of it, are busy in some way or other, preparatory to the approaching Tuesday.

Miss Grandison is the only idle person. I tell her, she is affectedly so.

The earl has presented her, in his son's name, with some very rich trinkets. Very valuable jewels are also bespoke by Lord G——, who takes Lady L——'s advice in everything; as one well read in the fashions. New equipages are bespoke; and gay ones they will be.

Miss Grandison confounded me this morning by an instance of her generosity. She was extremely urgent with me to accept, as her third sister, of her share of her mother's jewels. You may believe that I absolutely refused such a present. I was angry with her; and told her, she had but one way of making it up with me; and that was, that since she would be so completely set out from her lord, she would unite the two halves, by presenting hers to Lady L——, who had refused jewels from her lord on her marriage; and who then would make an appearance, occasionally, as brilliant as her own.

She was pleased with the hint; and has actually given them (unknown to anybody but me) to her jeweller; who is to dispose them in such figures, as shall answer those she herself is to have, which Lady L—— has not. And by this contrivance, which will make them in a manner useless to herself, she thinks she shall oblige her sister, however reluctant, to accept of them.

Lady Gertrude is also preparing some fine present for her niece elect: but neither the delighted approbation of the family she is entering into, nor the satisfaction expressed by her own friends, give the perverse Charlotte any visible joy, nor procure for Lord G—— the distinction which she ought to think of beginning to pay him. But, for his part, never was man so happy. He would, however, perhaps, fare better from her, if he could be more moderate in the outward expression of his joy; which she has taken it into her head to call an insult upon her.

She does not, however, give the scope she did before the day was fixed, to her playful captiousness. She is not quite so arch as she was. Thoughtfulness, and a seeming carelessness of what we are all employed in, appear in her countenance. She saunters about, and affects to be diverted by her harpsichord only. What a whimsical thing is Charlotte Grandison! But still she keeps Lord G—— at distance. I told her, an hour ago, that she knows not how to condescend to him with that grace which is so natural to her in her whole behaviour to everybody else.

I have been talking to Dr. Bartlett, about Sir Charles's journey to Italy. Nobody knows, he says, what a bleeding heart is covered by a countenance so benign and cheerful.

Sir Charles Grandison, said he, has a prudence beyond that of most young men; but he has great sensibilities.

I take it for granted, sir, said I, that he will for the future be more an Italian than Englishman.

Impossible, madam! A *prudent* youth, by travelling, reaps this advantage—From what he sees of other countries, he learns to prefer his own. An *imprudent* one the contrary. Sir Charles's country is endeared to him by his long absence from it. Italy, in particular, is called the garden of Europe; but it is rather to be valued for what it *was,* and *might be,* than what *it is.* I need not tell a lady, who has read and conversed as you have done, to what that incomparable difference is owing. Sir Charles Grandison is greatly sensible of it. He loves his country with the judgment of a wise man; and wants not the partiality of a patriot.

But doctor, he has offered, you know, to reside—There I stopt.

True, madam—And he will not recede from his offers, if they are claimed. But this uncertainty it is that disturbs him.

I pity my patron, proceeded he. I have often told you he is not happy. What has indiscretion to expect, when discretion has so much to suffer? His only consolation is, that he has nothing to reproach himself with. Inevitable evils he bears as a man should. He makes no ostentation of his piety: but, madam, Sir Charles Grandison is a CHRISTIAN.

You need not, sir, say more to me to exalt him: and, let me add, that I have no small pleasure in knowing that Clementina is a lady of strict piety, though a Roman Catholic.

And let me assure you, madam, that Sir Charles's regard for Miss Byron (his *more* than regard for her, why should I not say? since everybody sees it) is founded upon her piety, and upon the amiable qualities of her mind. Beauty, madam, is an accidental and transient good. No man better knows how to distinguish between *admiration* and *love* than my patron. His virtue is virtue upon *full proof,* and against sensibilities, that it is heroic to overcome. Lady Olivia knows this: and here I must acknowledge myself a debtor to you for three articles out of your ten. I hope soon to discharge the obligation.

Your own time, doctor: but I *must* say, that whenever you give me Lady Olivia's story, I shall be pained, if I find that a Clementina is considered by a beauty of an *unhappier* turn, as *her* rival in the love of Sir Charles Grandison.

Lady Olivia, madam, *admires* him for his virtues; but she cannot, as *he* has made it his study to do, divide *admiration* from *love*. What offers has she not refused?—But she declares, that she had rather be the *friend* of Sir Charles Grandison, than the wife of the greatest prince on earth.

This struck me: Have not *I* said something like it? But surely with innocence of heart. But here the doctor suggests, that Olivia has put his virtue to the proof: Yet I hope not.

The FRIEND, Dr. Bartlett!—I hope that no woman, who is not quite given up to dishonour, will pollute the sacred word, by affixing ideas to it, that cannot be connected with it. A *friend* is one of the highest characters that one human creature can shine in to another. There may be *love,* that though it has no view but to honour, yet, even in wedlock, ripens not into friendship. How poor are all such attachments! How much beneath the exalted notion I have of that noblest, that most delicate union of souls! You wonder at me, Dr. Bartlett. Let me repeat to you, sir (I have it by heart), Sir Charles Grandison's tender of friendship to the poor Harriet Byron, which has given me such exalted ideas of this disinterested passion; but you must not take notice that I have. I repeated those words, beginning, 'My heart demands alliance with hers'—and ending with these—'So long as it shall be 'consistent with her other attachments.'*

The doctor was silent for a few moments. At last, What a delicacy is there in the mind of this excellent man! Yet how consistent with the exactest truth! The friendship he offers you, madam, is *indeed* friendship. What you have repeated can want no explanation: yet it is expressive of his uncertain situation. It is——

He stopt of a sudden.

* See page 133 of this Volume.

Pray, doctor, proceed: I love to hear you talk.

My *good* young lady!—I may say too much. Sir Charles, in these nice points, must be left to himself. It is impossible for anybody to express his thoughts as *he* can express them. But let me say, that he justly, as well as greatly, admires Miss Byron.

My heart rose against itself. Bold Harriet, thought I, how darest thou thus urge a good man to say more than he has a mind to say of the secrets of a friend, which are committed to his keeping? Content thyself with the *hopes,* that the worthiest man in the world would wish to call thee his, were it not for an invincible obstacle. And noble, thrice noble Clementina, be thine the preference even in the heart of Harriet Byron, because justice gives it to thee; for, Harriet, hast thou not been taught to prefer right and justice to every other consideration? And, wouldst thou abhor the thought of a common theft, yet steal a heart that is the property, and that by the dearest purchase, of another?

LETTER XIX.

Miss Byron.—In continuation.

Friday Evening.

WE have had a great debate about the place in which the nuptial ceremony is to be performed.

Charlotte, the perverse Charlotte, insisted upon not going to church.

Lord G—— dared not to give his opinion; though his father and Lady Gertrude, as well as every other person, were against her.

Lord L—— said, that if fine ladies thought so slightly of the office, as that it might be performed anywhere, it would be no wonder if fine gentlemen thought still more slightly of the obligation it laid them under.

Being appealed to, I said, that I thought of marriage as one of the most solemn acts of a woman's life.

And if of a woman's, of a *man's,* surely, interrupted Lady L——. If your whimsey, Charlotte, added she, arises from modesty, you reflect upon your sister; and, what is worse, upon your mother.

Charlotte put up her pretty lip, and was unconvinced.

Lady Gertrude laid a heavy hand upon the affectation; yet admires her niece-elect. She distinguished between chamber vows and church-vows. She mentioned the word *decency.* She spoke plainer, on Charlotte's unfeeling perverseness. If a bride meant a compliment by it to the bridegroom, that was another thing; but then let her declare as much; and that she was in a hurry to oblige him.

Charlotte attempted to kill her by a look—She gave a worse to Lord G——. And why, whispered she to him, as he sat next her, must thou shew all thy teeth, man?—As Lady Gertrude meant to shame her, I thought I could as soon forgive that lady, as her who was the occasion of the freedom of speech.

But still she was perverse: she would not be married at all, she said, if she were not complied with.

I whispered her, as I sat on the other side of her, I wish, Charlotte, the knot were tied: till then, you will not do even right things, but in a wrong manner.

Dr. Bartlett was not present: he was making a kind visit to my cousins Reeves. When he came in, the debate was referred to him. He entered into it with her, with so much modesty, good sense, propriety, and steadiness, that at last the perverse creature gave way: but hardly would neither, had he not assured her, that her brother would be entirely against her; and that he himself must be excused performing the sacred office but in a sacred place. She has set her heart on the doctor's marrying her.

The Earl of G—— and Lady Gertrude, as also Lord and Lady L——, went away, not dissatisfied with Charlotte's compliance: she is the most ungraciously graceful young woman I ever knew in her compliances. But Lord G—— was to pay for all: she and I got together in the study: in bolted Lord G——, perhaps with *too* little ceremony. She coloured —Hey-day, sir! who expected you? His countenance immediately fell. He withdrew precipitately. Fie, Charlotte! said I; recollect yourself—and rising, stept to the door, My lord—calling after him.

He came back, but in a little ferment—I hoped, I hoped, madam, as you were not in your own apartment, that I might, that I might have been——

Wherever ladies are by themselves, it is a lady's apartment, my lord, said she, with a haughtiness that sat better on *her* features, than they would upon almost any other woman's.

He looked as if he knew not whether he should stay or go. Sit down, my lord, said I; we are not particularly engaged. He came nearer, his hat under his arm, bowing to her, who sat as stately as a princess on her throne: but yet looked disobliged. You give yourself pretty airs, my lord—don't you?

Pretty airs, madam!—Pretty airs!—By my soul, I think, madam—And with such a glow on your face, madam—Taking his laced hat from under his arm, and, with an earnest motion, swinging it backward and forward, as unknowing what he did——

What, sir, am I to be buffetted, sir?——

He put his hat under his arm again—*Buffetted*, madam!—Would to Heaven——

What has Heaven to do with your odd ways, Lord G——?

I beg pardon for intruding, madam—but I thought——

That you had a privilege, sir—But marriage itself, sir, shall not give you a privilege to break into my retirements. You *thought,* sir—You could *not think*—So much the worse if you did——

If I have really offended—I will be more circumspect for the future—I beg pardon, madam—Miss Byron, I hope will forgive me too.

He was going, in great discomposure, and with an air of angry humility.

Charlotte, whispered I, don't be silly——

Come, come, now *you* have broke in upon us, you may stay

—But another time, when you know me to be retired with a friend so dear to me, let it enter into your head, that no third person, unsent for, can be welcome.

Poor man!—How he loves her!—His countenance changed at once to the humble placid: he looked as if he had rather be in fault than she.

Oh! how *little* did she make him look!

But he has often, as well as in this instance, let her see her power over him. I am afraid she will use it. I now see it is and will be his misfortune, that she can vex him without being vexed herself: and what may he expect, who can be treated with feigned displeasure, which, while it seems to be in earnest to him, will be a jest to his wife?

I was very angry with her, when we were alone; and told her, that she would be an enemy, I was afraid, of her own happiness. But she only laughed at me: Happiness, my dear! said she: *that* only is happiness which we think so. If I can be as happy in my way, as you can be in yours, shall I not pursue it? Your happiness, child, is in the still life, I love not a dead calm: now a tempest, now a refreshing breeze, I shall know how to enjoy the difference—My brother will not be here to turn jest into earnest; as might, perhaps, be the effect of his mediation—But, heigh-ho, Harriet! that the first week were over, and I had got into my throne!

She ended with an Italian air, contrasted with another heigh-ho; and left me for a few moments.

Poor Lord G——! said I, looking after her.

She returned soon. *Poor Lord G——!* repeated she: those were the piteous words you threw after me—But if I should provoke him, do you think he would not give me a cuff, or so? —You know he can't return joke for joke; and he must revenge himself some way—If that should be the case, *Poor Charlotte,* I hope you would say——

Not if you deserved it.

Deserve a *cuff*, Harriet!—Well, but I am afraid I shall.

Remember next Tuesday, Charlotte!—You must vow obedience—Will you break your vow?—This is not a jesting matter.

True, Harriet. And that it is *not,* was, perhaps, one of the reasons that made me disinclined to go to so solemn a place as the church with Lord G——. Don't you think it one with those who insist upon being married in their own chamber?

I believe great people, said I, think they must not do right things in the common way: that seems to me to be one of their fantastic reasons: but the vow is the vow, Charlotte: God is everywhere.

Now you are so serious, Harriet, it is time to have done with the subject.

I HAVE no sleep in my eyes; and must go on. What keeps me more wakeful is, my real concern for this naughty Miss Grandison, and my pity for Lord G——; for the instance I have given you of her petulance is nothing to what I have seen: but I thought, so near the day, she would have changed her behaviour to him. Surely, the situation her brother is in, without any fault of his own, might convince her that she need not go out of her path to pick up subjects for unhappiness.

Such a kittenish disposition in her, I called it; for it is not so much the love of power that predominates in her mind, as the love of playfulness: and, when the fit is upon her, she regards not whether it is a china cup, or a cork, that she pats and tosses about. But her *sport* will certainly be the *death* of Lord G——'s happiness. Pity that Sir Charles, who only has power over her, is obliged to go abroad so soon! But she has principles: Lady Grandison's daughter, Sir Charles Grandison's sister, must have principles. The solemnity of the occasion; the office; the church; the altar;—must strike her: The vow—Will she not regard the vow she makes in circumstances so awful? Could but my Lord G—— assume dignity, and mingle raillery with it, and be able to laugh *with* her, and sometimes *at* her, she would not make *him* her sport: she would find somebody else: A butt she must have to shoot at: but I am afraid he will be too sensible of her smartness: and she will have her jest, let who will suffer by it.

Some of the contents of your last are very agreeable to me,

Lucy. I will begin in earnest to think of leaving London. Don't let me look silly in your eyes, my dear, when I come. It was not so *very* presumptuous in me (was it?) to hope—When all his relations—When he himself—Yet what room for hope did he, *could* he give me? He was honest; and I cheated myself: but then all you, my dearest friends, encouraged the cheat: nay, pointed my wishes, and my hopes, by yours, before I had dared (or shall I say, condescended?) to own them to myself.

You may let that Greville know, if you please, that there is no room for his *If's,* nor, of consequence, any for his *menaces.* You may own, that I shall soon be in Northamptonshire. This may prevent his and Fenwick's threatened journey to town.

But, Lucy, though my heart has been ever *dutifully,* as I may say, open to the venerable domestic circle; though it would not have been an honest heart, could it, circumstanced as I was, have concealed itself from Lady D——; and must have been an impenetrable one indeed, if it could have been disguised to the two sisters here—yet, I beseech you, my dear, almost on my knees I beseech you, let not the audacious, the insulting Greville, have ground given him to suspect a weakness in your Harriet, which indelicate minds know not how to judge of delicately. For sex-sake, for example-sake, Lucy, let it not be known, to any but the partial, friendly few, that our grandmamma Shirley's child, and aunt Selby's niece, has been a volunteer in her affections. How many still more forward girls would plead Mrs. Shirley's approbation of the hasty affection, without considering the circumstances, and the object! So the next girl that runs away to a dancing-master, or an ensign, would reckon herself one of Harriet's school.

Poor Mr. Orme! I am sorry he is not well. It is cruel in you, Lucy, at *this* time, to say (so undoubtingly), that his illness is owing to his love of me. You knew that such a suggestion would pain me. Heaven restore Mr. Orme!

But I am vexed, as it cannot be to purpose, that Sir Charles Grandison and I have been named together, and talked of, in your neighbourhood!—He will be gone abroad: I shall return to Northamptonshire: and shall look *so* silly! So like a refused girl!

'Everybody gives me to him,' you say—So much the worse. I wonder what business this everybody has to trouble itself about me.

One consolation, however, I shall have in my return; and this is, in my Nancy's recovered health; which was so precarious when I set out for London.

But I shall have nothing to entertain you with when I am with you: Sir Charles Grandison, Lord and Lady L——, Lady G—— (as now in three or four days she will be), my dear Miss Jervois, Dr. Bartlett, will be all my subject. And have I not exhausted that by pen and ink? Oh no! The doctor promises to correspond with me; and he makes no doubt but Sir Charles will correspond with him, as usual.

What can the unusually tender friendship be called which he professed for me, and, as I may say, claimed in return from me? I know that he has no notion of the love called *Platonic*. Nor have I: I think it, in general, a dangerous allowance; and, with regard to our sex, a very unequal one; since, while the man has nothing to fear, the woman has everything, from the privileges that may be claimed, in an *acknowledged* confidence, especially in presence. Miss Grandison thus interprets what he said, and strengthens her opinion by some of Dr. Bartlett's late intimations that he really loves me; but not being at liberty to avow his love, he knew not what to say; and so went as near to a declaration as was possible to do in his circumstances.

But might I not expect, from such a profession of friendship in Sir Charles, an offer of correspondence in absence? And if he made the offer, ought I to decline it? Would it not indicate too much on *my* side, were I to do so?—And does it not on *his,* if he make not the offer. He corresponds with Mrs. Beaumont: nobody thinks that anything can be meant by that correspondence on *either* side; because Mrs. Beaumont must be at least forty: Sir Charles but six or seven and twenty: but if he makes not the request to Harriet, who is but little more than twenty; what, after such professions of a friendship so tender, will be inferred from his forbearance?

But I shall puzzle myself, and you too, Lucy, if I go on with this sort of reasoning; because I shall not know how to put all I mean into words. Have I not already puzzled you? I think my expression is weak and perplexed—But this offered and accepted friendship between two persons not indelicate, must be perplexing; since he is the only young man in the world, from whom a woman has no dishonour to fear. —Ah, Lucy!—It would be vanity in me, would it not, to suppose that he had more to fear from Harriet, than she has from him; as the virtue of either, I hope, is not questionable? But the event of his Italian visit will explain and reconcile everything.

I will encourage a drowsy fit, that seems to be stealing upon me. If I have not written with the perspicuity I always aim at, allow, Lucy, for the time of night; for spirits not high; and for the subject, which having its delicacies, as well as uncertainties, I am not able to write clearly upon it.

LETTER XX.

Miss Byron.—In continuation.

Saturday Night, April 9.

SIR CHARLES is already returned! he arrived at Windsor on Friday morning; but found that Lord W—— had set out the afternoon of the day before, for the house of his friend Sir Joseph Lawrence, which is but fifteen miles from Mansfield House.

Upon this intelligence, Sir Charles, wanting to return to town as soon as he could, followed him to the knight's: and having time enough himself to reach Mansfield House that night, he, by his uncle's consent, pursued his journey thither to the great joy of the family, who wished for his personal introduction of my lord to Miss Mansfield.

My lord arrived by breakfast-time, unfatigued, and in high

spirits: stayed at Mansfield House all day; and promised so to manage as to be in town to-morrow, in order to be present at his niece's nuptials on Tuesday.

As for Sir Charles, he made the Mansfield family happy in his company the whole Friday evening; inquiring into their affairs relating to the oppression they lay under; pointing out measures for redress; encouraging Miss Mansfield; and informing the brothers, that the lawyers he had consulted on their deeds, told him, that a new trial might be hoped for; the result of which, probably, would be a means to do them justice, so powerfully protected and assisted as they would be now; for new lights had broken in upon them, and they wanted but to recover a deed, which they understood was in the hands of two gentlemen, named Hartley, who were but lately returned from the Indies. Thus prepared, the Mansfields also were in high spirits the next morning; and looked, Sir Charles said, on each other, when they met, as if they wanted to tell each other their agreeable dreams.

Sir Charles, in his way, had looked in upon Sir Harry Beauchamp and his lady. He found Sir Harry in high spirits expecting the arrival of his son; who was actually landed from Calais, having met there his father's letter, allowing him to return to England, and wishing in his own, and in Lady Beauchamp's name, his speedy arrival.

Sir Charles's impatience to see his friend, permitted him only to breakfast with my lord and the Mansfields; and to know the opinion each party formed of the other, on this first interview; and then he set out to Sir Harry Beauchamp's. What an activity!—Heaven reward him with the grant of his own wishes, whatever they be, and make him the happiest of men!

My lord is greatly taken with the lady, and her whole family. Well he may, Sir Charles says. He blessed him, and called himself blessed in his sister's son for his recommendation of each to the other. The lady thinks better of him, as her mother owned to Sir Charles, than she thought she should, from report.

I begin to think, Lucy, that those who set out for happiness, are most likely to find it, when they live single till the age of *fancy* is over. Those who marry while it lasts, are often disappointed of that which they propose so largely to themselves: while those who wed for convenience, and deal with tolerable honesty by each other, are at a greater certainty. *Tolerable,* I repeat, since, it seems, we are to expect that both parties will turn the best side of the old garment outward. Hence arises consolation to old maidens, and cautions against precipitation.—Expatiate, my dear, on this fruitful subject: I would, were I at leisure.

Sir Charles says, that he doubts not but Lord W—— will be as happy a man as he wishes to be, in less than a month.

The deuce is in this brother of mine, whispered Miss Grandison to me, for huddling up of marriages! He don't consider, that there may be two chances for one, that his honest folks may, in half a year's time, bless him the contrary way.

Sir Charles told us that he had desired Lord W—— to give out everywhere (that the adversaries of the Mansfield family might know it) his intended alliance; and that he and his nephew were both determined to procure a retrospection of all former proceedings.

Sir Charles got to Sir Harry Beauchamp's a little before his friend arrived. Sir Harry took him aside at his alighting, and told him, that Lady Beauchamp had had clouds on her brow all the day; and, he was afraid would not receive his son with the graciousness that once he hoped for from her: but that he left *him* to manage with her. She never, said he, had so high an opinion either of man or woman as she has of you.

Sir Charles addressed himself to her, as not doubting her goodness upon the foot of their former conversation; and praised her for the graces that however appeared but faintly in her countenance till his compliments lighted them up, and made them shine full out in it. He told her that his sister and Lord G—— were to be married on the following Tuesday. He himself, he said, should set out for Paris on Friday after: but hoped to see a family intimacy begun between his sisters and Lady Beauchamp; and between their lords, and Sir Harry, and Mr. Beauchamp. He applauded her on the generosity of her intentions, as declared to him in their former conference; and congratulated her on the power she had, of which she made so noble a use, of laying at the same time an obligation on the tenderest of husbands, and the most deserving of sons: whose duty to her he engaged for.

All this set her in high good humour; and she took to herself, and *bridled* upon it, to express myself in Charlotte's manner, the praises and graces this adroit manager gave her, as if they were her unquestionable due.

This agreeable way they were all in, Sir Harry transported with his lady's goodness, when Mr. Beauchamp arrived.

The young gentleman bent his knee to his stepmother, as well as to his father; and thanked her for the high favours which, his father had signified to him by letter, he owed to her goodness. She confirmed them; but, Sir Charles observed, with an ostentation, that showed she thought very highly of her own generosity.

They had a very cheerful evening. Not one cloud would hang on Lady Beauchamp's brow, though once or twice it seemed a little overshadowed, as Mr. Beauchamp displayed qualities for which his father was too ready to admire him. Sir Charles thought it necessary to caution Sir Harry on this subject; putting it in this light, that Lady Beauchamp loved her husband so well, that she would be too likely to dread a rivalry in his affections from a son so very accomplished. Sir Harry took the hint kindly.

Mr. Beauchamp was under a good deal of concern at Sir Charles's engagements to leave England so soon after his arrival; and asked his father's leave to attend him. Sir Harry declared that he could not part with him. Sir Charles chid his friend, and said, it was not quite so handsome a return as might have been expected from his Beauchamp to the joyful reception he had met with from his father and Lady Beauchamp. But she excused the young gentleman, and said, she wondered not, that anybody who was favoured with *his* friendship, should be unwilling to be separated from him.

Sir Charles expresses great satisfaction in Mr. Beauchamp's being arrived before his departure, that he may present to us himself, a man with whom he is sure we shall all be delighted, and leave *him* happy in the beloved society which he himself is obliged to quit.

A repining temper, Lucy, would consider only the hardship of meeting a long absent friend, just to feel the uneasiness of a second parting: but this man views everything in a right light. When his own happiness is not to be attained, he lays it out of his thoughts, and, as I have heretofore observed, rejoices in that of others. It is a pleasure to see how Sir Charles seems to enjoy the love which Dr. Bartlett expresses for this friend of them both.

Sir Charles addressed himself to me, on several occasions, in so polite, in so tender a manner, that every one told me afterwards, they are sure he loves me. Dr. Bartlett at the time, as he sat next me, whispered on the regret expressed by all on losing him so soon—Ah, madam!—I know and pity my patron's struggles!—*Struggles,* Lucy! What could the doctor mean by this whisper to *me?* But I hope he guesses not at mine! If he does, would he have whispered his pity of Sir Charles to me?—Come, Lucy, this is some comfort, however; and I will endeavour to be brave upon it, that I may not, by my weakness, lessen myself in the doctor's good opinion.

It was agreed for Charlotte (whose assent was given in these words—'Do as you will—or, rather, as my brother 'will—What signifies opposing *him?*') that the nuptials shall be solemnised, as privately as possible, at St. George's Church. The company is to drop in at different doors, and with as few attendants as may be. Lord W——, the Earl of G——, and Lady Gertrude, Lord and Lady L——, Miss Jervois, and your Harriet, are to be present at the ceremony. I was very earnest to be excused; till Miss Grandison, when we were alone, dropt down on one knee, and held up her hands, to beg me to accompany her. Mr. Everard Grandison, if he can be found, is to be also there at Sir Charles's desire.

Dr. Bartlett, as I before hinted, at *her* earnest request, is to perform the ceremony. Sir Charles wished it to be at his own parish church: but Miss Grandison thought it too near to be private. He was indifferent, as to the place, he said—

so it was at *church;* for he had been told of the difficulty we had to get Charlotte to desist from having it performed in her chamber; and seemed surprised.—Fie, Charlotte! said he —an office so solemn!—vows to receive and pay, as in the Divine Presence——

She was glad, she told me, that she had not left that battle to be fought with *him.*

———

Monday, April 10.

LORD W—— is come. Lord and Lady L—— are here. They, and Miss Grandison, received him with great respect. He embraced his niece in a very affectionate manner. Sir Charles was absent. Lord W—— is in person and behaviour a much more agreeable man than I expected him to be. Nor is he so decrepit with the gout, as I had supposed. He is very careful of himself, it seems. This world has been kind to him; and I fancy he makes a great deal of a little pain, for want of stronger exercises to his patience; and so is a sufferer by self-indulgence. Had I not been made acquainted with his free living, and with the insults he bore from Mrs. Giffard, with a spirit so poor and so low, I should have believed I saw not only the man of quality, but the man of sense, in his countenance. I endeavoured, however, as much as I could, to look upon him as the brother of the late Lady Grandison. Had he been worthy of that relation, how should I have reverenced him!

But, whatever I thought of *him,* he expressed himself highly in *my* favour. He particularly praised me for the modesty which he said was visible in my countenance. Free livers, Lucy, taken with that grace in a woman, which they make it their pride to destroy! But all men, good and bad, admire modesty in a woman; and I am sometimes out of humour with our sex that they do not as generally like modesty in men. I am sure that this grace in Sir Charles Grandison is one of his principal glories with me. It emboldens one's heart, and permits one to behave before him with ease;

and, as I may say, with *security*, in the consciousness of a right intention.

But what were Lord W———'s praises of his nephew! He called him, the glory of his sex and of human nature. How the cheeks of the dear Emily glowed at the praises given to her guardian!—She was the taller for them: when she moved, it was on tip-toe; stealing, as it were, across the floor, lest she should lose anything that was said on a subject so delightful to her.

My lord was also greatly pleased with her. He complimented her as the beloved ward of the best of guardians. He lamented, with us, the occasion that called his nephew abroad. He was full of his own engagements with Miss Mansfield, and declared that his nephew should guide and govern him as he pleased in every material case, respecting either the conduct of his future life, or the management and disposition of his estate; adding, that he had made his will, and, excepting only his lady's jointure, and a few legacies, had left everything to him.

How right a thing, even in policy, is it, my dear, to be good and generous!

I must not forget, that my lord wished, *with all his soul,* that was his expression, that he might have the honour of giving to his nephew *my* hand in marriage.

I could feel myself blush. I half suppressed a sigh: I would have wholly suppressed it, if I could. I recovered the little confusion, his too plainly expressed wish gave me, by repeating to myself the word CLEMENTINA.

This Charlotte is a great coward. But I dare not tell her so, for fear of a retort. I believe I should be as great a one in her circumstances, so few hours to one of the greatest events of one's life! But I *pretend* not to bravery: yet hope, that in the cause of virtue or honour I should be found to have a soul.

I write now at my cousin's. I came hither to make an alteration in my dress. I have promised to be with the sweet Bully early in the morning of her important day.

LETTER XXI.

Miss Byron.—In continuation.

Tuesday Night,
Wednesday Morning. } April 11, 12.

MISS GRANDISON is no longer to be called by that name. She is Lady G——. May she make Lord G—— as happy as I dare say he will make her, if it be not her own fault!

I was early with her, according to promise. I found her more affected than she was even last night with her approaching change of condition. Her brother had been talking to her, she said; and had laid down the duties of the state she was about to enter into, in such a serious manner, and made the performance of them of so much importance to her happiness, both here and hereafter, that she was terrified at the thoughts of what she was about to undertake. She had never considered matrimony in that formidable light before. He had told her, that he was afraid of her vivacity; yet was loath to discourage her cheerfulness, or to say anything that should lower her spirits. All he besought of her was, to regard times, tempers, and occasions; and then it would be impossible but her lively humour must give delight not only to the man whom she favoured with her hand, but to every one who had the pleasure of approaching her. If, Charlotte, said he, you would have the world around you respect your husband, *you* must set the example. While the wife gives the least room to suspect that she despises her husband, she will find that she subjects him to double contempt, if he resents it not; and if he does, can you be happy? Aggressors lay themselves open to severe reprisals. If you differ, you will be apt to make by-standers judges over you. They will remember, when you are willing to forget; and your fame will be the sport of those beneath you, as well in understanding as degree.

She believed, she told me, that Lord G—— had been making some complaints of her. *If he had——*

Hush, my dear, said I—not one word of threatening: are you more solicitous to conceal your fault than to amend it?

No—but you know, Harriet, for a man, before he has experienced what sort of a wife I shall make, to complain against me for foibles in courtship, when he can help himself if he *will,* has something so very little——

Your conscience, Charlotte, tells you, that he had *reason* for complaint; and therefore you think he *has* complained. Think the best of Lord G—— for *your own* reputation's sake, since you thought fit to go thus far with him. You have borne nothing from *him:* he has borne a great deal from *you.*

I am fretful, Harriet; I won't be chidden: I will be comforted by you: you *shall* sooth me: are you not my sister? She threw her arms around me, and kissed my cheek.

I ventured to rally her, though I was afraid of her retort, and met with it: but I thought it would divert her. I am glad, my dear, said I, that you are capable of this tenderness of temper: you blustering girls—but fear, I believe, will make cowards loving.

Harriet, said she, and flung from me to the window, remember *this:* may I soon see you in the same situation! I will then have no mercy upon you.

The subject, which Sir Charles led to at breakfast, was the three weddings of Thursday last. He spoke honourably of marriage, and made some just compliments to Lord and Lady L——; concluding them with wishes, that his sister Charlotte and Lord G—— might be neither more nor less happy than they were. Then turning to Lord W——, he said he questioned not his lordship's happiness with the lady he had so lately seen; for I cannot doubt, said he, of your lordship's affectionate gratitude to her, if she behaves as I am sure she will.

My lord had tears in his eyes. Never man had such a nephew as I have, said he. All the joy of my present prospects, all the comfort of my future life, are and will be owing to you.

Here had he stopt, would have been well: but turning to me, he unexpectedly said, Would to God, madam, that *you* could reward him! I cannot; and nobody *else* can.

All were alarmed for me; every eye was upon me. A sickishness came over my heart—I know not how to describe it. My head sunk upon my bosom. I could hardly sit; yet was less able to rise.

Sir Charles's face was overspread with blushes. He bowed to my lord. May the man, said he, who shall have the honour to call Miss Byron his, be, if *possible,* as deserving as *she* is! Then will they live together the life of angels.

He gracefully looked down; not at me; and I got a little courage to look up: yet Lady L—— was concerned for me: so was Lord L——: Emily's eye dropt a tear upon her blushing cheek.

Was it not, Lucy, a severe trial?—Indeed it was.

My lord, to mend the matter, lamented very pathetically, that Sir Charles was under an obligation to go abroad; and still more, that he could not stay to be present at the celebration of his nuptials with Miss Mansfield.

The Earl, Lord G——, Lady Gertrude, and the doctor, were to meet the bride and us at church. Lord and Lady L——, Sir Charles, and Emily, went in one coach: Miss Grandison and I in another.

As we went, I don't like this affair at all, Harriet, said she. My brother has long made all other men indifferent to me. Such an infinite difference!

Can anybody be happier than Lord and Lady L——, Charlotte? Yet Lady L—— admires her brother as much as you can do.

They happy!—and so they are. But Lady L——, soft soul! fell in love with Lord L—— before my brother came over. So the foundation was laid: and it being a first flame with her, she, in compliment to *herself,* could not but persevere. But the sorry creature Anderson, proving a sorry creature, made me despise the sex: and my brother's perfections contributed to my contempt of all other men.

Indeed, my dear, you are wrong. Lord G—— loves you: but were Sir Charles *not* your brother, it is not very certain that he would have returned your love.

Why, that's true. I believe he would not, in that case, have chosen *me.* I am sure he would not, if he had known *you:*

but for the man one loves, one can *do* anything, *be* everything, that he would wish one to be.

Do you think you cannot love Lord G——? For Heaven's sake, Charlotte, though you are now almost within sight of the church, do not think of giving your hand, if you cannot resolve to make Lord G—— as happy as I have no doubt he will make you, if it be not your own fault.

What will my brother say?—What will——

Leave that to me. I will engage Sir Charles and Dr. Bartlett to lend me their ear in the vestry; and I am sure your brother, if he knows that you have an antipathy to Lord G——, or that you think you cannot be happy with him, will undertake your cause, and bring you off.

Antipathy! That's a strong word, Harriet. The man is a good-natured silly man——

Silly! Charlotte!—Silly then he must be for loving you so well, who, really, have never yet given him an opportunity to show his importance with you.

I do pity him sometimes.

The coach stopt:—Ah, Lord! Harriet! The church! The church!

Say, Charlotte, before you step out—shall I speak to your brother, and Dr. Bartlett, in the vestry?

I shall look like a fool either way.

Don't *act* like one, Charlotte, on this solemn occasion. Say, you will deserve, that you will *try* to deserve, Lord G——'s love.

Sir Charles appeared. Lord help me!—My brother!—I'll try, I'll try what can be done.

He gave each his hand in turn: in we flew: the people began to gather about us. Lord G——, all rapture, received her at the entrance. Sir Charles led me: and the Earl and Lady Gertrude received us with joy in their countenances. I overheard the naughty one say, as Lord G—— led her up to the altar, You don't know what you are about, man. I expect to have all my way: remember that's one of my articles before marriage.

He returned her an answer of fond assent to her condition.

I am afraid, thought I, poor Lord G——, you will be more than *once* reminded of this previous article.

When she was led to the altar, and Lord G—— and she stood together, she trembled. Leave me not, Harriet, said she.—Brother! Lady L——!

I am sure she looked *sillier* than Lord G—— at that instant.

The good doctor began the office. *No dearly beloveds,* Harriet! whispered she, as I had said, on a really terrible occasion. I was offended with her in my heart: again, she whispered something against the office, as the doctor proceeded to give the reasons for the institution. Her levity did not forsake her even at that solemn moment.

When the service was over, every one (Sir Charles in a solemn and most affectionate manner) wished her happy. My Lord G—— kissed her hand with a bent knee.

She took my hand. Ah! Lord, what have I done?—And am I married? whispered she—and can it never be undone? —And is that the man to whom I am to be obedient?—Is *he* to be my lord and master?

Ah, Lady G——, said I, it is a solemn office. *You* have vowed: *he* has vowed.—It is a solemn office.

Lord G—— led her to the first coach. Sir Charles led me into the same. The people, to my great confusion, whispered, That's the bride! What a charming couple! Sir Charles handed Miss Emily next. Lord G—— came in: as he was entering, Harkee, friend, said Charlotte, and put out her hand, you mistake the coach: you are not of our company.

The whole world, replied my lord, shall not now divide us: and took his seat on the same side with Emily.

The man's a rogue, Harriet, whispered she: See! he gives himself airs already!

This, said Lord G——, as the coach drove on, taking one hand, and eagerly kissing it, is the hand that blessed me.

And that, said she, pushing him from her with the other, is the hand that repulses your forwardness. What came you in here for?—Don't be silly.

He was in raptures all the way.

When we came home, every one embraced and wished joy to the bride. The Earl and Lady Gertrude were in high spirits. The lady re-saluted her niece, as her *dear* niece: the earl recognised his beloved daughter.

But prepare to hear a noble action of Lord W——.

When he came up to compliment her—My dearest niece, said he, I wish you joy with all my soul! I have not been a kind uncle. There is no fastening anything on your brother. Accept of this: [and he put a little paper into her hand—it was a bank note of 1000*l.*:] *My* sister's daughter, and *your* brother's sister, merits more than this.

Was not this handsomely presented, Lucy?

He then in a manner becoming Lady Grandison's brother, stept to Lady L——. Ny niece Charlotte is not my *only* niece. I wish you, my dear, as if this was your day of marraige, all happiness: accept of these two papers: [the one, Lucy, was a note for 1000*l.* and the other for 100*l.*:] and he said, The lesser note is due to you for interest on the greater.

When the ladies opened their notes, and saw what they were, they were at first at a loss what to say.

It was most gracefully done. But see, Lucy, the example of a good and generous man can sometimes alter natures; and covetous men, I have heard it observed, when, their hearts are opened, often act nobly.

As soon as Lady G—— (so now I must call her) recovered herself from the surprise into which my lord's present and address had put her, she went to him: Allow me, my lord, said she, and bent one knee to him, to crave your blessing: and at the same time to thank you for your paternal present to your ever obliged Charlotte.

God bless you, my dear! saluting her—but thank your noble brother: you delight me with your graceful acceptance.

Lady L—— came up. My lord, you overcome me by your bounty.—How shall I——

Your brother's princely spirit, Lady L——, said he, makes this present look mean. Forgive me only, that it was not done before. And he saluted her.

Lord L—— came up. Lady L—— showed him the opened

notes—See here, my lord, said she, what Lord W—— has done: and he calls this the interest due on that.

Your lordship oppresses me with your goodness to your niece, said Lord L——. May health, long life, and happiness, attend you in your own nuptials!

There, there, said Lord W——, pointing to Sir Charles (who had withdrawn, and then entered), make your acknowledgment; his noble spirit has awakened mine; it was only asleep. My late sister's brother wanted but the force of such an example. That son is all his mother.

Sir Charles joining them, having heard only the last words —If I am thought a son not unworthy of the most excellent of mothers, said he, and by *her* brother, I am happy.

Then you *are* happy, replied my lord.

Her memory, resumed Sir Charles, I cherish; and when I have been tempted to forget myself, that memory has been a means of keeping me steady in my duty. Her precepts, my lord, were the guide of my early youth. Had I not kept them in mind, how much more blamable than most young men had I been!—My Charlotte! have that mother in your memory, on this great change of your condition! You will not be called to her trials.—His eyes glistened. Tender be our remembrance of my father.—Charlotte, be worthy of your mother.

He withdrew with an air *so* noble!—but soon returning, with a cheerful look, he was told what Lord W—— had done. —Your lordship was *before,* said he, entitled to our duty, by the ties of blood: but what is the relation of body to that of mind? You have bound me for my sisters, and that still more by the manner than by the act, in a bond of gratitude that never can be broken!

Thank yourself, thank yourself, my noble nephew.

Encourage, my lord, a family intimacy between your lady and her nieces and nephew. You will be delighted, my sisters, with Miss Mansfield; but when she obliges my lord with her hand, you will reverence your aunt. I shall have a pleasure, when I am far distant, in contemplating the family union. Your lordship must let me know your day in time;

and I will be joyful upon it, whatever of a contrary nature I may have to struggle with on my own account.

My lord wept—My *lord* wept, did I say?—Not *one* of us had a dry eye!—This was a solemn scene, you will say, for a wedding-day: but how delightfully do such scenes dilate the heart!

The day, however, was not forgotten as a day of festivity. Sir Charles himself, by his vivacity and openness of countenance, made every one joyful: and, except that now and then a sigh, which could not be checked, stole from some of us, to think that he would so soon be in another country (far distant from the friends he now made happy), and engaged in difficulties, perhaps in dangers, every heart was present to the occasion of the day.

O Charlotte! Dear Lady G——! Hitherto it is in your power to make every *future* day worthy of *this!*—' Have your mother, your noble mother, in your memory, my dear,' and give credit to the approbation of such a brother.

I should have told you, that my cousins Reeves came about two, and were received with the utmost politeness by everybody.

Sir Charles was called out just before dinner; and returned introducing a young gentleman, dressed as if for the day— This is an earlier favour than I had hoped for, said Sir Charles; and leading him to Lady G——. This, sir, is the queen of the day. My dear Lady G——, welcome (the house is yours—welcome) the man I love: welcome my Beauchamp.

Every one, except Emily and me, crowded about Mr. Beauchamp, as Sir Charles's avowedly beloved friend, and bid him cordially welcome; Sir Charles presenting him to each by name.

Then leading him to me—I am half ashamed, Lucy, to repeat—but take it as he spoke it—Revere, said he, my dear friend, that excellent young lady: but let not your admiration stop at her face and person: she has a mind as exalted, my Beauchamp, as your own: Miss Byron, in honour to my sister, and to us all, has gilded this day by her presence.

Mr. Beauchamp approached me with polite respect. The

lady whom Sir Charles Grandison admires, as he does you, madam, must be the first of women.

I might have said, that he, who was so eminently distinguished as the friend of Sir Charles Grandison, must be a most valuable man: but my spirits were not high. I courtesied to his compliment; and was silent.

Sir Charles presented Emily to him.—My Emily, Beauchamp. I hope to live to see her happily married. The man whose heart is but half so worthy as hers, must be an excellent man.

Modesty might look up, and be sensible to compliments from the lips of such a man. Emily looked at me with pleasure, as if she had said, Do you hear, Madam, what a fine thing my guardian has said of me?

Sir Charles asked Mr. Beauchamp, how he stood with my Lady Beauchamp?

Very well, answered he. After such an introduction as you had given me to her, I must have been to blame, had I *not*. She is my father's wife: I must respect her, were she ever so unkind to me: she is not without good qualities. Were every family so happy as to have Sir Charles Grandison for a mediator when misunderstandings happened, there would be very few lasting differences among relations. My father and mother tell me, that they never sit down to table together but they bless you: and to me they have talked of nobody else: but Lady Beauchamp depends upon your promise of making her acquainted with the ladies of your family.

My sisters, and their lords, will do honour to my promise in my absence. Lady L——, Lady G——, let me recommend to you Lady Beauchamp as more than a common visiting acquaintance. Do you, sir, to Mr. Beauchamp, see it cultivated.

Mr. Beauchamp is an agreeable, and, when Sir Charles Grandison is not in company, a handsome and genteel man. I think, my dear, that I do but the same justice that everybody would do, in this exception. He is cheerful, lively, yet modest, and not too full of words. One sees both love and respect in every look he casts upon his friend; and that he is delighted when he hears him speak, be the subject what it will.

He once said to Lord W——, who praised his nephew to him, as he does to everybody near him: The universal voice, my lord, is in his favour wherever he goes. Every one joins almost in the *same* words, in different countries, allowing for the different languages, that for sweetness of manners, and manly dignity, he hardly ever had his equal.

Sir Charles was then engaged in talk with his Emily; she before him; he standing in an easy genteel attitude, leaning against the wainscot, listening, smiling to her prattle, with looks of indulgent love, as a father might do to a child he was fond of; while she looked back every now and then towards me, *so* proud, poor dear! of being singled out by her guardian.

She tript to me afterwards, and, leaning over my shoulder, as I sat, whispered—I have been begging of my guardian to use his interest with you, madam, to take me down with you to Northamptonshire.

And what is the result?

She paused.

Has he denied your request?

No, madam.

Has he allowed you to go, my dear, if I comply, turning half round to her with pleasure.

She paused, and seemed at a loss. I repeated my question.

Why, no, he has not consented neither—but he has said such charming things, so obliging, so kind, both of you and of me, that I forgot to repeat my question, though it was so near my heart: but I will ask him again.

And thus, Lucy, can he decline complying, and yet send away a requester so much delighted with him, as to forget what her request was.

Miss Grandison—Lady G——, I would say—singled me out soon after—This Beauchamp is really a very pretty fellow, Harriet.

He is an agreeable man, answered I.

So I think.

She said no more of him at that time.

Between dinner and tea, at Lady L——'s motion, they made me play on the harpsichord; and, after one lesson, they besought Sir Charles to sing to my playing. He would not, he said, deny any request that was made him on that day.

He sung. He has a mellow manly voice, and great command of it.

This introduced a little concert. Mr. Beauchamp took the violin; Lord L——the bass-viol; Lord G—— the German flute; and most of the company joined in the chorus. The song was from 'Alexander's Feast;' the words:

> Happy, happy, happy pair!
> None but the *good* deserves the fair:

Sir Charles, though himself equally *brave* and *good,* preferring the latter word to the former.

Lady L—— had always insisted upon dancing at her sister's wedding. We were not company enough for country dances: but music having been ordered, and the performers come, it was insisted upon that we should have a dance, though we were engaged in a conversation, which I thought infinitely more agreeable.

Lord G—— began by dancing a minuet with his bride: she danced charmingly! but, on my telling her so afterwards, she whispered me that she should have performed better had she danced with her brother. Lord G—— danced extremely well.

Lord L—— and Lady Gertrude, Mr. Beauchamp and Mrs. Reeves, Mr. Reeves and Lady L——, danced all of them very agreeably.

The earl took me out: but we had hardly done, when asking pardon for disgracing me, as he too modestly expressed himself, he, and all but my cousins and Emily, called out for Sir Charles to dance with me.

I was abashed at the general voice calling upon us both: but it was obeyed.

He deserved all the praises that Miss Gran— Lady G——, I would say, gave him in her letter to me.

Lord bless me, my dear, this man is everything! but his conversation has ever been among the politest people of different nations.

Lord W—— wished himself able, from his gout, to take out Miss Jervois.

The bridegroom was called upon by Sir Charles: and he took out the good girl, who danced very prettily. I fancied that he chose to call out Lord G—— rather than Mr. Beauchamp. He is the most delicate and considerate of men.

Sir Charles was afterwards called upon by the bride herself: and she danced then with a grace indeed! I was pleased that she *could* perform so well at her own wedding.

Supper was not ready till twelve. Mr. Reeves's coach came about that hour; but we got not away till two.

Perhaps the company would not have broke up so soon, had not the bride been perverse, and refused to retire.

Was she not at home? she asked Lady L——, who was put upon urging her: and should she leave her company?

She would make me retire with her. She took a very affectionate leave of me.

Marriage, Lucy, is an awful rite. It is supposed to be a joyful solemnity: but, on the woman's side, it can be only so when she is given to the man she loves above all the men in the world; and, even to *her,* the anniversary day, when doubt is turned into certainty, must be much happier than the day itself.

What a victim must that woman look upon herself to be, who is compelled, or even *over-persuaded,* to give her hand to a man who has no share in her heart? Ought not a parent or guardian, in such a circumstance, especially if the child has a *delicate,* an *honest* mind, to be chargeable with all the unhappy consequences that may follow from such a cruel compulsion?

But this is not the case with Miss Grandison. Early she cast her eye on an improper object. Her pride convinced her in time of the impropriety. And this, as she owns, gave her an indifference to all men.

She hates not Lord G——. There is no man whom she prefers to him: and in this respect may, perhaps, be upon a par with eight women out of twelve who marry, and yet make not bad wives.

As she played with her passion till she lost it, she may be happy if she will: and since she intended to be, some time or other, Lady G——, her brother was kind in persuading her to shorten her days of coquetting and teasing, and to allow him to give her to Lord G—— before he went abroad.

LETTER XXII.

Miss Byron.—In continuation.

Wednesday, April 12.

DR. BARTLETT was so good as to breakfast with my cousins and me this morning. He talks of setting out for Grandison Hall on Saturday or Monday next. We have settled a correspondence; and he gives me hope, that he will make me a visit in Northamptonshire. I know you will all rejoice to see him.

Emily came in before the doctor went. She brought me the compliments of the bride and Lord W——, with their earnest request, that I, and my two cousins, would dine with them. Sir Charles was gone, she said, to make a farewell visit to the Danby set; but would be at home at dinner.

It would be better for me, I think, Lucy, to avoid all opportunities of seeing him: don't you think so?—There is no such thing as seeing him with indifference. But, so earnestly invited, how could I deny; especially as my cousins were inclinable to go?

Miss Jervois whispered me at parting: I never before, said she, had an opportunity to observe the behaviour of the new-married couple to each other: but is it customary, madam, for the bride to be more snappish, as the bridegroom is more obliging?

Lady G—— is very naughty, my dear, if she so behaves, as to give you reason to ask this question.

She does: and, upon my word, I see more *obedience* where it was not promised than where it was. Dear madam, is not what is said at church to be thought of *afterwards?* But why did not the doctor make her speak out? What signified bowing, except a woman was so bashful that she *could* not speak?

The bowing, my dear, is an assent. It is as efficacious as words. Lord G—— only bowed, you know. Could you like to be called upon, Emily, to speak out on such an occasion?

Why, no. But then I would be very civil and good-natured to my husband, if it were but for fear he should be cross to me: but I should think it my duty as well.

Sweet innocent!

She went away and left the doctor with me.

When our hearts are set upon a particular subject, how impertinent, how much beside the purpose, do we think every other! I wanted the doctor to talk of Sir Charles Grandison: but as he fell not into the subject, and as I was afraid he would think me to be always leading him into it, if I began it, I suffered him to go away at his first motion: I never knew him so shy upon it, however.

Sir Charles returned to dinner. He has told Lady L——, who afterwards told us, that he had a hint from Mr. Galliard, senior, that if he were not engaged in his affection, he was commissioned to make him a very great proposal in behalf of one of the young ladies he had seen the Thursday before; and that from her father.

Surely, Lucy, we may pronounce without doubt, that we live in an age in which there is a great dearth of good men, that so many offers fall to the lot of one.

But, I am thinking, 'tis no small advantage to Sir Charles, that his time is so taken up that he cannot stay long enough in any company to suffer them to cast their eyes on other objects, with distinction. He left the numerous assembly at

Enfield, while they were in the height of their admiration of him. Attention, love, admiration, cannot be always kept at the stretch. You will observe, Lucy, that on the return of a long-absent dear friend, the *rapture* lasts not more than an hour: gladdened as the heart is, the friend received, and the friends receiving, perhaps, in less than that time, can sit down quietly together, to hear and to tell stories, of what has happened to either in the long regretted absence. It will be so with us, Lucy, when I return to the arms of *my* kind friends: and now, does not Sir Charles's proposed journey to Italy endear his company to us?

The Earl of G——, Lady Gertrude, and two agreeable nieces of that nobleman, were here at dinner. Lady G—— behaved *pretty* well to her lord before them: but I, who understood the language of her eyes, *saw* them talk very saucily to him on several occasions. My lord is a little officious in his obligingness; which takes off from that graceful, that polite frankness, which so charmingly, on all occasions, distinguishes one happy man, who was then present. Lord G—— will, perhaps, appear more to advantage in that person's absence.

Mr. Beauchamp was also present. He is indeed an agreeable, a modest young man. He appeared to great advantage, as well in his conversation, as by his behaviour: and not the less for subscribing in both to the superiority of his friend; who, nevertheless, endeavoured to draw him out as the first man.

After dinner, Lady L——, Lady G——, and I, found an opportunity to be by ourselves for one half-hour. Lady G—— asked Lady L—— what she intended to do with the thousand pounds with which Lord W—— had so generously presented her?—Do with it, my dear!—what do you think I *intend* to do with it?—it is already disposed of.

I'll be hanged, said Lady G——, if this good creature has not given it to her husband.

Indeed, Charlotte, I have. I gave it to him before I slept.

I thought so! She laughed. And Lord L—— took it! Did he?

To be sure he did. I should otherwise have been displeased with him.

Dear, good soul!—And so you gave him a thousand pounds, to take part of it back from him by four or five paltry guineas at a time, at his pleasure?

Lord L—— and I, Charlotte, have but one purse. You may not, perhaps, know how we manage it.

Pray, good, meek, dependent creature! how *do* you manage it?

Thus, Charlotte: My lord knows that his wife and he have but one interest; and, from the first of our happy marriage, he would make me take one key, as he has another, of the private drawer, where his money and money-bills lie. There is a little memorandum-book in the drawer, in which he enters on one page the money he receives; on the opposite, the money he takes out: and, when I want money, I have recourse to my key. If I see but little in the drawer, I am the more moderate; or, perhaps, if my want is not urgent, defer the supplying of it till my lord is richer: but, little or much, I minute down the sum, as he himself does what he takes out: and so we know what we are about; and I never put it out of my lord's power, by my unseasonable expenses, to preserve that custom of his, for which he is as much respected as well served; not to suffer a demand to be twice made upon him where he is a debtor.

Good soul!—And, pray, don't you minute down, too, the *use* to which you put the money you take out?

Indeed I often do: always, indeed, when I take out more than five guineas at one time: I found my lord did so: and I followed the example of my own accord.

Happy pair! said I—O Lady G——, what a charming example is this!—I hope you will follow it.

Thank you, Harriet, for your advice. Why, I can't but say that this is one pretty way of coaxing each other into frugality: but don't you think, that where an honest pair are so *tender* of disobliging, and so *studious* of obliging each other, they seem to confess that the matrimonial good understanding hangs by very slender threads?

And do not the tenderest friendships, said I, hang by *as* slender? Can delicate minds be united to each other but by delicate observances?

Why *thou* art a good soul, too, Harriet!—and so you would both have me make a present to Lord G—— of my thousand pounds before we have chosen our private drawer; before he has got two keys made to it?

Let him know, Charlotte, what Lord L—— and I do, if you think the example worth following—and then——

Ay, and *then* give him my thousand pounds for a beginning, Lady L——? But see you not that this proposal should come from *him* and not from *me?*—And should we not let each other see a little of each other's merits first?

See, *first,* the merits of the man you have actually married, Charlotte!

Yes, Lady L——. But yesterday married, you know. Can there be a greater difference between any two men in the world, than there often is between the same man, a lover and a husband?—And now, my *generous* advisers, be pleased to continue silent. You cannot answer me fairly. And, besides, wot ye not the indelicacy of an early present, which you are not *obliged* to make?

We were both silent, each expecting the other to answer the strange creature.

She laughed at us both. Soft souls, and tender! said she, let me tell you, that there is more indeliacy in delicacy than you *very* delicate people are aware of.

You, Charlotte, said Lady L——, have odder notions than anybody else. Had you been a man you would have been a sad rake.

A rake, perhaps, I might have been; but not a *sad* one, Lady L——.

Lady G—— can't help being witty, said I: it is sometimes *her* misfortune, sometimes *ours,* that she cannot: however, I highly approve of the example set by Lord L——, and followed by Lady L——.

And so do I, Harriet. And when Lord G—— sets the example, I shall—consider of it. I am not a bad economist.

Vol. IV—15.

Had I *ten* thousand pounds in my hands, I would not be extravagant: had I but one hundred, I would not be mean. I value not money but as it enables me to lay an obligation, instead of being under the necessity of receiving one. I am my mother's daughter, and brother's sister, and *yours,* Lady L——, in this particular; and *yours* too, Harriet: different means may be taken to arrive at the same end. Lord G—— will have no reason to be dissatisfied with my prudence in money matters, although I should not make him one of my best courtesies, as if—as if—(and she laughed; but checking herself)—I were conscious—again she laughed—that I had signed and sealed to my absolute dependence on his bounty.

What a mad creature! said Lady L——; but, my Harriet, don't you think that she behaved pretty well to Lord G—— at table?

Yes, answered I, as those would think who observe not her arch looks: but she gave me pain for her several times: and, I believe, her brother was not without his apprehensions.

He had his eyes upon you, Harriet, replied Lady G——, more earnestly than he had upon me, or anybody else.

That's true, said Lady L——, I looked upon both him and you, my dear, with pity. My tears were ready to start more than once, to reflect how happy you two might be in each other, and how greatly you would love each other, were it not——

Not one word more on this subject, dear Lady L——! I cannot bear it. I thought my-*self,* that he often cast an eye of tenderness upon me. I cannot bear it. I am afraid of myself; of my *justice*——

His tender looks did not escape me, said Lady G——. Nor yet did my dear Harriet's. But we will not touch this string: it is *too* tender a one. I, for my part, was forced, in order to divert myself, to turn my eyes on Lord G——. He got nothing by that. The most *officious*——

Nay, Lady G——, interrupted I, you shall not change the discourse at the expense of the man you have vowed to

honour. I will take pain to myself, by the continuation of
the former subject, rather than that shall be.

Charming Harriet! said Lady L——. I hope your generosity will be rewarded. Yet, tell me, my dear, can you
wish Lady Clementina may be his? I have no doubt but
you wish her *recovery;* but can you wish her to be *his?*

I have debated the matter, my dear Lady L——, with
myself. I am sorry it has *admitted* of debate. So excellent
a creature! Such an honour to her sex! So nobly sincere!
so pious!—But I will confess the truth: I have called upon
justice to support me in my determination: I have supposed
myself in *her* situation, her unhappy malady excepted: I
have supposed *her* in *mine:* and ought I then to have hesitated to which to give the preference?—Yet——

What yet, most frank and most generous of women? said
Lady L——, clasping her arms about me: what yet——

Why, yet—Ah, ladies—Why, yet, I have many a pang;
many a twitch, as I may call it!—Why is your brother so
tender-hearted, so modest, so faultless?—Why did he not
insult me with his pity? Why does he on every occasion
show a tenderness for me, that is more affecting than pity?
And why does he give me a consequence that exalts, while
it depresses me?

I turned my head aside to hide my emotion. Lady G——
snatched my handkerchief from me; and wiped away a
starting tear; and called me by very tender names.

Am I dear, continued I, to the heart of such a man? You
think I am. Allow me to say, that he is indeed dear to
mine: yet I have not a wish but for his happiness whatever
becomes of me.

Emily appeared at the door—May I come in, ladies?—I
will come in!—My dear Miss Byron affected! My dear
Miss Byron in tears!

Her pity, without knowing the cause, sprung to her eyes.
She took my hand in both hers, and repeatedly kissed it!—
My guardian asks for you. Oh, with what tenderness of
voice—Where is you Miss Byron, love? He calls every one
by gentle names, when he speaks of *you*—his voice then is

the voice of love—*love,* said he, to *me!* Through *you,* madam, he will love his ward—and on your love will I build all my merit. But you sigh, dear Miss Byron! you sigh—forgive your prating girl!—you must not be grieved.

I embraced her. Grief, my dear, reaches not my heart at this time. It is the merit of your guardian that affects me.

God bless you, madam, for your gratitude to my guardian!

A Clementina and a Harriet! said Lady L——, two women so excellent! What a fate is *his!* How must his heart be divided!

Divided, say you, Lady L——? resumed Lady G——. The man who loves virtue, for virtue's sake, loves it wherever he finds it. Such a man may *distinguish* more virtuous women than one: and if he be of a gentle and beneficent nature, there will be tenderness in his distinction to every one, varying only according to the difference of circumstance and situation.

Let me embrace you, my Charlotte! resumed Lady L——, for that thought. Don't let me hear, for a month to come, one word from the same lips, that may be unworthy of it.

You have Lord G—— in your head, Lady L——; but never mind us. He must, now and then, be made to look about him. I'll take care to keep up my consequence with him, never fear: nor shall he have reason to doubt the virtue of his wife.

Virtue, my dear! said I: what is virtue only? She who will not be virtuous for *virtue's* sake is not worthy to be called a woman: but she must be something more than virtuous for her *husband's,* nay, for her *vow's* sake. Complacency, obligingness——

Obedience too, I warrant—Hush, hush, my sweet Harriet! putting her hand before my mouth; we will behave as well as we can: and that will be very well, if nobody minds us. And now let us go down together.

LETTER XXIII.

Miss Byron.—In continuation.

Thursday, April 13.

WE played at cards last night till supper-time. When that was over every one sought to engage Sir Charles in discourse. I will give you some particulars of our conversation, as I did of one before.

Lord W—— began it with a complaint of the insolence and profligateness of servants. What he said was only answered by Sir Charles, with the word, *Example, example,* my good lord, repeated.

You, Sir Charles, replied my lord, may, indeed, insist upon the force of example; for I cannot but observe, that all those of yours, whom I have seen, are entitled to regard. They have the looks of men at ease, and of men grateful for that ease: they know their duty, and need not a reminding look. A servant of yours, Sir Charles, looks as if he would one day make a figure as a master. How do you manage it?

Perhaps I have been peculiarly fortunate in worthy servants. There is nothing in my management deserving the attention of this company.

I am going to begin the world anew, nephew. Hitherto servants have been a continual plague to me. I must know how *you* treat them.

I treat them, my lord, as necessary parts of my family. I have no secrets, the keeping or disclosing of which might give them self-importance. I endeavour to set them no bad example. I am never angry with them but for wilful faults; if those are not habitual, I shame them into amendment by gentle expostulation and *forgiveness.* If they are not capable of a generous shame, and the faults are repeated, I part with them; but with such kindness, as makes their fellow-servants blame them, and take warning. I am fond of seeking occasions to praise them, and even when they mistake, if it be with a good intention, they have my approbation of the *intention,* and my endeavours to set them right as to the *act.* Sobriety is an indispensable qualification for my service; and, for the rest, if we receive them not quite good, we make them better than they were before. Generally speaking, a master may make a servant what he pleases. Servants judge by example rather than precept, and almost always by their feelings. One thing more permit me to add; I always insist upon my servants being kind and compassionate to one another. A compassionate heart cannot habitually be an unjust one. And thus do I make their good-nature contribute to my security as well as quiet.

My lord was greatly pleased with what his nephew said.

Upon some occasion, Lady G—— reflected upon a lady for *prudery,* and was going on, when Sir Charles interrupting her, said, Take care, Lady G——. You, ladies, take care; for I am afraid that MODESTY, under this name, will become ignominious, and be banished the hearts, at least the behaviour and conversation, of all those whose fortunes or inclinations carry them often to places of public resort.

Talk of places of public resort! said Lord L——: it is vexatious to observe at such, how men of real merit are neglected by the fine ladies of the age, while every distinction is shewn to fops and foplings.

But who, my lord, said Sir Charles, are those women? Are they not generally of a class with those men? Flippant women love empty men, because they cannot reproach them with a superiority of understanding, but keep their folly in countenance. They are afraid of a wise man: but I would by no means have such a one turn fool to please them: for they will despise the wise man's folly more than the silly man's, and with reason; because being uncharacteristic, it must sit more awkwardly upon him than the other's can do.

Yet wisdom itself, and the truest wisdom, *goodness,* said Mrs. Reeves, is sometimes thought to sit ungracefully, when it is uncharacteristic, not to the man, but to the times. She then named a person who was branded as a hypocrite for performing all his duties publicly.

He will be worse spoken of if he declines doing so, said

Dr. Bartlett. His enemies will *add* the charge of cowardice; and not acquit him of the other.

Lady Gertrude being withdrawn, it was mentioned as a wonder, that so agreeable a woman as she must have been in her youth, and still was for her years, should remain single. Lord G—— said that she had had many offers: and once, before she was twenty, had like to have stolen a wedding: but her fears, he said, since that, had kept her single.

The longer, said Sir Charles, a woman remains unmarried, the more apprehensive she will be of entering into the state. At *seventeen* or *eighteen* a girl will plunge into it, sometimes without either fear or wit; at *twenty,* she will begin to think; at *twenty-four* will weigh and discriminate; at *twenty-eight* will be afraid of venturing; at *thirty* will turn about and look down the hill she has ascended; and, as occasions offer, and instances are given, will sometimes repent, sometimes rejoice, that she has gained that summit *sola.*

Indeed, said Mrs. Reeves, I believe in England many a poor girl goes up the hill with a companion she would little care for, if the state of a single woman were not here so peculiarly unprovided and helpless: for girls of slender fortunes, if they have been genteelly brought up, how can they, when family connexions are dissolved, support themselves? A man can rise in a profession, and, if he acquires wealth in a trade, can get above it, and be respected. A woman is looked upon as demeaning herself, if she gains a maintenance by her needle, or by domestic attendance on a superior; and without them where has she a retreat?

You speak, good Mrs. Reeves, said Sir Charles, as if you would join with Dr. Bartlett and me in wishing the *establishment* of a scheme we have often talked over, though the name of it would make many a lady start. We want to see established in every county, *Protestant Nunneries,* in which single women of small or no fortunes, might live with all manner of freedom, under such regulations as it would be a disgrace for a modest or good woman not to comply with, were she absolutely on her own hands; and to be allowed to quit it whenever they pleased.

Well, brother, said Lady G——, and why could you not have got all this settled a fortnight ago (you that can carry every point) and have made poor me a lady abbess?

You are still better provided for, my sister. But let the doctor and me proceed with our scheme. The governesses or matrons of the society I would have to be women of family, of unblamable characters from infancy, and noted equally for their prudence, good-nature, and gentleness of manners. The attendants, for the slighter services, should be the hopeful female children of the honest industrious poor.

Do you not, ladies, imagine, said Dr. Bartlett, that such a society as this, all women of unblemished reputation, employing themselves as each (consulting her own genius), at her admission, shall undertake to employ herself, and supported genteelly, some at more, some at less expense to the foundation, according to their circumstances, might become a *national* good; and particularly a seminary for good wives and the institution a stand for virtue, in an age given up to luxury, extravagance, and amusements little less than riotous?

How could it be supported? said Lord W——.

Many of the persons, of which each community would consist, would be, I imagine, replied Sir Charles, no expense to it at all; as numbers of young women, joining their small fortunes, might be able, in such a society, to maintain themselves genteelly on their own income; though each, singly in the world, would be distressed. Besides, liberty might be given for wives, in the absence of their husbands, in this maritime country; and for widows, who, on the deaths of theirs, might wish to retire from the noise and hurry of the world, for three, six, or twelve months, more or less; to reside in this well-regulated society: and such persons, we may suppose, would be glad, according to their respective abilities, to be benefactresses to it. No doubt but it would have, besides, the countenance of the well-disposed of both sexes; since every family in Britain, in their connexions and relations, near or distant, might be benefited by so reputable and useful an institution: to say nothing of the works of the ladies in it, the profits of which, perhaps, will be thought proper to be carried towards the support of a foundation that so genteelly supports them. Yet I would have a number of hours in each day, for the encouragement of industry, that should be called their own; and what was produced in them, to be solely appropriated to their own use.

A truly worthy divine, at the appointment of the bishop of the diocese, to direct and animate the devotion of such a society, and to guard it from that superstition and enthusiasm which soars to wild heights in almost all nunneries, would confirm it a blessing to the kingdom.

I have another scheme, my lord, proceeded Sir Charles— An hospital for female penitents: for such unhappy women, as having been once drawn in, and betrayed by the perfidy of men, find themselves, by the cruelty of the world, and principally by that of their own sex, unable to recover the path of virtue, when, perhaps (convinced of the wickedness of the men in whose honour they confided), they would willingly make their first departure from it the last.

These, continued he, are the poor creatures who are eminently entitled to our pity, though they seldom meet with it. Good nature; and *credulity,* the child of good-nature; are generally, as I have the charity to believe, rather than viciousness, the foundation of their crime. Those men who pretend they would not be the first destroyers of a woman's innocence, look upon these as fair prize. But what a wretch is he, who, seeing a poor creature exposed on the summit of a dangerous precipice, and unable, without an assisting hand, to find her way down, would rather push her into the gulf below, than convey her down in safety!

Speaking of the force put upon a daughter's inclinations in wedlock; Tyranny and ingratitude, said Sir Charles, from a man beloved, will be more supportable to a woman of strong passions, than even kindness from a man she loves not: shall not parents, then, who hope to see their children happy, avoid compelling them to give their hands to a man who has no share in their hearts?

But would you allow young ladies to be their own choosers, Sir Charles? said Mr. Reeves.

Daughters, replied he, who are earnest to choose for themselves, should be *doubly* careful that prudence justifies their choice. Every widow who marries imprudently (and very many there are who do), furnishes a strong argument in favour of a parent's authority over a maiden daughter. A designing man looks out for a woman who has an independent fortune, and has no questions to ask. He seems *assured* of finding indiscretion and rashness in such a one, to befriend him. But ought not she to think herself affronted, and resolve to disappoint him?

But how, said Lady G——, shall a young creature be able to judge——

By his application to *her,* rather than to her natural friends and relations; by his endeavouring to alienate her affections from them; by wishing her to favour private and clandestine meetings (conscious that his pretensions will not stand discussion); by the inequality of his fortune to hers: and has not our excellent Miss Byron, in the letters to her Lucy (bowing to me), which she has had the goodness to allow us to read, helped us to a criterion? 'Men in their 'addresses to young women,' she very happily observes, 'forget not to set forward the advantages by which they are 'distinguished, whether hereditary or acquired; while love, 'love, is all the cry of him who has no other to boast of.'

And by that means, said Lady Gertrude, setting the silly creature at variance with all her friends, he makes her fight his battles for him; and become herself the cat'spaw to help him to the ready roasted chestnuts.

But, dear brother, said Lady G——, do you think love is such a staid deliberate passion, as to allow a young creature to take time to ponder and weigh all the merits of the cause?

Love at first sight, answered Sir Charles, must indicate a mind *prepared* for impression, and a sudden gust of passion, and that of the least noble kind; since there could be no opportunity of knowing the *merit* of the object. What women would have herself supposed capable of such a *tindery fit?* In a *man,* it is an indelicate paroxysm: but in a *woman,* who expects protection and instruction from a man, much more so. Love, at first, may be only fancy. Such a young love may be easily given up, and ought, to a parent's judgment. Nor is the conquest, so difficult as some young creatures think it. One thing, my good Emily, let me say to *you,* as a rule of some consequence in the world you are just entering into—Young persons, on arduous occasions, especially in love-cases, should not presume to advise young persons; because they seldom can divest themselves of passion, partiality, or prejudice; that is, indeed, of *youth;* and forbear to mix their own concerns and biases with the question referred to them. It should not be put from young friend to young friend, What would *you* do in such a case? but, What *ought* to be done?

How the dear girl blushed, and how pleased she looked, to be particularly addressed by her guardian!

Lady Gertrude spoke of a certain father, who, for interested views, obliged his daughter to marry at fifteen, when she was not only indifferent to the man, but had formed no right notions of the state.

And are they not unhappy? asked Sir Charles.

They are, replied she.

I knew such an instance, returned he. The lady was handsome, and had her full share of vanity. She believed every man who said civil things to her was in love with her; and had she been single, that he would have made his addresses to her. She supposed that she might have had *this* great man, or *that,* had she not been precipitated. And this brought her to slight the man who had, as she concluded, deprived her of better offers. They were unhappy to the end of their lives. Had the lady lived single long enough to find out the difference between compliment and sincerity, and that the man who flattered her vanity meant no more than to take advantage of her folly, she would have thought herself not unhappy with the very man with whom she was so dissatisfied.

Lady L—— speaking afterwards of a certain nobleman,

who is continually railing against matrimony, and who makes a very indifferent husband to an obliging wife: I have known more men than one, said Sir Charles, inveigh against matrimony, when the invective would have proceeded with a much better grace from their wives' lips than from theirs. But let us inquire, would this complainer have been, or deserved to be, happier in *any* state than he now is?

A state of suffering, said Lady L——, had probably humbled the spirit of the poor wife into perfect meekness and patience.

You observe rightly, replied Sir Charles: and surely a most kind disposition of Providence it is that adversity, so painful in itself, should conduce so peculiarly as it does to the improvement of the human mind: it teaches modesty, humility, and compassion.

You speak feelingly, brother, said Lady L——, with a sigh. Do you think, Lucy, nobody sighed but she?

I do, said he. I speak with a sense of gratitude. I am naturally of an imperious spirit: but I have reaped advantages from the early stroke of a mother's death. Being for years, against my wishes, obliged to submit to a kind of exile from my native country, which I considered as a heavy evil, though I thought it my duty to acquiesce, I was determined, as much as my capacity would allow, to make my advantage of the compulsion, by qualifying myself to do credit, rather than discredit, to my father, my friends, and my country. And, let me add, that if I have in any tolerable manner succeeded, I owe much to the example and precepts of my dear Dr. Bartlett.

The doctor blushed and bowed, and was going to disclaim the merit which his patron had ascribed to him; but Sir Charles confirmed it in still stronger terms. You, my dear Dr. Bartlett, said he, as I have told Miss Byron, was a second conscience to me in my earlier youth: your precepts, your excellent life, your pure manners, your sweetness of temper, could not but open and enlarge my mind. The soil, I hope I may say, was not barren; but you, my dear paternal friend, was the cultivator: I shall ever acknowledge it—and he bowed to the good man, who was covered with modest confusion, and could not look up.

And think you, Lucy, that this acknowledgment lessened the excellent man with any one present? No! It raised him in every eye: and I was the more pleased with it, as it helped me to account for that deep observation, which otherwise one should have been at a loss to account for in so young a man. And yet I am convinced, that there is hardly a greater difference in intellect between angel and man, than there is between man and man.

LETTER XXIV.

Lady G—— to Miss Byron.

Thursday, April 13.

FOR Heaven's sake, my dearest Harriet, dine with us to-day, for two reasons: one relates to myself; the other you shall hear by and by: to myself, first, as is most fit—this silly creature has offended me, and presumed to be sullen upon my resentment. Married but two days, and show his airs? —Were I in fault, my dear (which, upon my honour, I am not), for the man to lose his patience with me, to forget his obligations to me, in two days!—What an ungrateful wretch is he! What a poor powerless creature your Charlotte!

Nobody knows of the matter, except he has complained to my brother—*If* he has! But what if he has?—Alas! my dear, I am married; and cannot help myself.

We seem, however, to be drawing up our forces on both sides—one struggle for my dying liberty, my dear! The success of one pitched battle will determine which is to be the general, which the subaltern, for the rest of the campaign. To *dare* to be sullen already!—as I hope to live, my dear, I was in high good humour within myself; and when he was *foolish,* only intended a little play with him;

and he takes it in earnest. He worships you: so I shall rally him before you: but I charge you, as the man by his sullenness has taken upon him to fight his own battle, either to be on my side, or be silent. I shall take it very ill of my Harriet, if she strengthen his hands.

Well, but enough of this husband—HUSBAND! What a word! Who do you think is arrived from abroad?—You cannot guess for your life—Lady OLIVIA!—True as you are alive! accompanied, it seems, by an aunt of hers; a widow, whose years and character are to keep the niece in countenance in this excursion. The pretence is, making the tour of Europe; and England was not to be left out of the scheme. My brother is excessively disturbed at her arrival. She came to town but last night. He had notice of it but this morning. He took Emily with him to visit her: Emily was known to her at Florence. She and her aunt are to be here at dinner. As she *is* come, Sir Charles says, he must bring her acquainted with his sisters, and their lords, in order to be at liberty to pursue the measures he has unalterably resolved upon: and this, Harriet, is my second reason for urging you to dine with us.

Now I do wish we had known her history at large. Dr. Bartlett shall tell it us. Unwelcome as she is to my brother, I long to see her. I hope I shall not hear something in *her* story, that will make me pity her.

Will you come?

I wonder whether she speaks English, or not. I don't think I can converse in Italian.

I won't forgive you, if you refuse to come.

Lady L—— and her good man will be here. We shall therefore, if *you* come, be our whole family together.

My brother has presented this house to me, till his return. He calls himself Lord G——'s guest and mine: so you can have no punctilio about it. Besides, Lord W—— will set out to-morrow morning for Windsor. He dotes upon you: and perhaps it is in your power to make a new-married man penitent and polite.

So you must come.

Hang me, if I sign by any other name, while this man is in fits, than that of

CHARLOTTE GRANDISON.

LETTER XXV.

Miss Byron to Miss Selby.

Thursday, April 13.

I SEND you enclosed a letter I received this morning from Lady G———. I will suppose you have read it.

Emily says that the meeting between Sir Charles and the lady mentioned in it, was very polite on both sides: but more cold on his than on hers. She made some difficulty, however, of dining at his house; and her aunt, Lady Maffei, more. But on Sir Charles's telling them, that he would bring his elder sister to attend them thither, they complied.

When I went to St. James's Square, Sir Charles and Lady L——— were gone in his coach to bring the two ladies.

Lady G——— met me on the stairs-head leading into her dressing-room. Not a word, said she, of the man's sullens: he repents: a fine figure, as I told him, of a bridegroom, would he make in the eyes of foreign ladies, at dinner, were he to retain his gloomy airs. He has begged my pardon; as good as promised amendment; and I have forgiven him.

Poor Lord G———, said I.

Hush, hush! He is within: he will hear you: and then perhaps repent of his repentance.

She led me in: my lord had a glow in his cheeks, and looked as if he had been nettled, and was but just recovering a smile, to help to carry off the petulance. Oh how saucily did her eyes look! Well, my lord, said she, I hope— but you say, I misunderstood—

No more, madam, no more, I beseech you—

Well, sir, not a word more, since you are—

Pray, madam—

Well, well, give me your hand—you must leave Harriet and me together.

She humorously courtesied to him as he bowed to me, taking the compliment as to herself. She nodded her head to him, as he turned back his when he was at the door; and when he was gone, If I can but make this man orderly, said she, I shall not quarrel with my brother for hurrying me, as he has done.

You are wrong, excessively wrong, Charlotte. You call my lord a silly man, but have no proof that he is so, but by his bearing this treatment from you.

None of your grave airs, my dear. The man is a good sort of man, and will be so, if you and Lady L—— don't spoil him. I have a vast deal of roguery, but no ill-nature in my heart. There is luxury in jesting with a solemn man, who wants to assume airs of privilege, and thinks he has a right to be impertinent. I'll tell you how I will manage—I believe I shall often try his patience, and when I am conscious that I have gone too far, I will be patient if he is angry with me; so we shall be quits. Then I'll begin again: he will resent: and if I find his aspect very solemn—Come, come, no glouting, friend, I will say, and perhaps smile in his face: I'll play you a tune, or sing you a song—Which, which? Speak in a moment, or the humor will be off.

If he was ready to cry before, he will laugh then, though against his will: and as he admires my finger, and my voice, shall we not be instantly friends?

It signified nothing to rave at her: she will have her way. Poor Lord G——! At my first knowledge of her, I thought her very lively; but imagined not that she was indiscreetly so.

Lord G——'s fondness for his saucy bride was, as I have reason to believe, his fault. I dared not to ask for particulars of their quarrel: and if I had, and *found* it so, could not, with such a rallying creature, have entered into his defence, or censured her.

I went down a few moments before her. Lord G—— whispered me, that he should be the happiest man in the world, if I, who had such an influence over her, would stand his friend.

I hope, my lord, said I, that you will not want any influence but your own. She has a thousand good qualities. She has charming spirits. You will have nothing to bear with but from them. They will not last always. Think only, that she can mean nothing by the exertion of them, but innocent gaiety; and she will every day love your lordship the better for bearing with her. You know she is generous and noble.

I see, madam, said he, she has led you into——

She has not acquainted me with the particulars of the little misunderstanding; only has said, that there had been a slight one; which was quite made up.

I am ashamed, replied he, to have it thought by Miss Byron, that there *could* have been a misunderstanding between us, especially so early. She knows her power over me. I am afraid she despises me.

Impossible, my lord! Have you not observed, that she spares nobody when she is in a lively humour?

True—but here she comes!—Not a word, madam!—I bowed assenting silence. Lord G——, said she, approaching him, in a low voice, I shall be jealous of your conversations with Miss Byron.

Would to Heaven, my dearest life! snatching at her withdrawn hand, that——

I were half as good as Miss Byron: I understand you: but time and patience, sir; nodding to him, and passing him.

Admirable creature! said he, how I adore her!

I hinted to her, afterwards, his fear of her despising him. Harriet, answered she, with a serious air, I will do my duty by him. I will abhor my own heart, if I ever find in it the shadow of a regard for any man in the world, inconsistent with that which he has a right to expect from me.

I was pleased with her. And found an opportunity to communicate what she said, in confidence, to my lord; and had his blessings for it.

But now for some account of Lady Olivia. With which I will begin a new letter.

LETTER XXVI.

Miss Byron.—In continuation.

SIR CHARLES returned with the ladies. He presented to Lady Olivia and her aunt, Lady G——, Lord L——, and Lord W——. I was in another apartment talking with Dr. Bartlett.

Lady Olivia asked for the doctor. He left *me* to pay his respects to *her*.

Sir Charles being informed that I was in the house, told Lady Olivia, that he hoped he should have the honour of presenting to her one of our English beauties; desiring Lady G—— to request my company.

Lady G—— came to me—A lovely woman, I assure you, Harriet; let me lead you to her.

Sir Charles met me at the entrance of the drawing-room: Excuse me, madam, said he, taking my hand, with profound respect, and allow me to introduce to you a very amiable Italian lady, one who does so much honour to Britain.—Miss Byron, madam, addressing himself to her, salutes you. The advantages of person are her least perfection.

Her face glowed, Miss Byron, said she, in French, is all loveliness. A relation, sir? In Italian.

He bowed; but answered not her question.

I would sooner forgive you *here,* whispered Lady Olivia to Sir Charles, in Italian, looking at me, than at Bologna.

I heard her; and by my confusion showed that I understood her. She was in confusion too.

Mademoiselle, said she, in French, understands Italian.— I am ashamed, monsieur.

Miss Byron does, answered Sir Charles; and French too.

I must have the honour, said she, in French, to be better known to you, mademoiselle.

I answered her as politely as I could in the same language.

Lady OLIVIA is really a lovely woman. Her complexion is fine. Her face oval. Every feature of it is delicate. Her hair is black; and, I think, I never saw brighter black eyes in my life: if possible, they are brighter, and shine with a more piercing lustre, than even Sir Charles Grandison's: but yet I give his the preference; for we see in them a benignity, that hers, though a woman's, has not; and a thoughtfulness, as if something lay upon his mind, which nothing but patience could overcome; yet mingled with an air that shows him to be equal to anything that can be undertaken by man; while Olivia's eyes show more fire and impetuosity than sweetness. Had I not been *told* it, I should have been sure that she has a violent spirit: but on the whole she is a very fine figure of a woman.

She talked of taking a house, and staying in England a year at least; and was determined, she said, to perfect herself in the language, and to become an Englishwoman: but when Sir Charles, in the way of discourse, mentioned his obligation to leave England, as on next Friday morning, how did she and her aunt look upon each other! And how was the sunshine that gilded her fine countenance, shut in: Surely, sir, said her aunt, you are not in earnest!

After dinner, the two ladies retired with Sir Charles, at his motion. Dr. Bartlett, at Lady G——'s request, then gave us this short sketch of her history. He said, she had a vast fortune: she had had indiscretions; but none that had affected her character as to virtue: but her spirit could not bear control. She had shown herself to be vindictive, even to a criminal degree. Lord bless me, my dear! the doctor has mentioned to me in confidence, that she always carries a poniard about her; and that once she used it. Had the person died, she would have been called to public account for it. The man, it seems, was of rank, and offered some slight affront to her. She now comes over, the doctor said, as he had reason to believe, with a resolution to sacrifice even her religion, if it were insisted upon, to the passion she had so long in vain endeavoured to conquer.

She has, he says, an utter hatred to Lady Clementina; and will not be able to govern her passion, he is sure, when Sir Charles shall acquaint her, that he is going to attend that lady, and her family: for he has only mentioned his obligation to go abroad; but not said whither.

Lord W—— praised the person of the lady, and her majestic air. Lord L—— and Lord G—— wished to be within hearing of the conference between her and Sir Charles: so did Lady G——: and while they were thus wishing, in came Sir Charles, his face all in a glow; Lady L——, said he, be so good as to attend Lady Olivia.

She went to her; Sir Charles stayed not with us, yet went not to the lady, but into his study. Dr. Bartlett attended him there: the doctor returned soon after to us. His noble heart is vexed, said he; Lady Olivia has greatly disturbed him: he chooses to be alone.

Lady L—— afterwards told us, that she found the lady in violent anguish of spirit, her aunt endeavouring to calm her: she, however, politely addressed herself to Lady L——, and begging her aunt to withdraw for a few moments, she owned to her, in French, her passion for her brother: She was not, she said, ashamed to own it to his sister, who must know that his merit would dignify the passion of the noblest woman. She had endeavoured, she said, to conquer hers: she had been willing to give way to the prior attachments that he had pleaded for a lady of her own country, Signora Clementina della Porretta, whom she allowed to have had great merit; but who, having irrecoverably been put out of her right mind, was shut up at Naples by a brother, who vowed eternal enmity to Sir Charles; and from whom his life would be in the utmost hazard, if he went over. She owned that her chief motive for her coming to England was to cast her fortune at her brother's feet; and, as she knew him to be a man of honour, to comply with any terms he should propose to her. He had offered to the family della Porretta to allow their daughter her religion, and her confessor, and to live with her every other year in Italy. She herself, not inferior in birth, in person, in mind, as she said, she presumed, and superior in fortune, the riches of three branches of her family, all rich, having centered in *her*, insisted not now upon such conditions. Her aunt, she said, knew not that she proposed, on conviction, a change of her religion; but she was resolved not to conceal anything from Lady L——. She left her to judge how much she must be affected, when he declared his obligation to leave England; and especially when he owned that it was to go to Bologna, and that so suddenly, as if, as she apprehended at first, it was to avoid *her*. She had been in tears, she said, and even would have kneeled to him to induce him to suspend his journey for one month, and then to have taken her over with him, and seen her safe in her own palace, if he *would* go upon so hated, and so fruitless, as well as so hazardous an errand: but he had denied her this poor favour.

This refusal, she owned, had put her out of all patience. She was unhappily passionate; but was the most placable of her sex. What, madam, said she, can affect a woman, if slight, indignity, and repulse, from a favoured person, is not able to do it? A woman of my condition to come over to England, to solicit—how can I support the thought—and to be refused the protection of the man she prefers to all men; and her request to see her safe back again, though but as the fool she came over!—You may blame me, madam —but you must pity me, even were you to have a heart the sister heart of your inflexible brother.

In vain did Lady L—— plead to her Lady Clementina's deplorable situation; the reluctance of his own relations to part with him; and the magnanimity of his self-denial in a hundred instances, on the bare possibility of being an instrument to restore her: she could not bear to hear her speak highly of the unhappy lady. She charged Clementina with the pride of her family, to which she attributed the deserved calamity: [*Deserved!* Cruel lady! How could her pitiless heart allow her lips to utter such a word!] and imputed meanness to the noblest of human minds, for yielding to the entreaties of a family, some of the principals of which, she said, had entreated him with an arrogance that a man of his spirit ought not to bear.

Lady Maffei came in. She seems dependent upon her niece. She is her aunt by marriage only: and Lady L——

speaks very favourably of her, from the advice she gave, and her remonstrances to her kinswoman. Lady Maffei besought her to compose herself, and return to the company.

She could not bear, she said, to return to the company, the slighted, the contemned object, she must appear to be to every one in it. I am an intruder, said she haughtily; a beggar, with a fortune that would purchase a sovereignty in some countries. Make my excuses to your sister, to the rest of the company—and to that fine young lady—whose eyes, by their officious withdrawing from his, and by the consciousness that glowed in her face whenever he addressed her, betrayed, at least to a jealous eye, more than she would wish to have seen—but tell her, that all lovely and blooming as she is, she must have no hope, while Clementina lives.

I hope, Lucy, it is *only* to a jealous eye that my *heart* is so discoverable!—I thank her for her caution. But I can say what she cannot; that from my heart, cost me what it may, I do subscribe to a preference in favour of a lady, who has acted, in the most arduous trials, in a greater manner than I fear either Olivia or I could have acted, in the same circumstances. We see that her reason, but not her piety, deserted her in the noble struggle between her love and her religion. In the most affecting absences of her reason, the soul of the man she loved was the object of her passion. However hard it is to prefer another to one's self, in such a case as this; yet if my judgment is convinced, my acknowledgment shall follow it. Heaven will enable me to be reconciled to the event, because I pursue the dictates of that judgment, against the biases of my more partial heart. Let that Heaven, which only *can,* restore Clementina, and dispose as it pleases of Olivia and Harriet. We cannot either of us, I humbly hope, be so unhappy as the lady has been whom I rank among the first of women; and whose whole family deserves almost equal compassion.

Lady Olivia asked Lady L——, if her brother had not a very tender regard for me? He had, Lady L—— answered; and told her, that he had rescued me from a very great distress; and that mine was the most grateful of human hearts.

She called me sweet young creature (supposing me, I doubt not, younger than I am); but said that the graces of my person and mind alarmed her not, as they would have done, had not his attachment to Clementina been what now she saw, but never could have believed it was; having supposed, that compassion only was the tie that bound him to her.

But compassion, Lucy, from such a heart as his, the merit so great in the lady, must be love; a love of the nobler kind —and if it were *not,* it would be unworthy of Clementina's.

Lady Maffei called upon her dignity, her birth, to carry her above a passion that met not with a grateful return. She advised her to dispose herself to stay in England some months, now she was here. And as her friends in Italy would suppose what her view was in coming to England, their censures would be obviated by her continuing here for some time, while Sir Charles was abroad, and in Italy: and that she should divert herself with visiting the court, the public places, and in seeing the principal curiosities of this kingdom, as she had done those of others; in order to give credit to an excursion that might otherwise be freely spoken of, in her own country.

She seemed to listen to this advice. She bespoke, and was promised, the friendship of the two sisters: and included in her request, through their interests, mine; and Lady G—— was called in, by her sister, to join in the promise.

She desired that Sir Charles might be requested to walk in; but would not suffer the sisters to withdraw, as they would have done, when he returned. He could not but be polite; but, it seems, looked still disturbed. I beg you to excuse, sir, said she, my behaviour to you: it was passionate; it was unbecoming. But, in compliment to your own consequence, you *ought* to excuse it. I have only to request one favour of you: That you will suspend for *one* week, in regard to me, your proposed journey; *but* for one week; and I will, now I am in England, stay some months; perhaps till you return.

Excuse me, madam.

I will *not* excuse you—but *one* week, sir. Give me so

much importance with myself, as for one week's suspension. You will. You must.

Indeed I cannot. My soul, I own to you, is in the distresses of the family of Porretta. Why should I repeat what I said to you before?

I have bespoken, sir, the civilities of your sisters, of your family: you forbid them not?

You expect not an answer, madam, to that question. My sisters will be glad, and so will their lords, to attend you wherever you please, with a hope to make England agreeable to you.

How long do you propose to stay in *Italy*, sir?

It is not possible for me to determine.

Are you not apprehensive of danger to your person?

I am not.

You *ought* to be.

No danger shall deter me from doing what I think to be right. If my motives justify me, I cannot fear.

Do you wish me, sir, to stay in England till your return?

A question so home put, disturbed him. Was it a prudent one in the lady? It must either subject her to a repulse; or him, by a polite answer, to give her hope, that her stay in England might not be fruitless as to the view she had in coming. He reddened. It is fit, answered he, that your own pleasure should determine you. It did, pardon me, madam, in your journey hither.

She reddened to her very ears. Your brother, ladies, has the reputation of being a polite man: bear witness to this instance of it. I am ashamed of myself!

If I am unpolite, madam, my sincerity will be my excuse: at least to my own heart.

Oh, that inflexible heart! But, ladies, if the inhospitable Englishman refuse his protection in his own country, to a foreign woman, of no mean quality; do not you, his sisters, despise her.

They, madam, and their lords, will render you every cheerful service. Let me request you, my sisters, to make England as agreeable as possible to this lady. She is of the first consideration in her own country: she will be of such wherever she goes. My Lady Maffei deserves likewise your utmost respect. Then addressing himself to them; Ladies, said he, encourage my sisters: they will think themselves honoured by your commands.

The two sisters confirmed, in an obliging manner, what their brother had said; and both ladies acknowledged themselves indebted to them for their offered friendship: but Lady Olivia seemed not at all satisfied with their brother: and it was with some difficulty he prevailed on her to return to the company, and drink coffee.

I could not help reflecting, on occasion of this lady's conduct, that fathers and mothers are great blessings, to *daughters,* in particular, even when women grown. It is not every woman that will shine in a state of independency. Great fortunes are snares. If independent women escape the machinations of men, which they have often a difficulty to do, they will frequently be hurried by their own imaginations, which are said to be livelier than those of men, though their judgments are supposed less, into inconveniences. Had Lady Olivia's parents or uncles lived, she hardly would have been permitted to make the tour of Europe: and not having so great a fortune to support vagaries, would have shone, as she is well qualified to do, in a dependent state, in Italy, and made some worthy man and herself happy.

Had she a mind great enough to induce her to pity Clementina, I should have been apt to pity *her;* for I saw her soul was disturbed. I saw that the man she loved was not able to return her love: a pitiable case!—I saw a starting tear now and then with difficulty dispersed. Once she rubbed her eye, and, being conscious of observation, said something had got into it: so it had. The something was a tear. Yet she looked with haughtiness, and her bosom swelled with indignation ill-concealed.

Sir Charles repeated his recommendation of her to Lord L—— and Lord G——. They offered their best services: Lord W—— invited her and all of us to Windsor. Different parties of pleasure were talked of: but still the enlivener of every party was not to be in any one of them. She tried to look pleased; but did not always succeed in the trial: an eye of love and anger mingled was often cast upon the man whom everybody loved. Her bosom heaved, as it seemed sometimes, with indignation against herself: that was the construction which I made of some of her looks.

Lady Maffei, however, seemed pleased with the parties of pleasure talked of. She often directed herself to me in Italian. I answered her in it as well as I could. I do not talk it well: but as I am not an Italian, and little more than book-learned in it (for it is a long time ago since I lost my grandpapa, who used to converse with me in it, and in French), I was not scrupulous to answer in it. To have forborne, because I did not excel in what I had no opportunity to excel in, would have been false modesty, nearly bordering upon pride. Were any lady to laugh at me for not speaking well *her* native tongue, I would *not* return the smile, were she to be less perfect in mine, than I am in hers. But Lady Olivia made me a compliment on my faulty accent, when I acknowledged it to be so. Signora, said she, you show us that a pretty mouth can give beauty to a defect. A *master* teaching you, added she, would perhaps find some fault; but a *friend* conversing with you, must be in love with you for the very imperfection.

Sir Charles was generously pleased with the compliment, and made a fine one on her observation.

He attended the two ladies to their lodgings in his coach. He owned to Dr. Bartlett, that Lady Olivia was in tears all the way, lamenting her disgrace in coming to England, just as he was quitting it; and wishing she had stayed at Florence. She would have engaged him to correspond with her: he excused himself. It was a very afflicting thing to him, he told the doctor, to deny any request that was made to him, especially by a lady: but he thought he ought in conscience and honour to forbear giving the shadow of an expectation that might be improved into hope, where none was intended to be given. Heaven, he said, had, for laudable ends, implanted such a regard in the sexes towards each other, that both man and woman who hoped to be innocent, could not be too circumspect in relation to the friendships they were so ready to contract with each other. He thought he had gone a great way, in recommending an intimacy between her and his sisters, considering her views, her spirit, her perseverance, and the free avowal of her regard for him, and her menaces on his supposed neglect of her. And yet, as she *had* come over, and he was obliged to leave England so soon after her arrival; he though he could not do less: and he hoped his sisters, from whose example she might be benefited, would, while she behaved prudently, cultivate her acquaintance.

The doctor tells me, that now Lady Olivia is so unexpectedly come hither in person, he thinks it best to decline giving me, as he had once intended, her history at large; but will leave so much of it as may satisfy my curiosity, to be gathered from my own observation; and not only from the violence and haughtiness of her temper, but from the freedom of her declarations. He is sure, he said, that his patron will be best pleased, that a veil should be thrown over the weaker part of her conduct; which, were it known, would indeed be glorious to Sir Charles, but not so to the lady; who, however, never was suspected, even by her enemies, of giving any other man reason to tax her with a thought that was not strictly virtuous: and she had engaged his pity and esteem, for the sake of her other fine qualities, though she could not his love. Before she saw *him* (which, it seems, was at the opera at Florence for the first time, when he had an opportunity to pay her some slight civilities) she set all men at defiance.

To-morrow morning Sir Charles is to breakfast with *me*. My cousins and I are to dine at Lord L——'s. The Earl and Lady Gertrude are also to be there. Lord W—— has been prevailed upon to stay, and be there also, as it is his nephew's last day in England—'Last day in England!' Oh, my Lucy! what words are those! Lady L—— has invited Lady Olivia and her aunt, at her own motion, Sir Charles (his time being so short) not disapproving.

I thank my grandmamma and aunt for their kind summons. I will soon set my day: I will, my dear, soon set my day.

LETTER XXVII.

Miss Byron.—In continuation.

Friday, Noon, April 14.

NOT five hours in bed; not one hour's rest for many uneasy nights before; I was stupid till Sir Charles came: I then was better. He inquired, with tender looks and voice, after my health; as if he thought I did not look well.

We had some talk about Lord and Lady G——. He was anxious for their happiness. He complimented me with hopes from my advice to her. Lord G——, he said, was a good-natured honest man. If he thought his sister would make him unhappy, he should himself be so.

I told him, that I dared to answer for her heart. My lord must bear with some innocent foibles, and all would be well.

We then talked of Lady Olivia. *He* began the subject, by asking my opinion of her. I said she was a very fine woman in her person; and that she had an air of grandeur in her mien.

And she has good qualities, said he; but she is violent in her passions. I am frequently grieved for her. She is a fine creature in danger of being lost, by being made too soon her own mistress.

He said not one word of his departure to-morrow morning: I could not begin it; my heart would not let me; my spirits were not high: and I am afraid, if that key had been touched, I should have been too visibly affected. My cousins forbore, upon the same apprehension.

He was excessively tender and soothing to me, in his air, his voice, his manner. I thought of what Emily said; that his voice, when he spoke of me, was the voice of love. Dear flattering girl!—But *why* did she flatter me?

We talked of *her* next. He spoke of her with the tenderness of a father. He besought me to love her. He praised her heart.

Emily, said I, venerates her guardian. She never will do anything contrary to his advice.

She is very young, replied he. She will be happy, madam, in yours. She both loves and reverences you.

I greatly love the dear Emily, sir. She and I shall be always sisters.

How happy am I, in your goodness to her! Permit me, madam, to enumerate to you my own felicities in those of my dearest friends.

Mr. Beauchamp is now in the agreeable situation I have long wished him to be in. His prudence and obliging behaviour to his mother-in-law have won her. His father grants him everything through her; and she, by this means, finds that power enlarged, which she was afraid would be lessened, if the son were allowed to come over. How just is this reward of his filial duty!

Thus, Lucy, did he give up the merit to his Beauchamp, which was solely due to himself.

Lord W——, he hoped, would soon be one of the happiest men in England: and the whole Mansfield family had now fair prospects opening before them.

Emily [not *he,* you see] had made it the interest of her mother to be quiet.

Lord and Lady L—— gave him pleasure whenever he saw them, or thought of them.

Dr. Bartlett was in heaven while on earth. He would retire to his beloved Grandison Hall, and employ himself in distributing, as objects offered, at least a thousand pounds of the three thousand bequeathed to charitable uses by his late friend Mr. Danby. His sister's fortune was paid. His estates in both kingdoms were improving.—See, madam, said he, how, like the friend of my soul, I claim your attention to affairs that are of consequence to myself; and in some of which your generosity of heart has interested you.

I bowed. Had I spoken, I had burst into tears. I had

something arose in my throat, I know not what. Still, thought I, excellent man, you are not yourself happy!—Oh pity! pity! Yet, Lucy, he plainly had been enumerating all these things, to take off from my mind that impression which I am afraid he too well knows it is affected with, from his difficult situation.

And now, madam, resumed he, how are all my dear and good friends, whom you more particularly call yours?—I hope to have the honour of a personal knowledge from them. When heard you of our good friend Mr. Deane? He is well, I hope.

Very well, sir.

Your grandmamma Shirley, that ornament of advanced years?

I bowed: I dared not to trust to my voice.

Your excellent aunt Selby?

I bowed again.

Your uncle, your Lucy, your Nancy: Happy family! all harmony! all love!—how do they?

I wiped my eyes.

Is there any service in my power to do them, or any of them? Command me, good Miss Byron, if there be: my Lord W—— and I are one. Our influence is not small.—Make me still *more* happy, in the power of serving any one favoured by you.

You oppress me, sir, by your goodness!—I cannot speak my grateful sensibilities.

Will you, my dear Mr. Reeves, will you, madam (to my cousin), employ me in any way that I can be of use to you, either abroad or at home? Your acquaintance has given me great pleasure. To what a family of worthies has this excellent young lady introduced me!

Oh, sir! said Mrs. Reeves, tears running down her cheeks, that you were not to leave people whom you have made so happy in the knowledge of the best of men.

Indispensable calls must be obeyed, my dear Mrs. Reeves. If we cannot be as happy as we wish, we will rejoice in the happiness we *can* have. We must not be our own carvers.—

But I make you all serious. I was enumerating, as I told you, my present felicities! I was rejoicing in your friendships. I *have* joy; and, I presume to say, I *will* have joy. There is a bright side in every event; I will not lose sight of it: and there is a dark one; but I will endeavour to see it only with the eye of prudence, that I may not be involved by it at unawares. Who, that is not reproached by his own heart, and is blessed with health, can grieve for inevitable evils; evils that can be only evils as we make them so? Forgive my seriousness: my dear friends, you *make* me grave. Favour me, I beseech you, my good Miss Byron, with one lesson: we shall be too much engaged, perhaps, by and by.

He led me (I thought it was with a *cheerful* air; but my cousins both say, his eyes glistened) to the harpsichord: he sung unasked, but with a low voice; and my mind was calmed. O Lucy! How can I part with such a man? How can I take my leave of him?—But, perhaps, he has taken his leave of me already, as to the solemnity of it, in the manner I have recited.

LETTER XXVIII.

Miss Byron.—In continuation.

Saturday Morning, April 15.

O Lucy, Sir Charles Grandison is gone! Gone, indeed! He set out at three this morning; on purpose, no doubt, to spare his sisters, and friends, as well as himself, concern.

We broke not up till after two. Were I in the writing humour, which I have never known to fail me till now, I could dwell upon a hundred things, some of which I can now only briefly mention.

Dinner-time, yesterday, passed with tolerable cheerfulness: every one tried to be cheerful. Oh, what pain attends loving too well, and being too well beloved! He must have pain, as well as we.

Lady Olivia was the most thoughtful, at dinner-time; yet poor Emily! Ah, the poor Emily! she went out four or five times to weep; though only I perceived it.

Nobody was cheerful after dinner but Sir Charles. He seemed to exert himself to be so. He prevailed on me to give them a lesson on the harpsichord. Lady L—— played: Lady G—— played: we *tried* to play, I should rather say. He himself took the violin, and afterwards sat down to the harpsichord, for one short lesson. He was not known to be such a master: but he was long in Italy. Lady Olivia, indeed, knew him to be so. She was induced to play upon the harpsichord: she surpassed everybody. Italy is the land of harmony.

About seven at night he singled me out, and surprised me greatly by what he said. He told me, that Lady D—— had made him a visit. I was before low: I was then ready to sink. She has asked me questions, madam.

Sir, sir! was all I could say.

He himself trembled as he spoke—Alas! my dear, he surely loves me! Hear how solemnly he spoke—God Almighty be your director, my dear Miss Byron! I wish not more happiness to my own soul, than I do to you.—In discharge of a promise made, I mentioned this visit to you: I might otherwise have spared you and myself——

He stopt there—then resumed; for I was silent. I could not speak—Your friends will be entreated for a man that loves you; a very worthy young nobleman.—I give you emotion, madam.—Forgive me.—I have performed my promise. He turned from me with a seeming cheerful air. How *could* he appear to be cheerful!

We made parties at cards. I knew not what I played. Emily sighed, and tears stole down her cheeks, as she played. Oh, how she loves her guardian! Emily, I say—I don't know what I write!

At supper we were all very melancholy. Mr. Beauchamp was urgent to go abroad with him. He changed the subject, and gave him an *indirect* denial, as I may call it, by recommending the two Italian ladies to his best services.

Sir Charles, kind, good, excellent! wished to Lord L——

to have seen Mr. Grandison:—unworthy as that man has made himself of his attention.

He was a few moments in private with Lady Olivia. She returned to company with red eyes.

Poor Emily watched an opportunity to be spoken to by him alone—so diligently! He led her to the window—about one o'clock it was—he held both her hands. He called her, she says, *his* Emily. He charged her to write to him.

She could not speak; she could only sob; yet thought she had a thousand things to say to him.

He contradicted not the hope his sisters and their lords had of his breakfasting with them. They invited me; they invited the Italian ladies: Lady L——, Lord L——, did go, in expectation: but Lady G——, when she found him gone, sent me and the Italian ladies word, that he was. It would have been cruel if she had not. How *could* he steal away so! I find, that he intended that his morning visit to me (as, indeed, I half suspected) should be a taking leave of my cousins, and your Harriet. How many things did he say then —how many questions ask—in tender woe—he wanted to do us all service—he seemed not to know what to say.—Surely he hates not your poor Harriet—What struggles in his noble bosom!—But a man cannot complain; a man cannot ask for compassion, as a woman can. But, surely, his is the gentlest of manly minds!

When we broke up, he handed my cousin Reeves into her coach. He handed me. Mr. Reeves said, We see you again Sir Charles, in the morning? He bowed. At handing me in, he sighed—he pressed my hand—I think he did—that was all—he saluted nobody. He will not meet his Clementina as he parted with us.

But, I doubt not, Dr. Bartlett was in the secret.

HE *was*. He has just been here. He found my eyes swelled. I had had no rest; yet knew not, till seven o'clock, that he was gone.

It was very good of the doctor to come: his visit soothed me: yet he took no notice of my red eyes. Nay, for that matter, Mrs. Reeves's eyes were swelled, as well as mine. Angel of a man! how is he beloved!

The doctor says, that his sisters, their lords, Lord W——, are in as much grief as if he were departed for ever—and who knows—but I will not torment myself with supposing the worst: I will endeavour to bear in mind what he said yesterday morning to us, no doubt for an instruction, that he *would* have joy.

And did he then think that I should be so much grieved as to want such an instruction?—and, therefore, did he vouchsafe to give it?—But, vanity, be quiet—lie down, hope—hopelessness, take place!—Clementina shall be his. He shall be hers.

Yet his emotion, Lucy, at mentioning Lady D——'s visit—Oh! but that was only owing to his humanity. He saw *my* emotion; and acknowledged the tenderest friendship for me! Ought I not to be satisfied with that? I *am*. I *will be* satisfied. Does he not love me with the love of mind? The poor Olivia has not this to comfort herself with. The poor Olivia! if I see her sad and afflicted, how I shall pity her! All her expectations frustrated; the expectations that engaged her to combat difficulties, to travel, to cross many waters, and to come to England—to come just time enough to take leave of him; he hastening on the wings of love and compassion to a dearer, a *deservedly* dearer object, in the country she had quitted on purpose to visit him in his—is not hers a more grievous situation than mine?—It is. Why, then, do I lament?

But here, Lucy, let me in confidence hint, what I have gathered from several intimations from Dr. Bartlett, though as tenderly made by him as possible, that had Sir Charles Grandison been a man capable of taking advantage of the violence of a lady's passion for him, the unhappy Olivia would not have scrupled, great, haughty, and noble as she is, by birth and fortune, to have been his, without conditions, if she could not have been so with: the Italian world is of this opinion, at least. Had Sir Charles been a Rinaldo, Olivia had been an Armida.

Oh, that I could hope, for the honour of the sex, and of the lady, who is so fine a woman, that the Italian world is mistaken!—I will presume that it is.

My good Dr. Bartlett, will you allow me to accuse you of a virtue too rigorous? That is sometimes the fault of very good people. You own that Sir Charles has not, even to *you,* revealed a secret so disgraceful to her. You own, that he has only blamed her for having too little regard for her reputation, and for the violence of her temper: yet how patiently, for one of such a temper, has she taken his departure, almost on the day of her arrival! *He* could not have given her an *opportunity* to indicate to him a concession so criminal: *she* could not, if he *had,* have made the overture. Wicked, wicked world! I will not believe you! And the less credit shall you have with me, Italian world, as I have *seen* the lady. The innocent heart will be a charitable one. Lady Olivia is only too intrepid. Prosperity, as Sir Charles observed, has been a snare to her, and set her above a proper regard to her reputation.—Merciless world! I do not love you. Dear Dr. Bartlett, you are not yet absolutely perfect! These hints of yours against Olivia, gathered from the malevolence of the envious, are proofs (the first, indeed, that I have met with) of *your* imperfection!

Excuse me, Lucy: how have I run on! Disappointment has mortified me, and made me good-natured.—I will welcome adversity, if it enlarge my charity.

The doctor tells me, that Emily, with her half-broken heart, will be here presently. If I can be of comfort to her—but I want it myself, from the same cause. We shall only weep over each other.

As I told you, the doctor, and the doctor only, knew of his setting out so early. He took leave of him. Happy Dr. Bartlett!—Yet I see, by his eyes, that this parting cost him some paternal tears.

Never father better loved a son than this good man loves Sir Charles Grandison.

Sir Charles, it seems, had settled all his affairs three days before. His servants were appointed.

The doctor tells me, that he had last week presented the elder Mr. Oldham with a pair of colours, which he had purchased for him. Nobody had heard of this.

Lord W——, he says, is preparing for Windsor; Mr. Beauchamp for Hampshire, for a few days; and then he returns to attend the commands of the noble Italians.

Lady Olivia will soon have her equipage ready.

She will make a great appearance.—But SIR CHARLES GRANDISON will not be with her. What is grandeur to a disturbed heart?

The Earl of G—— and Lady Gertrude are setting out for Hertfordshire. Lord and Lady L—— talk of retiring, for a few weeks, to Colnebrook: the doctor is preparing for Grandison Hall; your poor Harriet for Northamptonshire—bless me, my dear, what a dispersion!—But Lord W——'s nuptials will collect some of them together at Windsor.

EMILY, the dear weeping girl! is just come. She is with my cousin. She expects my permission for coming up to me. Imagine us weeping over each other; praying for, blessing the guardian of us both. Your imagination cannot form a scene too tender.—Adieu, my Lucy.

LETTER XXIX.

Miss Byron.—In continuation.

Sunday, April 16.

OH, what a blank, my dear!—But I need not say what I was going to say. Poor Emily!—but, to mention her grief, is to paint my own.

Lord W—— went to Windsor yesterday.

A very odd behaviour of Lady Olivia. Mr. Beauchamp went yesterday, and offered to attend her to any of the public places, at her pleasure; in pursuance of Sir Charles's reference to him, to do all in his power to make England agreeable to her: and she thought fit to tell him, before her aunt, that she thanked him for his civility; but she should not trouble him during her stay in England. She had *gentlemen* in her train; and one of them had been in England before——

He left her in disgust.

Lady L—— making her a visit in the evening, she told her of Mr. Beauchamp's offer, and of her answer. The gentleman, said she, is a polite and very agreeable man; and *this* made me treat his kind offer with abruptness: for I can hardly doubt your brother's view in it. I *scorn* his view: and, if I were sure of it, perhaps I should find a way to make him repent of the indignity. Lady L—— was sure, she said, that neither her brother, nor Mr. Beauchamp, had any other views than to make England as agreeable to her as possible.

Be this as it may, madam, said she, I have no service for Mr. Beauchamp: but if your ladyship, your sister, and your two lords, will allow me to cultivate your friendship, you will do me honour. Dr. Bartlett's company will be very agreeable to me likewise, as often as he will give it to me. To Miss Jervois I lay some little claim. I would have had her for my companion in Italy; but your cruel brother—no more, however, of him. Your English beauty, too, I admire her: but, poor young creature, I admire her the more, because I can pity *her*. I should think myself very happy to be better acquainted with her.

Lady L—— made her a very polite answer for herself and her sister, and their lords. But told her, that I was very soon to set out for my own abode in Northamptonshire: and that Dr. Bartlett had some commissions, which would oblige him, in a day or two, to go to Sir Charles's seat in the country. She herself offered to attend her to Windsor, and to every other place, at her command.

Lady L—— took notice of her wrist being bound round with a broad black ribband, and asked, if it were hurt? A kind of sprain, said she. But you little imagine how it came; and must not ask.

This made Lady L—— curious; and Olivia requesting that

Emily might be allowed to breakfast with her as this morning, she has bid the dear girl endeavour to know how it came, if it fell in her way: for Olivia reddened, and looked up, with a kind of consciousness, to Lady L——, when she told her that she must not ask questions about it.

Lady G—— is very earnest with me to give into the town diversions for a month to come: but I have now no desire in my heart so strong, as to return to all my dear Northamptonshire friends.

I am only afraid of my uncle. He will rally his Harriet; yet only, I know, in hopes to divert her, and us all: but my jesting days are over: my situation will not bear it. Yet, if it will divert him, let him rally.

I shall be so much importuned to stay longer than I ought, or *will* stay, that I may as well fix a peremptory day at once. Will you, my ever-indulgent friends, allow me to set out for Selby House on Friday next? Not on a Sunday, as Lady Betty Williams advises, for fear of the *odious waggons*. But I have been in a different school. Sir Charles Grandison, I find, makes it a *tacit* rule with him, never to *begin* a journey on a Sunday; nor, except when in pursuit of works of mercy or necessity, to travel in time of divine service. And this rule he observed last Sunday, though he reached us here in the evening. Oh, my grandmamma! How much is he what you all are, and ever have been!—but he is now pursuing a work of mercy. God succeed to him the end of his pursuit!

But why *tacit?* you will ask. Is Sir Charles Grandison ashamed to make an open appearance in behalf of his Christian duties? He is not. For instance; I have never seen him sit down at his own table, in the absence of Dr. Bartlett, or some other clergyman, but he himself says grace; and that with such an easy dignity as commands every one's reverence; and which is succeeded by a cheerfulness that looks as if he were the better pleased for having shown a thankful heart.

Dr. Bartlett has also told me, that he begins and ends every day, either in his chamber, or in his study, in a manner worthy of one who is in earnest in his Christian profession. But he never frights gay company with grave maxims. I remember one day, Mr. Grandison asked him, in his absurd way, Why he did not *preach* to his company now and then? Faith, Sir Charles, said he, if you did, you would reform many a poor ignorant sinner of us; since you could do it with more weight, and more certainty of attention, than any parson in Christendom.

It would be an affront, said Sir Charles, to the understanding, as well as education, of a man who took rank above a peasant, in such a country as this, to seem to question whether he *knew* his general duties, or not, and the necessity of practising what he knew of them. If he should be at a loss, he *may* once a week be reminded, and his heart kept warm. Let you and me, cousin Everard, show our conviction by our practice; and not invade the clergyman's province.

I remember that Mr. Grandison showed his conviction by his blushes; and by repeating the three little words, *You and me!* Sir Charles.

Sunday Evening.

OH, my dear friends! I have a strange, a shocking piece of intelligence to give you! Emily has just been with me in tears: she begged to speak with me in private. When we were alone she threw her arms about my neck: Ah, madam! said she, I am come to tell you, that there is a person in the world that I hate, and must and will hate, as long as I live. It is Lady Olivia—take me down with you into Northamptonshire, and let me never see her more.

I was surprised.

Oh, madam! I have found out, that she would, on Thursday last, have killed my guardian.

I was astonished, Lucy.

They retired together, you know, madam: my guardian came from her, his face in a glow; and he sent in his sister to her, and went not in himself till afterwards. She would have had him put off his journey. She was enraged because he would not; and they were high together; and, at last, she pulled out of her stays, in a fury, a poniard, and vowed to plunge it into his heart. He should never, she said, see his Clementina more. He went to her. Her heart failed her. Well it might, you know, madam. He seized her hand. He took it from her. She struggled, and, in struggling, her wrist was hurt; that's the meaning of the broad black ribband!—Wicked creature! to have such a thought in her heart!—He only said, when he had got it from her, Unhappy, violent woman! I return not this instrument of mischief! You will have no use for it in England—and would not let her have it again.

I shuddered. Oh, my dear! said I, he has been a sufferer, we are told, by good women: but this is *not* a good woman. But can it be true? Who informed you of it?

Lady Maffei herself. She thought that Sir Charles must have spoken of it: and when she found *he* had not, she was sorry *she* had, and begged I would not tell anybody: but I could not keep it from you. And she says that Lady Olivia is grieved on the remembrance of it; and arraigns herself and her wicked passion; and the more, for his noble forgiveness of her on the spot, and recommending her afterwards to the civilities of his sisters, and their lords. But I hate her, for all that.

Poor unhappy Olivia! said I. But what, my Emily, are we women, who should be the meekest and tenderest of the whole animal creation, when we give way to passion! But if she is so penitent, let not the shocking attempt be known to his sisters, or their lords. I may take the liberty of mentioning it, in *strict confidence*, [observe that, Lucy,] to those from whom I keep not any secret: but let it not be divulged to any of the relations of Sir Charles. Their detestation of her, which must follow, would not be concealed; and the unhappy creature, made desperate, might—who knows what she might do?

The dear girl ran on upon what might have been the consequence, and what a loss the world would have had, if the horrid fact had been perpetrated. Lady Maffei told her, however, that had not her heart relented, she might have done him mischief; for he was too rash in approaching her. She

She pulled out of her stays, in fury, a poniard, and vowed to plunge it into his heart.

R. Vinkeles, inv. del and sc.

fell down on her knees to him, as soon as he had wrested the poniard from her. I forgive, and pity you, madam, said he, with an air that had, as Olivia and her aunt have recollected since, both majesty and compassion in it: but, against her entreaty, he would withdraw: yet, at her request, sent in Lady L—— to her; and, going into his study, told not even Dr. Bartlett of it, though he went to him there immediately.

From the consciousness of this violence, perhaps, the lady was more temperate afterwards, even to the very time of his departure.

LORD bless me, what shall I do? Lady D—— has sent a card to let me know, that she will wait upon Mrs. Reeves and me to-morrow to breakfast. She comes, no doubt, to tell me, that Sir Charles, having no thoughts of Harriet Byron, Lord D—— may have hopes of succeeding with her: and, perhaps, her ladyship will plead Sir Charles's recommendation and interest in Lord D——'s favour. But should this plea be made, good Heaven, give me patience! I am afraid I shall be uncivil to this excellent woman.

LETTER XXX.

Miss Byron.—In continuation.

Monday, April 17.

THE countess is just gone.

Mr. Reeves was engaged before to breakfast with Lady Betty Williams; and we were only Mrs. Reeves, Lady D——, and I.

My heart ached at her entrance; and every moment still more, as we were at breakfast. Her looks, I thought, had such a particular kindness and meaning in them, as seemed to express, 'You have no hopes, Miss Byron, anywhere else; and I will have you to be mine.'

But my suspense was over the moment the tea-table was removed. I see your confusion, my dear, said the countess; [Mrs. Reeves, you must not leave us;] and I have sat in pain for you, as I saw it increase. By this I know that Sir Charles Grandison has been as good as his word. Indeed I doubted not but he would. I don't wonder, my dear, that you love him. He is the finest man in his manners, as well as person, that I ever saw. A woman of virtue and honour cannot *but* love him. But I need not praise him to you; nor to *you*, neither, Mrs. Reeves; I see that. Now you must know, proceeded she, that there is an alliance proposed for my son, of which I think very well; but still should have thought better, had I never seen you, my dear. I have talked to my lord about it: you know I am very desirous to have him married. His answer was; I never can think of any proposal of this nature, while I have any hope that I can make myself acceptable to Miss Byron.

What think you, my lord, said I, if I should directly apply to Sir Charles Grandison to know his intentions; and whether he has any hopes of obtaining her favour? He is said to be the most unreserved of men. He knows our characters to be as unexceptionable as his own; and that our alliance cannot be thought a discredit to the first family in the kingdom. It is a free question, I own, as I am unacquainted with him by person: but he is such a man, that, methinks, I can take pleasure in addressing myself to him on *any* subject.

My lord smiled at the freedom of my motion; but, not disapproving it, I directly went to Sir Charles; and, after due compliments, told him my business.

The countess stopped. She is very penetrating. She looked at us both.

Well, madam, said my cousin, with an air of curiosity—pray, your ladyship——

I could not speak for very impatience——

I never heard in my life, said the countess, such a fine character of any mortal, as he gave you. He told me of his engagements to go abroad as the very next day. He highly extolled the lady, for whose sake, principally, he was obliged to go abroad; and he spoke as highly of a brother of hers, whom he loved as if he were his own brother; and mentioned very affectionately the young lady's whole family.

'God only knows,' said he, 'what may be *my* destiny!— 'As generosity, as justice, or rather as Providence leads, I 'will follow.'

After he had generously opened his heart, proceeded the countess, I asked him if he had any hope, should the foreign lady recover her *health,* of her being his?

'I can promise myself nothing,' said he. 'I go over with- 'out one selfish hope. If the lady recover *her* health, and 'her brother can be amended in *his,* by the assistance I shall 'carry over with me, I shall have joy inexpressible. To 'Providence I leave the rest. The result cannot be in my '*own* power.'

Then, sir, proceeded the countess, you cannot in honour be under any engagements to Miss Byron?

I arose from my seat. Whither, my dear?—I have *done,* if I oppress you. I moved my chair behind her, but so close to hers, that I leaned on the back of it, my face hid, and my eyes running over. She stood up. Sit down again, madam, said I, and proceed—pray proceed. You have excited my curiosity. Only let me sit here, *unheeded,* behind you.

Pray, madam, said Mrs. Reeves (burning also with curiosity as she has since owned), go on; and indulge my cousin in her present seat. What answer did Sir Charles return?

My dear love, said the countess (sitting down, as I had requested), let me first be answered one question. I would not do mischief.

You cannot do mischief, madam, replied I. What is your ladyship's question?

Has Sir Charles Grandison ever directly made his addresses to you, my dear?

Never, madam.

It is not for want of love, I dare aver, that he has not. But thus he answered my question: 'I should have thought my- 'self the unworthiest of men, knowing the difficulties of my 'own situation, how great soever were the temptation from

'Miss Byron's merit, if I had sought to engage her affec-
'tions.'

[O Lucy! How nobly is his whole conduct towards me justified!]

'She has, madam,' (proceeded the countess, in his words),
'a prudence that I never knew equalled in a woman so young.
'With a frankness of mind, to which hardly ever young lady
'before her had pretensions, she has such a command of her
'affections, that no man, I dare say, will ever have a share
'in them, till he has courted her favour by assiduities which
'shall convince her that he has no heart but for *her*.'

Oh, my Lucy! What an honour to me would these sentiments be, if I deserved them! And *can* Sir Charles Grandison think I *do?*—I hope so. But if he does, how much am I indebted to his favourable, his generous opinion! Who knows but I have reason to rejoice, rather than to regret, as I used to do, his frequent absences from Colnebrook?

The countess proceeded.

Then, sir, you will not take amiss, if my son, by *his* assiduities, can prevail upon Miss Byron to think that he *has* merit, and that his heart is *wholly* devoted to her.

'Amiss, madam!—No!—In justice, in honour, I cannot.
'May Miss Byron be, as she deserves to be, one of the hap-
'piest women on earth in her nuptials. I have heard a great
'character of Lord D——. He has a very large estate. He
'may boast of his mother—God forbid, that *I,* a man *divided*
'*in myself,* not knowing what I *can* do, hardly sometimes
'what I *ought* to do, should seek to involve in my own uncer-
'tainties the friend I revere; the woman I so greatly admire:
'her beauty so attracting; so proper for her, therefore, to en-
'gage a generous protector in the married state.'

Generous man! thought I. Oh, how my tears ran down my cheeks, as I hid my face behind the countess's chair!

But will you allow me, sir, proceeded the countess, to ask you, Were you freed from all your uncertainties——

'Permit me, madam,' interrupted he, 'to spare you the
'question you were going to put. As I know not what will
'be the result of my journey abroad, I should think myself a

'very *selfish* man, and a very dishonorable one to *two* ladies
'of equal delicacy and worthiness, if I sought to involve, as
'I hinted before, in my own uncertainties, a young lady,
'whose prudence and great qualities must make herself and
'*any* man happy, whom she shall favour with her hand.

'To be still more explicit, proceeded he, With what face
'could I look up to a woman of honour and delicacy, such a
'one as the lady before whom I now stand, if I could own a
'wish, that while my honour has laid me under obligation
'to *one lady,* if she shall be permitted to accept of me, I
'should presume to hope, that *another,* no less worthy, would
'hold her favour for me suspended, till she saw what would
'be the issue of the first obligation? No, madam; I could
'sooner die than offer such indignity to BOTH! *I* am fettered,
'added he; but Miss Byron is free: and so is the lady abroad.
'My attendance on her at this time is indispensable; but I
'make not any conditions for myself—my reward will be in
'the consciousness of having discharged the obligations that
'I think myself under as a man of honour.'

The countess's voice changed in repeating this speech of
his: and she stopt to praise him; and then went on.

You are *THE* man indeed, sir!—But then give me leave
to ask you, as I think it very likely that you will be married
before your return to England, whether, now that you have
been so good as to speak favourably of my son, and that you
call Miss Byron sister, you will oblige him with a recommendation to that sister?

'The Countess of D—— shows, by this request, her value
'for a young lady who deserves it; and the *more,* for its be-
'ing, I think (excuse me, madam), a pretty extraordinary
'one. But what a presumption would it be in me, to suppose
'that I had *such* an interest with Miss Byron, when she has
'relations as worthy of *her,* as she is of *them?*'

You may guess, my dear, said the countess, that I should
not have put this question, but as a trial of his heart. However, I asked his pardon; and told him, that I would not believe he gave it me, except he would promise to mention to
Miss Byron, that I had made him a visit on this subject.

[Methinks, Lucy, I should have been glad that he had not let *me* know that he was so forgiving!]

And now, my dear, said the lady, let me turn about. She did; and put one arm round my neck, and with my own handkerchief wiped my eyes, and kissed my cheek: and when she saw me a little recovered, she addressed me as follows:

Now, my good young creature [Oh that you would let me call you daughter in my way! for I think I must always call you so, whether you do, or not], let me ask you, as if I were your real mother, ' Have you any expectation that Sir Charles ' Grandison will be yours?'

Dear madam, is not this as hard a question to be put to me, as that which you put to him?

Yes, my dear—full as hard. And I am as ready to ask your pardon, as I was his, if you are really displeased with me for putting it. Are you, Miss Byron? Excuse me, Mrs. Reeves, for thus urging your lovely cousin; I am at least entitled to the excuse Sir Charles Grandison made for me, that it is a demonstration of my value for her.

I have declared, madam, returned I, and it is from my heart, that I think he ought to be the husband of the lady abroad: and though I prefer him to all the men I ever saw, yet I have resolved, if possible, to conquer the particular regard I have for him. He has in a very noble manner offered me his friendship, so long as it may be accepted without interfering with any other attachments on my part: and I will be satisfied with that.

A friendship so pure, replied the countess, as that of such a man, is consistent with *any other* attachments. My Lord D—— will, with his whole soul, contribute all in his power to strengthen it: he admires Sir Charles Grandison: he would think it a double honour to be acquainted with him through you. Dearest Miss Byron, take another worthy young man into your friendship, but with a tenderer name: I shall then claim a fourth place in it for myself. Oh my dear! What a quadruple knot will you tie!

Your ladyship does me too much honour, was all I could just then reply.

I *must* have an answer, my dear: I will not take up with a compliment.

This, then, madam, is my answer—I hope I am an honest creature:—I have *not* a heart to give.

Then you have expectations, my dear.—Well, I will call you *mine,* if I can. Never did I think that I could have made the proposal, that I am going to make you: but in my eyes, as well as in my lord's, you are an incomparable young woman. This is it. We will not think of the alliance proposed to us (it is yet but a proposal, and to which we have not returned any answer) till we see what turn the affair Sir Charles is gone upon takes. You once said, you could prefer my son to any of the men that had hitherto applied to you for your favour. Your affections to Sir Charles were engaged before you knew us. Will you allow my son this preference, which will be the *first* preference, if Sir Charles engages himself abroad?

Your ladyship surprises me: shall I not improve by the example you have just now set before me? Who was it that said (and a *man* too) 'With what face could I look up to a 'woman of honour and delicacy, such a one as the lady before 'whom I now stand, if I could own a wish, that, while' my heart leaned to one person, I should think of keeping another in suspence till I saw whether I could or could not be the other's? 'No madam, I would sooner die,' as Sir Charles said, 'than offer such an indignity to *both*.' But I know, madam, that you only made this proposal, as you did another to Sir Charles Grandison, as a *trial of my heart.*

Upon my word, my dear, I should, I think, be glad to be entitled to such an excuse: but I was really in earnest; and now take a little shame to myself.

What charming ingenuousness in this lady!

She clasped her arms about me, and kissed my cheek again. I have but one plea, said she, to make for myself! I could not have fallen into such an error (the example so recently given to the contrary), had I not wished you to be, before any woman in the world, Countess of D——. Noble creature: no title can give you dignity. May your own wishes be granted!

The countess asked, when I returned to Northamptonshire? I told her my intention. She charged me to see her first. But I can tell you, said she, my lord shall not be present when you come: not once more will I trust him in your company; and if he should steal a visit, unknown to me, let not your cousin see him, Mrs. Reeves. He does *indeed* admire you, love.

I acknowledged, with a grateful heart, her goodness to me. She engaged me to correspond with her when I got home. Her commands were an honour done me, that I could not refuse myself. Her son, she smilingly told me, should no more see my letters, than my person.

At her going away—I will tell you one thing, said she; I never before, in a business which my heart was set upon, was so effectually silenced by precedent produced by myself in the same conversation. I came with an assurance of success. When our *hearts* are engaged in a hope, we are apt to think every step we take for the promoting it, reasonable: our passions, my dear, will evermore run away with our judgment. But, now I think of it, I must, when I say *our*, make two exceptions; one for you, and one for Sir Charles Grandison.

But, Lucy, tell me—may I, do you think, explain the meaning of the word SELFISH used by Sir Charles in the conclusion of the library conference at Colnebrook (and which puzzled me then to make out), by his disclaiming of *selfishness* in the conversation with the countess above recited? If I may, what an opening of his heart does that word give in my favour, were he at liberty? Does it not look, my dear, as if his *honour* checked him, when his *love* would have prompted him to wish me to preserve my heart disengaged till his return from abroad? Nor let it be said that it was dishonourable in him to have such a thought, as it was *checked* and *overcome;* and as it was succeeded by such an emotion, that he was obliged to depart abruptly from me. Let me repeat the words—you may not have my letter at hand which relates that affecting address to me; and it is impossible for me, while I have memory, to forget them. He had just concluded his brief history of Clementina—'and now, madam, what can I say?—Honour forbids 'me!—yet honour bids me—yet I cannot be unjust, un-'generous, *selfish!*'—If I may flatter myself, Lucy, that he did love me when he said this, and that he had a conflict in his noble heart between the love on one side so *hopeless* (for I could not forgive him, if he did not *love,* as well as *pity,* Clementina), and on the other *not so* hopeless, were there to have been no bar between—shall we not pity him for the arduous struggle? Shall we not see that honour carried it, even in favour of the *hopeless* against the *hopeful,* and applaud him the more for being able to overcome? How shall we call virtue by its name, if it be not tried; and if it hath no contest with inclination?

If I am a vain self-flatterer, tell me, chide me, Lucy; but allow me, however, at the same time, this praise, if I can make good my claim to it, that *my* conquest of my passion is at least as glorious for me, as *his* is for him, were he to love me ever so well; since I can most sincerely, however painfully, subscribe to the preference which honour, love, compassion, unitedly, give to CLEMENTINA.

LETTER XXXI.

Miss Byron.—In continuation.

Monday Night.

MY cousins and I, by invitation, supped with Lady G—— this evening. Lord and Lady L—— were there; Lady Olivia also, and Lady Maffei.

I have set them all into a consternation, as they expressed themselves, by my declaration of leaving London on my return home early on Friday morning next. I knew, that were I to pass the whole summer here, I must be peremptory at last. The two sisters vow, that I shall not go so soon. They say, that I have seen so few of the town diversions—

town diversions, Lucy!—I have had diversions enough, of one sort! But in your arms, my dear friends, I shall have consolation—and I want it.

I have great regrets, and shall have hourly more, as the day approaches, on the leaving of such dear and obliging friends: but I am determined.

My cousin's coach will convey me to Dunstable; and there, I know, I shall meet with my indulgent uncle, or your brother. I would not have it publicly known, because of the officious gentlemen in the neighbourhood.

Dr. Bartlett intended to set out for Grandison Hall tomorrow: but, from the natural kindness of his heart, he has suspended his journey to Thursday next. No consideration, therefore, shall detain me, if I am well.

My cousins are grieved: they did not expect that I would be a word and a blow, as they phrase it.

Lady Olivia expressed herself concerned, that she, in particular, was to lose me. She had proposed great pleasure, she said, in the parties she should make in my company. But, after what Emily told me, she appears to me as a Medusa; and were I to be thought by her a formidable rival, I might have as much reason to be afraid of the potion, as the man she loves of the poniard. Emily has kept the secret from everybody but me. And I rely on the inviolable secrecy of all you, my friends.

Lord and Lady L—— had designed to go to Colnebrook tomorrow, or at my day, having hopes of getting me with them; but now, they say, they will stay in town till they can see whether I am to be prevailed upon, or will be *obdurate*.

Lady Olivia inquired after the distance of Northamptonshire. She will make the tour of England, she says, and visit me there. I was obliged to say I should take her visit as an honour.

Wicked politeness! Of how many falsehoods, dost thou make the people, who are called *polite,* guilty!

But there is one man in the world, who is remarkable for his truth, yet is unquestionably polite. He censures not others for complying with fashions established by custom; but he gives not into them. He never perverts the meaning of words. He never, for instance, suffers his servants to deny him when he is at home. If he is busy, he just finds time to say he is, to unexpected visitors; and if they will stay, he turns them over to his sisters, to Dr. Bartlett, to Emily, till he can attend them. But then he has *always* done so. Every one knows that he lives to his own heart, and they *expect* it of him; and when they *can* have his company, they have double joy in the ease and cheerfulness that attend his leisure: they then have him *wholly.* And he can be the more polite, as the company then is all his business.

Sir Charles might the better do so, as he came over so few months ago, after so long an absence; and his reputation for politeness was so well established, that people rather looked for rules from him, than a conformity to theirs.

His denials of complimenting Lady Olivia (though she was but just arrived in his native country, where she never was before) with the suspending of his departure for one week, or but for one day—who but he could have given them? But he was convinced, that it was right to hasten away, for the sake of Clementina and his Jeronymo; and that it would have been wrong to show Olivia, even for her *own* sake, that in *such* a competition she had consequence with him; and all her entreaties, all her menaces, the detested poniard in her hand, could not shake his steady soul, and make him delay his well-settled purpose.

LETTER XXXII.

Miss Byron.—In continuation.

Tuesday Morning, April 18.

This naughty Lady G——! She is excessively to blame. Lord L—— is out of patience with her. So is Lady L——. Emily says she loves her dearly, but she does not love her ways. Lord G——, as Emily tells me, talks of coming to me;

the cause of quarrel supposed to be not great: but trifles, insisted upon, make frequently the widest breaches. Whatever it be, it is between themselves: and neither cares to tell: but Lord and Lady L—— are angry with her, for the ludicrous manner in which she treats him.

The misunderstanding happened after my cousin and I left them last night. I was not in spirits, and declined staying to cards. Lady Olivia and her aunt went away at the same time. Whist was the game. Lord and Lady L——, Dr. Bartlett and Emily, were cast in. In the midst of their play, Lady G—— came hurrying down stairs to them, warbling an air. Lord G—— followed her, much disturbed. Madam, I must tell you, said he—Why MUST, my lord? I don't bid you.

Sit still child, said she to Emily; and took her seat behind her—Who wins? Who loses?

Lord G—— walked about the room—Lord and Lady L—— were unwilling to take notice, hoping it would go off; for there had been a few livelinesses on her side at dinner-time, though all was serene at supper.

Dr. Bartlett offered her his cards. She refused them—No, doctor, said she, I will play my own cards: I shall have enough to do to play *them* well.

As you manage it, so you will, madam, said Lord G——.

Don't expose yourself, my lord: we are before company. Lady L——, you have nothing but trumps in your hand.

Let me say a word or two to you, madam, said Lord G—— to her.

I am all obedience, my lord.

She arose. He would have taken her hand: she put it behind her.

Not your *hand,* madam?

I can't spare it.

He flung from her, and went out of the room.

Lord bless me, said she, returning to the card-table with a gay unconcern, what strange passionate creatures are these men!

Charlotte, said Lady L——, I *wonder* at you.

Then I give you joy——

What do you mean, sister?

We women love wonder, and the wonderful!

Surely, Lady G——, said Lord L——, you are wrong.

I give your lordship joy, too.

On what?

That my sister is always right.

Indeed, madam, were I Lord G——, I should have no patience.

A good hint for you, Lady L——. I hope you will take this for a warning, and continue good.

When I behave as you do, Charlotte——

I understand you, Lady L——, you need not speak out—every one in their way.

You would not behave thus, were my brother——

Perhaps not.

Dear Charlotte, you are excessively wrong.

So I think, returned she.

Why then do you not——

Mend, Lady L——? All in good time.

Her woman came in with a message expressing her lord's desire to see her.—The deuce is in these men! They will neither be satisfied with us nor without us. But I am all obedience: no *vow* will I break—and out she went.

Lord G—— not returning presently, and Lord and Lady L——'s chariot being come, they both took this opportunity, in order to show their displeasure, to go away without taking leave of their sister. Dr. Bartlett retired to his apartment. And when Lady G—— came down, she was surprised, and a little vexed, to find only Emily there. Lord G—— came in at another door—Upon my word, my lord, this is strange behaviour in you: you frighten away, with your husband-like airs, all one's company.

Good God!—I am astonished at you, madam.

What *signifies* your astonishment when you have scared everybody out of the house?

I, madam?

You, sir. Yes, you!—Did you not lord it over me in my dressing-room?—To be easy and quiet, did I not fly to our company in the drawing-room? Did you not follow me there —with looks—very pretty looks for a new-married man, I assure you! Then did you not want to take me aside—would not anybody have supposed it was to express your sorrow for your odd behaviour? Was I not all obedience?—Did you not, with very *mannish* airs, slight me for my compliance, and fly out of the room? All the company could witness the calmness with which I returned to them, that they might not be grieved for me; nor think our misunderstanding a deep one. Well, then, when your stomach came down, as I supposed, you sent for me out: no doubt, thought I, to express his concern now.—I was all obedience again.

And did I not beseech you, madam——

Beseech me, my lord!—yes—but with such looks!—I married, sir, let me tell you, a man with another face.—See, see, Emily—he is gone again.

My lord flew out of the room in a rage.—Oh these men, my dear! said she to Emily.

I know, said Emily, what I could have answered, if I dared: but it is ill meddling, as I have heard say, between man and wife.

Emily says the quarrel was not made up; but was carried higher still in the morning.

She had but just finished her tale, when the following billet was brought me, from Lady G——:

Tuesday Morning.

HARRIET,—If you love me, if you pity me, come hither this instant: I have great need of your counsel. I am resolved to be unmarried; and therefore subscribe myself by the beloved name of   CHARLOTTE GRANDISON.

I instantly despatched the following:

I KNOW no such person as Charlotte Grandison. I love Lady G——, but can pity only her lord. I will not come near you. I have no counsel to give you, but that you will not jest away your own happiness.   HARRIET BYRON.

Soon after, came a servant from Lady G—— with the following letter:

So, then, I have made a blessed hand of wedlock. My brother gone: my man excessive unruly: Lord and Lady L—— on his side, without inquiring into merits or demerits: lectured by Dr. Bartlett's grave face: Emily standing aloof; her finger in her eye: and now my Harriet renouncing me: and all in one week!

What can I do?—War seems to be declared: and will you not turn mediatrix?—You won't, you say. Let it alone. Nevertheless, I will lay the whole matter before you.

I was last night, the week from the wedding-day not completed, that Lord G—— thought fit to break into my retirement without my leave—by the way, he was a little impertinent at dinner-time; but that I passed over——

What boldness is this? said I—Pray, sir, begone—Why do you leave your company below?

I come, my dearest life! to make a request to you.

The man began with civility enough, had he had a little less of his odious rapture; for he flung his arms about me, Jenny in presence. A husband's fondness is enough to ruin these girls. Don't you think, Harriet, that there is an immorality in it, before them?

I refuse your request, be it what it will. How dare you invade me in my retirement?—You may believe, that I intended not to stay long above, my sister below. Does the ceremony, so lately past, authorise want of breeding?

Want of breeding, madam!—and he did *so* stare!

Leave me this instant!—I looked good-natured, I suppose, in my anger: for he declared he would not; and again throwing his arms about me as I sat, joined his sharp face to mine, and presumed to kiss me; Jenny still in the room.

Now, Harriet, you never will desert me in a point of delicacy, I am sure. You cannot defend these odious freedoms in a matrimony so young, unless you would be willing to be served so yourself.

You may suppose, that then I let loose my indignation upon

him. And he stole out, daring to mutter and be displeased. The word *devil* was in his mouth.

Did he call *me* devil, Jenny?

No, indeed, madam, said the wench—and, Harriet, see the ill example of such a free behaviour before her: she presumed to prate in favour of the man's fit of fondness; yet at other times, is a prude of a girl.

Before my anger was gone down, in again [It is truth, Harriet,] came the bold wretch. I will not, said he, as you are not *particularly* employed, leave you—Upon my soul, madam, you don't use me well. But if you will oblige me with your company to-morrow morning——

Nowhere, sir——

Only to breakfast with Miss Byron, my *dear*—As a mark of your obligingness, I request it.

His dear!—Now I hate a hypocrite, of all things. I knew that he had a design to make a show of his bride, as his property, at another place; and seeing me angry, thought he would name a visit agreeable to me, and which at the same time would give him a merit with you, and preserve to himself the consequence of being obliged by his obedient wife, at the word of authority.

From this foolish beginning arose our mighty quarrel. What vexed me was, the *art* of the man, and the evident design he had to get you of his side. He, in the course of it, threatened me with appealing to you.—To intend to ruin me in the love of my dearest friend! Who, that valued that friend, could forgive it? You may believe, that if *he* had not proposed it, and after such accumulated offences, it was the very visit that I should have been delighted with.

Indeed, sir—Upon my word, my lord—I do assure you, sir,—with a moderate degree of haughtiness—was what the quarrel arose to, on my side—and, at last, to a declaration of rebellion—I *won't*.

On his side, Upon my soul, madam—Let me perish, if—and then hesitating—You use me ill, madam. I have not deserved—and give me leave to say—I *insist* upon being obliged, madam.

There was no bearing of this, Harriet.—It was a cool evening; but I took up my fan—Hey-day! said I, what language is this?—You *insist upon it*, my lord!—I think I am married; am I not?—And I took my watch, half an hour after ten on Monday night—the—what day of the month is this?—Please the Lord, I will note down this beginning moment of your authoritative demeanour.

My dear Lady G—— [The wretch called me by his own name, perhaps farther to insult me], if I could bear this treatment, it would be impossible for me to love you as I do.

So it is in *love* to me, that you are to put on already all the husband!—Jenny! [Do you see, my lord, affecting a whisper, how you dash the poor wench? How like a fool she looks at our folly!] Remember, Jenny, that to-morrow morning you carry my wedding-suits to Mrs. Arnold; and tell her, she has forgot the hanging-sleeves to the gowns. Let her put them on directly.

I was proceeding—but he rudely, gravely, and even with an air of scorn [There was no bearing *that*, you know], admonished me. A little less wit, madam, and a little more discretion, would perhaps better become you.

This was too *true* to be forgiven. *You'll* say it, Harriet, if *I* don't. And to come from a man that was not over-burdened with either—but I had too great a command of myself to say so. My dependence, my lord [this I did say] is upon your *judgment;* that will always be a balance to my *wit;* and, with the assistance of your *reproving love*, will in time teach me *discretion*.

Now, my dear, was not this a high compliment to him? Ought he not to have taken it as such? Especially as I looked grave, and dropt him a very fine courtesy. But either his conscience or ill-nature (perhaps you'll say both), made him take it as a reflection [True as you are alive, Harriet!] He bit his lip. Jenny, begone! said he—Jenny, don't go, said I —Jenny knew not which to obey. Upon my word, Harriet, I began to think the man would have cuffed me.—And while he was in his airs of mock-majesty, I stept to the door, and whipt down to my company.

As married people are not to expose themselves to their friends (who, I once heard you sagely remark, would remember disagreeable things, when the honest pair had forgot them), I was determined to be prudent. You would have been charmed with me, my dear, for my discretion. I will cheat by-standers, thought I; I will make my Lord and Lady L——, Dr. Bartlett, and Emily, whom I had before set in at cards, think we are egregiously happy—and down I sat, intending, with a lamb-like peaceableness, to make observations on the play. But soon after, in whipt my indiscreet lord, his colour heightened, his features working: and though I *cautioned* him not to expose himself, yet he assumed airs that were the occasion, as you shall hear, of frighting away my company. He withdrew, *in consequence of those airs;* and, after a little while (repenting, as I hoped), he sent for me out. Some wives would have played the queen Vashti on their tyrant, and refused to go: but I, all obedience (my vow, so recently made, in my head), obeyed, at the very first word: yet you must think that I (meek as I am naturally) could not help recriminating. He was too lordly to be expostulated with.—There was, 'I tell you, madam,' and 'I won't be told, sir;' and when I broke from the passionate creature, and hoped to find my company, behold! they were all gone! None but Emily left. And thus poor Lady L—— was sent home, weeping, perhaps, for such an early marriage-tyranny exerted on her meek sister.

Well, and don't you think that we looked like a couple of fools at each other, when we saw ourselves left alone, as I may say, to fight it out? I *did* expostulate with him as mildly as I could: he would have made it up with me afterwards; but, no! there was no doing that, as a girl of your nice notions may believe, after he had, by his violent airs, exposed us both before so many witnesses. In *decency,* therefore, I was obliged to keep it up: and now our misunderstanding blazes, and is at such a comfortable height, that if we meet by accident, we run away from each other by design. We have already made two breakfast-tables: yet I am meek; he is sullen: I make courtesies; he returns not bows.—Sullen creature, and a rustic!—I go to my harpsichord; melody enrages him. He is worse than Saul; for Saul could be gloomily pleased with the music even of the man he hated.

I would have got *you* to come to us: that I thought was *tending* to a compliance; for it would have been condescending *too much,* as he is so *very* perverse, if I had accompanied him to you. He has a great mind to appeal to you; but I have half rallied him out of his purpose. I sent to you. What an answer did you return me!—Cruel Harriet! to deny your requested mediation in a difference that has arisen between man and wife.—But let the fire glow. If it spares the house, and only blazes in the chimney, I can bear it.

Cross creature, adieu! If you know not such a woman as *Grandison,* Heaven grant that I *may;* and that my wishes may be answered as to the *person;* and then I will not know a *Byron.*

See, Lucy, how high this dear flighty creature bribes? But I will not be influenced, by her bribery, to take her part.

LETTER XXXIII.

Miss Byron.—In continuation.

Tuesday Night.

I AM just returned from St. James's Square.

But, first, I should tell you, that I had a visit from Lady Olivia and Lady Maffei. Our conversation was in Italian and French. Lady Olivia and I had a quarter of an hour's discourse in private; you may guess at our subject. She is not without that tenderness of heart, which is the indispensable characteristic of a woman. She lamented the violence of her temper, in a manner so affecting, that I cannot help pitying her, though at the instant I had in my head a certain attempt, that makes me shudder whenever I think of it. She regrets my going to Northamptonshire so soon. I have promised to return her visit to-morrow in the afternoon.

She sets out on Friday next for Oxford. She wished I could accompany her. She resolves to see all that is worth seeing in the western circuit, as I may call it. She observes, she says, that Sir Charles Grandison's sisters, and their lords, are very particularly engaged at present; and are in expectation of a call to Windsor, to attend Lord W——'s nuptials: she will therefore, having attendants enough, and two men of consideration in her train, one of whom is not unacquainted with England, take cursory tours over the kingdom; having a taste for travelling, and finding it a great relief to her spirits: and when Lady L—— and Lady G—— are more disengaged, will review the seats and places which she shall think worthy of a second visit, in their company.

She professed to like the people here, and the face of the country; and talked favourably of the religion of it: but, poor woman! she likes all those the better, I doubt not, for the sake of one Englishman. Love, Lucy, gilds every object which bears a relation to the person beloved.

Lady Maffei was very free in blaming her niece for this excursion. She took her chiding patiently; but yet, like a person that thought it too much in her *power* to gratify the person blaming her, to pay much regard to what she said.

I took a chair to Lady G——'s. Emily ran to meet me in the hall. She threw her arms about me: I rejoice you are come, said she. Did you not meet the house in the square?—What means my Emily?—Why, it has been flung out of the window, as the saying is. Ah, madam! we are all to pieces. One *so* careless, the other *so* passionate!—But, hush! Here comes Lady G——.

Take, Lucy, in the dialogue-way, particulars.

Lady G. Then you are come, at last, Harriet. You wrote, that you would not come near me.

Har. I did; but I could not stay away. Ah, Lady G——, you will destroy your own happiness!

Lady G. So you wrote. Not one word, on the subject you

hint at, that you have ever said or written before. I hate repetitions, child.

Har. Then I must be silent upon it.

Lady G. Not of necessity. You can say new things upon old subjects.—But hush! Here comes the man—She ran to her harpsichord—Is this it, Harriet? and touched the keys —repeating

" Softly sweet, in *Lydian* measures
Soon she sooth'd————"

Enter Lord G————.

Lord G. Miss Byron, I am your most obedient servant. The sight of you rejoices my soul.—Madam (to his lady), you have not been long enough together to begin a tune. I know what this is for————

Lady G. Harmony! harmony! is a charming thing! But I, poor I! know not any but what this simple instrument affords me.

Lord G. [Lifting up his hands]. Harmony, madam! God is my witness—But I will lay everything before Miss Byron.

Lady G. You need not, my lord: she knows as much as she can know, already; except the fine colourings be added to the woeful tale, that your unbridled spirit can give it.—Have you my long letter about you, Harriet?

Lord G. And could you, madam, have the *heart* to write————

Lady G. Why, my lord, do you mince the matter? For *heart,* say *courage.* You may speak as plain in Miss Byron's presence, as you did before she came: I know what you mean.

Lord G. Let it be *courage,* then.

Har. Fie, fie, Lord G————! Fie, fie, Lady G————! What lengths do you run! If I understand the matter right, you have both, like children, been at play till you have fallen out.

Lord G. If, Miss Byron, you know the truth, and can blame me————

Har. I blame you only, my lord, for being in a passion. You see my lady is serene: she keeps her temper: she looks as if she wanted to be friends with you.

Lord G. Oh that cursed serenity!—When my soul is torn by a whirlwind——

Lady G. A good tragedy rant!—But, Harriet, you are mistaken: my Lord G—— is a very passionate man. So humble, so—what shall I call it? before marriage—did not the man see what a creature I was?—To bear with me, when he had no obligation to me; and not now, when he has the highest—a miserable sinking! O Harriet, Harriet! Never, never marry!

Har. Dear Lady G——, you know in your own heart you are wrong—*indeed* you are wrong——

Lord G. God for ever reward you, madam!—I will tell you how it began——

Lady G. 'Began!' She knows *that* already, I tell you, my lord. But what has passed within these *four hours,* she knows not: you may entertain her with *that,* if you please.—It was just about the time this day is a week, that we were altogether, mighty comfortable, at St. George's, Hanover Square——

Lord G. Every tittle of what you promised there, madam——

Lady G. And I, my lord, could be your echo in this, were I not resolved to keep my temper: as you cannot but say I have done, all along.

Lord G. You could not, madam, if you did not despise me.

Lady G. You are wrong, my lord, to think so: but you don't believe yourself: if you *did,* the pride of your heart ought not to permit you to own it.

Lord G. Miss Byron, give me leave——

Lady G. Lord bless me! that people are so fond of exposing themselves! had you taken my advice, when you pursued me out of my dressing-room into company—My lord, said I, as mildly as I now speak, *don't* expose yourself. But he was not at all the wiser for my advice.

Lord G. Miss Byron, you see—but I had not come down but to make my compliments to you. He bowed, and was about to withdraw.

I took him by the sleeve—My lord, you must not go. Lady

G——, if your own heart justifies you for your part in this misunderstanding, say so; I challenge you to say so—she was silent.

Har. If otherwise, own your fault, promise amendment ——ask pardon.

Lady G. Hey-day!

Har. And my lord will asks yours, for mistaking you—for being too easily provoked——

Lord G. Too easily, madam——

Har. What generous man would not smile at the foibles of a woman, whose heart is only gay with prosperity and lively youth; but has not the least malice in it? Has not she made choice of your lordship in preference to any other man? she rallies every one; she can't help it; she is to blame.—Indeed, Lady G——, you are. Your *brother* felt your edge; he once smarted by it, and was angry with you.—But afterwards, observing that it was her way, my lord, that it was a kind of constitutional gaiety of heart, and exercised on those she loved best, he forgave, rallied her again, and turned her own weapons upon her; and every one in company was delighted with the spirit of *both*.—You love her, my lord——

Lord G. Never man more loved a woman. I am not an ill-natured man——

Lady G. But a captious, a passionate one, Lord G——. Who'd have thought it!

Lord G. Never was there, my dear Miss Byron, such a strangely aggravating creature! She *could* not be so, if she did not despise me.

Lady G. Fiddle-faddle, silly man! And so you said before. If you thought so, you take the way (don't you?) to mend the matter, by dancing and capering about, and putting yourself into all manner of disagreeable attitudes; and even sometimes being ready to foam at the mouth?—I told him, Miss Byron —there he stands, let him deny it, if he can—that I married a man with another face. Would not any other man have taken this for a compliment to his natural undistorted face, and instantly have pulled off the ugly mask of passion, and shown his own?——

Lord G. You see, you see, the air, Miss Byron!—How ludicrously does she now, even now——

Lady G. See, Miss Byron!—How captious!—Lord G—— ought to have a termagant wife: one who could return rage for rage.—Meekness is *my* crime.—I cannot be put out of temper. Meekness was never before attributed to woman as a fault.

Lord G. Good God!—Meekness!—Good God!

Lady G. But, Harriet, do you judge on which side the grievance lies. Lord G—— presents me with a face for his, that I never saw him wear before marriage: he has cheated me, therefore. I show him the same face that I ever wore, and treat him pretty much in the same manner (or I am mistaken) that I ever did: and what reason can he give, that will not demonstrate him to be the most ungrateful of men, for the airs he gives himself? Airs that he would not have presumed to put on eight days ago. Who then, Harriet, has reason to complain of grievance; my lord, or I?

Lord G. You *see,* Miss Byron. Can there be any arguing with a woman who knows herself to be in jest, in all she says?

Har. Why then, my lord, make a jest of it. What will not bear an argument will not be worth one's anger.

Lord G. I leave it to Miss Byron, Lady G——, to decide between us, as she pleases.

Lady G. You'd better leave it to me, sir.

Har. Do, my lord.

Lord G. Well, madam!—And what is your decree?

Lady G. You, Miss Byron, had best be Lady Chancellor, after all. I should not bear to have my decree disputed after it is pronounced.

Har. If I must, my decree is this:—You, Lady G——, shall own yourself in fault; and promise amendment. My lord shall forgive you; and promise that he will, for the future, endeavour to distinguish between your good and your ill-nature: that he will sit down to jest with your jest, and never be disturbed at what you say, when he sees it accompanied with that archness of eye and lip which you put on to your brother, and to every one whom you best love, when you are disposed to be teazingly facetious.

Lady G. Why, Harriet, you have given Lord G—— a clue to find me out, and spoil all my sport.

Har. What say *you,* my lord?

Lord G. Will Lady G—— own herself in fault, as you propose?

Lady G. Odious recrimination!—I leave you together. I never was in fault in my life. Am I not a *woman?* If my lord will ask pardon for his froppishness, as we say of children——

She stopt, and pretended to be going——

Har. That my lord shall *not* do, Charlotte. You have carried the jest too far already. My lord shall preserve his dignity for his *wife's* sake. My lord, you will not permit Lady G—— to leave us, however?

He took her hand, and pressed it to his lips: For God's sake, madam, let us be happy! It is in your power to make us both so: it ever *shall* be in your power. If I have been in fault, impute it to my love. I cannot bear your contempt; and I never will deserve it.

Lady G. Why could not this have been said some hours ago? —Why, slighting my early caution, would you *expose* yourself?

I took her aside. Be generous, Lady G——. Let not your *husband* be the only person to whom you are not so.

Lady G. [Whispering.] Our quarrel has not run half its length. If we make up here, we shall make up clumsily. One of the silliest things in the world is a quarrel that ends not, as a coachman after a journey comes in, with a spirit. We shall certainly renew it.

Har. Take the caution you gave to my lord: Don't *expose* yourself. And another; that you cannot more effectually do so, than by exposing your husband. I am more than half ashamed of you. You are not the Charlotte I once thought you were. Let me see, if you have and regard to *my* good opinion of you, that you can own an error with some grace.

Lady G. I am a meek, humble, docible creature. She turned to me, and make me a rustic courtesy, her hands before her: I'll try for it; tell me, if I am right. Then stepping towards my lord, who was with his back to us looking out at the window—and he turning about to her bowing—My lord, said she, Miss Byron has been telling me more than I knew before of my duty. She proposes herself one day to make a won-der-ful obedient wife. It would have been well for you, perhaps, had I had *her* example to walk by. She seems to say, that now I am married, I must be grave, sage, and passive: that *smiles* will hardly become me: that I must be prim and formal, and reverence my husband. If you think this behaviour will become a married woman, and expect it from me, pray, my lord, put me right by your *frowns,* whenever I shall be wrong. For the future, if I ever find myself disposed to be very light-hearted, I will ask your leave before I give way to it. And now, what is next to be done? humorously courtesying, her hands before her.

He clasped her in his arms: Dear provoking creature! This, this is next to be done—I ask you but to love me half as much as I love you, and I shall be the happiest man on earth.

My lord, said I, you ruin all by this condescension on a speech and air so ungracious. If this is all you get by it, never, never, my lord, fall out again. O Charlotte! If you are not generous, you come off much, *much* too easily.

Well now, my lord, said she, holding out her hand, as if threatening me, let you and me, man and wife like, join against the interposer in our quarrels.—Harriet, I will not forgive you for this last part of your lecture.

And thus was this idle quarrel made up. All that vexes me on the occasion is, that it was not made up with dignity on my lord's part. His honest heart so overflowed with joy at his lips, that the naughty creature, by her arch leers, every now and then showed that she was sensible of her consequence to his happiness. But, Lucy, don't let her sink *too* low in your esteem: she has many fine qualities.

They prevailed on me to stay supper. Emily rejoiced in the reconciliation: her heart was, as I may say, visible in her joy. *Can* I love her better than I do? If I *could,* she would, every time I see her, give me reason for it.

LETTER XXXIV.

Miss Byron.—In continuation.

Wednesday, Noon, April 29.

It would puzzle you to guess at a visitor I had this morning. —Honest Mr. Fowler. I was very glad to see him. He brought me a letter from his worthy uncle. Good Sir Rowland! I had a joy that I thought I should not have had while I stayed in London, on its being put into my hand, though the contents gave me sensible pain. I enclose it. It is dated from Caermarthen. Be pleased to read it here.

Caermarthen, April 11.

How shall I, in fit manner, inscribe my letter to the loveliest of women! I don't mean *because* of your loveliness; but whether as *daughter* or not, as you did me the honour to call yourself. Really, and truly, I must say, that I had rather call you by *another* name, though a little more remote as to consanguinity. Lord have mercy upon me, how have I talked of you! How many of our fine Caermarthen girls have I filled with envy of your peerless perfections!

Here am I settled to my heart's content, could I but obtain —you know whom I mean.—A town of gentry: a fine country round us—a fine estate of our own. Esteemed, nay for that matter, *beloved* by all our neighbours and tenants. Who so happy as Rowland Meredith, if his poor boy could be happy! —Ah, madam!—And can't it be so? I am *afraid* of asking. Yet I understand that, notwithstanding all the jack-a-dandies that have been fluttering about you, you are what you were when I left town. Some whispers have gone out of a fine gentleman indeed, who had a great kindness for you; but yet that something was in the way between you. The Lord bless and prosper my dear *daughter,* as I must then call you, and not *niece,* if you have any kindness for him. And if as how you have, it would be wonderfully gracious if you would but give half a hint of it to my nephew; or if so be, you will not to him, to me, your *father* you know, under your own precious hand. The Lord be good unto me! But I shall never see the she that will strike my fancy, as you have done. But what a dreadful thing would it be, if you, who are so much courted and admired by many fine gallants, should at last be taken with a man who could not be yours! God forbid that such a disastrous thing should happen! I profess to you, madam, that a tear or two have strayed down my cheeks at the thoughts of it. For why? Because you played no tricks with any man: you never were a coquette, as they call them. You dealt plainly, sincerely, and tenderly too, to all men; of which my nephew and I can bear witness.

Well, but what now is the end of my writing?—Lord love you, cannot, cannot you at last give comfort to two honest hearts? Honester you never knew! and yet, if you could, I dare say you would. Well, then, and if you can't, we must sit down as contented as we can; that's all we have for it.—But, poor young man! Look at him, if you read this before him. *Strangely* altered! Poor young man!—And if as how you cannot, why then, God bless my *daughter!* that's all. And I do assure you, that you have our prayers every Lord's day, from the bottom of our hearts.

And now, if you will keep a secret, I will tell it you; and yet, when I began I did not intend it: the poor youth must not know I do. It is done in the singleness of our hearts; and if you think we mean to gain your love for us by it, I do assure you that you wrong us.—My nephew declares, that he never will marry, if it be not *somebody;* and he has made his will, and so have I his uncle; and, let me tell you, that if as how I cannot have a *niece,* my *daughter* shall be the better for having known, and treated as kindly as power was lent her,

Her true friend, loving father, and obedient servant,

ROWLAND MEREDITH.

Love and service to Mr. and Mrs. Reeves, and all friends who inquire after me. Farewell. God bless you! Amen.

HAVE you, could you, Lucy, read this letter with dry eyes? Generous, worthy, honest man! I read but half way before Mr. Fowler—glad I was that I read no farther. I should not have been able to have kept his uncle's secret, if I had; had it been but to disclaim the acceptance of the generous purpose. The carrying it into effect would exceedingly distress me, besides the pain the demise of the honest man would give me; and the more, as I bespoke the fatherly relation from him myself. If such a thing were to be, Sir Charles Grandison's behaviour to the Danbys should be my example.

Do you know, Mr. Fowler, said I, the contents of the letter you have put into my hand?

No farther than that my uncle told me it contained professions of fatherly love; and with *wishes* only—but without so much as expressing his *hopes.*

Sir Rowland is a good man, said I: I have not read above half his letter. There seems to be too much of the *father* in it for me to read farther before my *brother.* God bless my *brother* Fowler, and reward the *fatherly* love of Sir Rowland to his *daughter* Byron! I must write to him.

Mr. Fowler, poor man! profoundly sighed; bowed; with *such* a look of respectful acquiescence—Bless me, my dear, how am I to be distressed on all sides! by *good* men too; as Sir Charles could say he was by good women.

Is there nothing less than giving myself to either, that I can do to show Mr. Orme and Mr. Fowler my true value for them?

Poor Mr. Fowler!—Indeed he looks to be, as Sir Rowland hints, not well.—Such a modest, such a humble, such a silent lover!—He cost me tears at parting: I could not hide them. He heaped praises and good wishes upon me, and hurried away at last, to hide his emotion, with a sentence unfinished.— God preserve you, dear and worthy sir! was all I could *try* to say. The last words stuck in my throat, till he was out of hearing; and then I prayed for blessings upon him and his uncle: and repeated them, with fresh tears, on reading the rest of the affecting letter.

Mr. Fowler told Mr. Reeves, before I saw him, that he is

to go to Caermarthen for the benefit of his native air, in a week. He let him know where he lodged in town. He had been riding for his health and diversion about the country, ever since his uncle went; and has not been yet at Caermarthen.

I wish Mr. Fowler had once, if *but* once, called me *sister:* it would have been such a *kind* acquiescence, as would have given me some little pleasure, on recollection. Methinks I don't know how to have done writing of Sir Rowland and Mr. Fowler.

I sat down, however, while the uncle and nephew filled my thoughts, and wrote to the former. I have enclosed the copy of my letter. Adieu, my Lucy.

LETTER XXXV.

Miss Byron to Sir Rowland Meredith.

Wednesday, April 19.

IT was with great pleasure that I received this day the kindest letter that ever was written by a real father to his dearest child. I was resolved that I would not go to rest till I had acknowledged the favour.

How sweet is the name of *father* to a young person who, out of near one-and-twenty years of life, has for more than half the time been bereaved of hers; and who was also one of the best of men!

You gave me an additional pleasure in causing this remembrance of your promised paternal goodness to be given me by Mr. Fowler in person. Till I knew you and him, I had no father, no brother.

How good you are in your apprehensions that there may be a man on whom your daughter has cast her eye, and who cannot look upon *her* with the same distinction—Oh that I had been near you when you wrote that sweetly compassionating, that indulgent passage! I would have wiped the tears from your eyes, myself, and reverenced you as my true father.

You demand of me, *as* my father, a hint, or half a hint, as you call it, to be given to my brother Fowler; or, if not to him, to you. To him, whom I call father, I *mean* all the duty of a child. I call him not father *nominally* only: I will, irksome as the subject is, own, without reserve, the truth to you —[in tenderness to my brother, how could I to him?]—There is a man whom, and whom only, I could love as a good wife ought to love her husband. He is the best of men. Oh, my good Sir Rowland Meredith! if you knew him, you would love him yourself, and own him for your son. I will not conceal his name from my father; Sir Charles Grandison is the man. Inquire about him. His character will rise upon you from every mouth. He engaged first all your daughter's gratitude, by rescuing her from a great danger and oppression; for he is as brave as he is good: and how could she help suffering a tenderness to spring up from her gratitude, of which she was never before sensible to any man in the world? There *is* something in the way, my good sir; but not that proceeds from his slights or contempts. Your daughter could not live, if it were so. A glorious creature is in the way! who has suffered for him, who *does* suffer for him: he ought to be hers, and only hers; and if she can be recovered from a fearful malady that has seized her mind, he probably will. My daily prayers are, that God will restore her!

But yet, my dear sir, my friend, my father! my esteem for this noblest of men is of such a nature, that I cannot give my hand to any other: My father Meredith would not wish me to give a hand without a heart.

This, sir, is the case. Let it, I beseech you, rest within your own breast, and my brother Fowler's. How few minds are there delicate and candid enough to see circumstances of this kind in the light they ought to appear in! and pray for me, my good Sir Rowland; not that the way may be smoothed to what once would have crowned my wishes as to this life; but that Sir Charles Grandison may be happy with the lady that is, and ought to be, dearest to his heart; and that your daughter may be enabled to rejoice in their felicity. What, my good sir, is this span of life, that a passenger through it should seek to overturn the interests of others to establish her own? And can the single life be a grievance? Can it be destitute of the noblest tendernesses? No, sir. You that have lived to an advanced age, in a fair fame, surrounded with comforts, and as tender to a worthy nephew, as the most indulgent father could be to the worthiest of sons, can testify for me, that it is not.

But now, sir, one word—I disclaim, but yet, in all thankfulness, the acceptance of the favour signified to be intended me in the latter part of the paternal letter before me. Our acquaintance began with a hope, on your side, that I could not encourage. As I could not, shall I accept of the benefit from you, to which I could only have been entitled (and that as I had behaved) had I been able to oblige you?—No, sir! I will not, in this case, be benefited, when I cannot benefit. Put me not, therefore, I beseech you, sir, if such an event (deplored by me, as it would be!) should happen, upon the necessity of inquiring after your other relations and friends. Sir Rowland Meredith my father, and Mr. Fowler my brother, are all to me of the family they distinguish by their relation that I know at present. Let me not be made known to the rest by a distinction that would be unjust to them, and to yourself, as it must deprive you of the grace of obliging those who have more than a stranger's claim; and must, in the event, lay them under the appearance of an obligation to that stranger for doing them common justice.

I use the word *stranger* with reference to those of your family and friends to whom I must really appear in that light. But, laying these considerations aside, in which I am determined not to interfere with *them,* I am, with the tenderest regard, dear and good sir, your ever-dutiful and affectionate daughter, HARRIET BYRON.

LETTER XXXVI.

Miss Byron to Miss Selby.

Wednesday, April 19.

I SHALL despatch this by your Gibson early in the morning. It was kind in you to bid him call, in his way down; for now I shall be almost sure of meeting (if not my uncle) your brother, and who knows, but my Lucy herself, at Dunstable, where, barring accidents, I shall be on Friday night.

You will see some of the worthiest people in the world, my dear, if you come, all prepared to love you; but let not anybody be put to inconvenience to meet me at Dunstable. My noble friends here will proceed with me to Stratford, or even to Northampton, they say; but they will see me safe in the protection of somebody I love, and whom they must love for my sake.

I don't wonder that Sir Charles Grandison loves Mr. Beauchamp: he is a very worthy and sensible man. He, as everybody else, idolises Sir Charles. It is some pleasure to me, Lucy, that I stand high in his esteem. To be respected by the worthy, is one of the greatest felicities in this life; since it is to be ranked as one of them. Sir Harry and his lady are come to town. All, it seems, is harmony in that family. They cannot bear Mr. Beauchamp's absence from them for three days together. All the neighbouring gentlemen are in love with him. His manners are so gentle; his temper so even; so desirous to oblige; so genteel in his person; so pleasing in his address: he must undoubtedly make a good woman very happy.

But Emily, poor girl! sees only Sir Charles Grandison with eyes of love. Mr. Beauchamp is, however, greatly pleased with Emily. He told Lady G—— that he thought her a fine young creature, and that her mind was still more amiable than her person. But his behaviour to her is extremely prudent. He says finer things *of* her than *to* her: yet, surely, I am mistaken if he meditates not in her his future wife.

Mr. Beauchamp will be one of my escort.

Emily has made it her request to go to Colnebrook with Lady L—— after I am gone.

Mr. Reeves will ride. Lord L—— and Lord G—— will also oblige me with their company on horseback.

Mrs. Reeves is forbidden to venture; but Lady L—— and Lady G—— will not be denied coming with me.

I shall take leave of Lady Olivia and Lady Maffei to-morrow morning when they will set out for their projected tour. To-morrow we and the whole Grandison family are to dine together at Lord L——'s, for the last time. It will be a mournful dining-time, on that account.

Lady Betty Williams, her daughter, and Miss Clements, supped with us this night, and took leave of me in the tenderest manner. They greatly regret my going down so soon, as they call it.

As to the public diversions which they wish me to stay and give into, to be sure I should have been glad to have been better qualified to have entertained you with the performances of this or that actor, this or that musician, and the like: but, frightened by the vile plot upon me at the masquerade, I was thrown out of that course of diversion, and, indeed, into more affecting, more interesting engagements; into the knowledge of a family that had no need to look out of itself for entertainments: and, besides, are not all the company we see, as visitors or guests, full of these things! I have seen the principal performers, in every way, often enough to give me a notion of their performances, though I have not troubled you with such common things as revolve every season.

You know I am far from slighting the innocent pleasures in which other delight—it would have been happier for me, perhaps, had I had more leisure to attend those amusements, than I have found. Yet I am not sure neither: for, methinks, with all the pangs that my suspenses have cost me, I would not but have known Sir Charles Grandison, his sisters, his Emily, and Dr. Bartlett.

I could only have wished to have been spared Sir Hargrave Pollexfen's vile attempt: then, if I had come acquainted with this family, it would have been as I came acquainted with others: my gratitude had not been engaged so deeply.

Well—but what signify if's?—What has been, has: what must be, must. Only love me, my dear friend, as you *used* to love me. If I was a good girl when I left you, I hope I am not a bad one now that I am returning to you. My heart is not corrupted by the vanities of the great town: I have a little more experience than I had: and if I have severely paid for it, it is not at the price of my reputation. And I hope, if nobody has benefited by me, since I have been in town, that no one has suffered by me. Poor Mr. Fowler!—I could not help it, you know. Had I, by little snares, follies, coquetries, sought to draw him on, and entangle him, his future welfare would, with reason, be more the subject of my solicitude than it is now *necessary* it should be; though, indeed, I cannot *help* making it a good deal so.

Thursday Morning.

DR. BARTLETT has just now taken leave of me, in my own dressing-room. The parting scene between us was tender.

I have not given you my opinion of Miss Williams. Had I seen her at my first coming to town, I should have taken as much notice of her, in my letters to you, as I did of the two Miss Brambers, Miss Darlington, Miss Cantillon, Miss Allestree, and others of my own sex; and of Mr. Somner, Mr. Barnet, Mr. Walden, of the other; who took my first notice, as they fell early in my way, and with whom it is possible, as well as with the town diversions, I had been more intimate, had not Sir Hargrave's vile attempt carried me out of their acquaintance into a much higher; which, of necessity, as well as choice, entirely engrossed my attention. But *now* how insipid would any new characters appear to you, if they were but of a like cast with those I have mentioned, were I to make *such* the subjects of my pen, and had I time before me, which I cannot have, to write again, before I embrace you all, my dear, my ever dear and indulgent friends!

I will only say, that Miss Williams is a genteel girl; but will hardly be more than one of the *better* sort of modern women of condition; and that she is to be classed so *high*, will be more owing to Miss Clement's lessons, than, I am afraid, to her mother's example.

Is it, Lucy, that I have more experience and discernment now, or less charity and good-nature, than when I first came to town? for then I thought well, in the main, of Lady Betty Williams. But though she is a good-natured, obliging woman, she is so immersed in the love of public diversions! so fond of routs, drums, hurricanes—bless me, my dear! how learned should I have been in all the gaieties of the modern life; what a fine lady, possibly; had I not been carried into more rational (however to me they have been more painful) scenes; and had I followed the lead of this lady, as she (kindly, as to her intention) had designed I should!

In the afternoon Mr. Beauchamp is to introduce Sir Harry and Lady Beauchamp, on their first visit to the two sisters.

I had almost forgot to tell you, that my cousins and I are to attend the good Countess of D——, for one half hour, after we have taken leave of Lady Olivia and her aunt.

And now, my Lucy, do I shut up my correspondence with you from London. My heart beats high with the hope of being as indulgently received by all you, my dearest friends, as I used to be after a shorter absence: for I am, and ever will be,

The grateful, dutiful, and affectionate

HARRIET BYRON.

LETTER XXXVII.

Miss Byron to Lady G——.

Selby House, Monday, April 24.

THOUGH the kind friends with whom I parted at Dunstable were pleased, one and all, to allow that the correspondence which is to pass between my dear Lady G—— and their Harriet, should answer the just expectations of each upon her, in the writing way; and though (at *your* motion, remember, not at mine) they promised to be contented with hearing read to them such parts of my letters as you shall think proper to communicate; yet cannot I dispense with my duty to Lady L——, my Emily, my cousin Reeves, and Dr. Bartlett. Accordingly, I write to them by this post; and I charge *you*, my dear, with my sincere and thankful compliments to your lord, and to Mr. Beauchamp, for their favours.

What an agreeable night, in the main, was Friday night! Had we not been to separate next morning, it would have been an agreeable one indeed!

Is not my aunt Selby an excellent woman? But you all admired her. She admires you all. I will tell you, another time, what she said of *you,* my dear, in particular.

My cousin Lucy, too—*is* she not an amiable creature? Indeed you all were delighted with her. But I take pleasure in recollecting your approbations of one I so dearly love. She is as prudent as Lady L——, and now our Nancy is so well recovered, as cheerful as Lady G——. You said you would provide a good husband for her: don't forget. The man, whoever he be, cannot be too good for my Lucy. Nancy is such another good girl: but so I told you.

Well, and pray, did you ever meet with so pleasant a man as my uncle Selby? What should we have done, when we talked of your brother, when we talked of our parting, had it not been for him? You looked upon me every now and then, when he returned your smartness upon him, as if you thought I had let him know some of your perversenesses to Lord G——. And do you think I did not? Indeed I did. Can you imagine that your frank-hearted Harriet, who hides not from her friends her own faults, should conceal yours?—But what a particular character is yours! Everybody blames you, that knows of your over-livelinesses; yet everybody loves you —I think, for your very faults. Had it not been so, do you imagine I could ever have loved you, after you had led Lady L—— to join with you, on a certain teasing occasion?—My uncle dotes upon you!

But don't tell Emily that my cousin James Selby is in love with her. That he may not, on the score of the dear girl's fortune, be thought presumptuous, let me tell you, that he is almost of age; and, when he is, comes into possession of a handsome estate. He has many good qualities. I have, in short, a very great value for him; but not enough, though he is my relation, to wish him my still more beloved Emily. Dear creature! methinks I still feel her parting tears on my cheek!

You charge me to be as minute, in the letters I write to you, as I used to be to my friends here: and you promise to be as circumstantial in yours. I will set you the example: do you be sure to follow it.

We baited at Stoney Stratford. I was *afraid* how it would be: there were the two bold creatures, Mr. Greville and Mr. Fenwick, ready to receive us. A handsome collation, as at our setting out, so now, bespoke by them, was set on the table. How they came by their intelligence, nobody knows: we were all concerned to see them. They seemed half mad for joy. My cousin James had alighted to hand us out; but Mr. Greville was so earnest to offer his hand, and though my cousin was equally ready, I thought I could not deny to his solicitude for the poor favour, such a mark of civility. Besides, if I had, it would have been distinguishing him for more than a common neighbour, you know. Mr. Fenwick took the other hand, when I had stept out of the coach, and then (with so much pride, as made me ashamed of myself) they hurried me between them, through the inn yard, and into the room they had engaged for us; blessing themselves, all the way, for my coming down Harriot Byron.

I looked about, as if for the dear friends I had parted with at Dunstable. This is not, thought I, so delightful an inn as they made that; now they, thought I, are pursuing their road to London, as we are ours to Northampton. But, ah! where, where is Sir Charles Grandison at this time? And I sighed! But don't read this, and such strokes as this, to anybody but Lord and Lady L——. You won't, you say—Thank you, Charlotte.—I will call you *Charlotte,* when I think of it, as you commanded me.

The joy we had at Dunstable was easy, serene, deep, full,

as I may say; it was the joy of sensible people: but the joy here was made by the two gentlemen, mad, loud, and even noisy. They hardly were able to contain themselves; and my uncle and cousin James were forced to be loud, to be heard.

Mr. Orme, good Mr. Orme, when we came near his park, was on the highway side, perhaps near the very spot where he stood to see me pass to London so many weeks ago—poor man!—When I first saw him, (which was before the coach came near, for I looked out only, as thinking I would mark the place where I last beheld him), he looked with so *disconsolate* an air, and so fixed, that I compassionately said to myself, Surely the worthy man has not been there ever since!

I twitched the string just in time: the coach stopt. Mr. Orme, said I, how do you? Well, I hope?—How does Miss Orme?

I had my hand on the coach-door. He snatched it. It was not an unwilling hand. He pressed it with his lips. God be praised, said he (with a countenance, oh, how altered for the better!) for permitting me once more to behold that face—that *angelic* face, he said.

God bless you, Mr. Orme! said I: I am glad to see you. Adieu.

The coach drove on. Poor Mr. Orme! said my aunt.

Mr. Orme, Lucy, said I, don't look so ill as you wrote he was.

His joy to see you, returned she—but Mr. Orme is in a declining way.

Mr. Greville, on the coach stopping, rode back just as it was going on again—and with a loud laugh—How the d—l came Orme to know of your coming, madam?—Poor fellow! It was very kind of you to stop your coach to speak to the statue. And he laughed again.—Nonsensical! At what?

My grandmamma Shirley, dearest of parents! her youth, as she was pleased to say, renewed by the expectation of so soon seeing her darling child, came (as my aunt told us, you know) on Thursday night to Selby House, to charge her and Lucy with her blessing to me; and resolving to stay there to receive me. Our beloved Nancy was also to be there; so were two other cousins, Kitty and Patty Holles, *good* young creatures; who, in my absence, had attended my grandmamma at every convenient opportunity, and whom I also found here.

When we came within sight of this house, Now, Harriet, said Lucy, I see the same kind of emotions beginning to arise in your face and bosom, as Lady G—— told us you showed when you first saw your aunt at Dunstable. My grandmamma! said I, I am in sight of the dear house that holds her: I hope she is here. But I will not surprise her with my joy to see her. Lie still, throbbing, impatient heart.

But when the coach set us down at the inner gate, *there,* in the outward-hall, sat my blessed grandmamma. The moment I beheld her, my intended caution forsook me: I sprang by my aunt, and before the foot-step could be put down, flew as it were out of the coach, and threw myself at her feet, wrapping my arms about her: Bless, bless, said I, your Harriet! I could not at the moment say another word.

Great God! said the pious parent, her hands and eyes lifted up, Great God! I thank thee! Then folding her arms about my neck, she kissed my forehead, my cheek, my lips—God bless my love! Pride of my life! the most precious of a hundred daughters! How does my child—my Harriet—Oh my love!—After such dangers, such trials, such harassings! Once more, God be praised, that I clasp to my fond heart my Harriet!

Separate them, separate them, said my facetious uncle (yet he had tears in his eyes), before they grow together!—Madam, to my grandmamma, she is *our* Harriet as well as *yours:* let us welcome the *saucy* girl on her re-entrance into these doors! —Saucy, I suppose, I shall soon find her.

My grandmamma withdrew her fond arms: Take her, take her, said she, each in turn: but I think I never can part with her again.

My uncle saluted me, and bid me very kindly welcome home —so did every one.

How can I return the obligations which the love of all my friends lays upon me? To be good, to be grateful, is not enough; since *that* one ought to be for one's own sake. Yet how can I be even grateful to them with half a heart. Ah, Lady G——, don't you think I look silly to myself? You bid me be free in my confessions. You promise to look my letters over before you read them to anybody, and to mark passages proper to be kept to yourself—pray do.

Mr. Greville and Mr. Fenwick were here separately, an hour ago: I thanked them for their civility on the road, and not *ungraciously,* as Mr. Greville told my uncle, as to him. He was not, he said, without hopes, yet; since I knew not how to be ungrateful. Mr. Greville builds, as he always did, a merit on his civility; and by that means sinks, in the narrower lover, the claim he might otherwise make to the title of the generous neighbour.

Miss Orme has just been here. She could not help throwing in a word for her brother.

You will guess, my dear Lady G——, at the subject of our conversations here, and what they *will be,* morning, noon, and night, for a week to come. My grandmamma is better in health than I have known her for a year or two past. The health of people in years *can* mend but slowly; and they are slow to acknowledge it in their own favour. My grandmamma, however, allows that she is better within these few days past; but attributes the amendment to her Harriet's return.

How do they all bless, revere, extol your noble brother!—How do they wish—and how do they regret—you know what—yet how ready are they to applaud your Harriet, if she can hold her magnanimity, in preferring the happiness of Clementina to her own!—My grandmamma and aunt are of opinion that I *should;* and they praise me for the generosity of my effort, whether the superior merits of the man will or will not allow me to succeed in it. But my uncle, my Lucy, and my Nancy, from their unbounded love of me, think a little, and *but* a little, narrower; and, believing it will go hard with me, say, It *is* hard. My uncle, in particular, says, The very pretension is flight and nonsense: but, however, if the girl, added he, can *parade* away her passion for an object so worthy, with all my heart: it will be but just, that the romancing elevations, which so often drive headstrong girls into difficulties, should now and then help a more discreet one out of them.

Adieu, my beloved Lady G——! *Repeated* compliments, love, thanks, to my Lord and Lady L——, to my Emily, to Dr. Bartlett, to Mr. Beauchamp, and particularly to my Lord G——. Dear, dear Charlotte, be good! Let me beseech you be good! If you are *not,* you will have every one of *my* friends against you; for those of them who met you at Dunstable find but one fault in my lord: it is, that he seems too fond of a wife, who by her archness of looks, and half-saucy turns upon him, even before them, evidently showed—shall I say what?

But I stand up for you, my dear. Your gratitude, your generosity, your honour, I say (and why should I not add your *duty?*) will certainly make you one of the most obliging of wives, to the most affectionate of husbands.

My uncle says, he hopes so: but though he adores you for a friend, and the companion of a lively hour; yet he does not know but his *dame* Selby is *still* the woman whom a man should prefer for a wife: and she, said he, is full as saucy as a wife need to be; though I think, Harriet, that she has not been the less dutiful of late for *your* absence.

Once more, adieu, my dear Lady G——, and continue to love your   HARRIET BYRON.

LETTER XXXVIII.

Lady G—— to Miss Byron.

Thursday, April 27.

EVERY one of the Dunstable party says that you are a grateful and good girl. Beauchamp can talk of nobody else of our sex: I believe in my conscience he is in love with you. I think all the unprovided-for young women, wherever you come, must hate you. Were you never by surprise carried into the chamber of a friend labouring with the small pox, in the infectious stage of it?—Oh, but I think you once said you had had that distemper. But your mind, Harriet, were your face to be ruined, would make you admirers. The fellows who could think of preferring even such a face to such a heart, may be turned over to the class of insignificants.

Is not your aunt Selby, you ask, an excellent woman?—She is. I admire her. But I am very angry with you for deferring to another time acquainting me with what she said of *me*. When we are taken with anybody, we love they should be taken with us. Teasing Harriet! You know what an immoderate quantity of curiosity I have. Never serve me so again!

I am in love with your cousin Lucy. Were either Fenwick or Greville good enough—but they are not. I think she shall have Mr. Orme. Nancy, you say, is such another good girl. I don't doubt it. Is she not your cousin, and Lucy's sister? But I cannot undertake for every good girl who wants a husband. I wish I had seen Lucy a fortnight ago: then Nancy might have had Mr. Orme, and Lucy should have had Lord G——. He admires her greatly. And do you think that a man, who at that time professed for me so much love and service, and all that, would have scrupled to oblige me, had I (as I easily should) proved to him, that he would have been a much happier man than he could hope to be with somebody else?

Your uncle is a pleasant man: but tell him I say, that the man would be out of his wits, that did not make the preference he does in favour of his *dame* Selby, as he calls her. Tell him also, if you please, in return for his plain dealing, that I say, he *studies* too much for his pleasantries: he is continually hunting for occasions to be smart. I have heard my father say, that this was the fault of some wits of his acquaintance, whom he ranked among the witlings for it. If you think it will mortify him more, you may tell him (for I am very revengeful when I think myself affronted), that were I at liberty, which, God help me, I am not! I would sooner choose for a husband the man I *have* (poor soul, as I now and then think him), than such a teasing creature as himself, were *both* in my power, and both of an age. And I should have this good reason for my preference: your uncle and I should have been too much alike, and so been jealous of each other's wit; whereas I can make my honest Lord G—— look about him, and admire me strangely, whenever I please.

But I am, it seems, a person of a particular character. Every one, you say, loves me, yet blames me. Odd characters, my dear, are needful to make even characters shine. You good girls would not be valued as you are, if there were not bad ones. Have you not heard it said, that all human excellence is but comparative? Pray allow of the contrast. You, I am sure, ought. You are an ungrateful creature, if whenever you think of my over-livelinesses, as you call 'em, you don't drop a courtesy, and say, you are obliged to me.

But still the attack made upon you in your dressing-room at Colnebrook, by my sister and me, sticks in your stomach— and why so? We were willing to show you, that we were *not* the silly people you must have thought us, had we not been able to distinguish light from darkness. You, who ever were, I believe, one of the frankest-hearted girls in Britain, and admired for the ease and dignity given you by that frankness, were growing awkward, nay dishonest. Your gratitude! your gratitude! was the dust you wanted to throw into our eyes, that we might not see that you were governed by a stronger motive. You called us your friends, your sisters, but treated us not as either; and this man, and that, and t'other, you could refuse; and why? No reason given for it; and we were to be popt off with your gratitude, truly!—We were to believe just what you said, and no more; nay, not so much as you said. But we were not so implicit. Nor would *you,* in our case, have been so.

But 'you, perhaps, would not have violently broken in upon 'a poor thing, who thought we were blind, because she was 'not willing we should see.'—May be not; but then, in that case, we were honester than you would have been; that's all.

Here, said I, Lady L——, is this poor girl awkwardly struggling to conceal what everybody sees; and, seeing, applauds her for, the man considered: [Yes, Harriet, the man considered; be pleased to take that in:] let us, in pity, relieve her. She is thought to be frank, open-hearted, communicative; nay, she passes herself upon us in those characters: she sees we keep nothing from her. She has been acquainted with *your* love before wedlock; with *my* folly, in relation to Anderson: she had carried her head above a score or two of men not contemptible. She sits enthroned among *us,* while *we* make but common figures at her footstool: she calls us sisters, friends, and twenty pretty names. Let us acquaint her, that we see into her heart; and why Lord D—— and others are so indifferent with her. If she is ingenuous, let us spare her; if not, leave *me* to punish her: yet we will keep up her punctilio as to our brother; we will leave him to make his own discoveries. She may confide in his politeness; and the result will be happier for her; because she will then be under no restraint to us, and her native freedom of heart may again take its course.

Agreed, agreed, said Lady L——. And, arm-in-arm, we entered your dressing-room, dismissed the maid, and began the attack—and, O Harriet! how you hesitated, paraded, fooled on with us, before you came to confession! Indeed you deserved not the mercy we showed you—so, child, you had better to have let this part of your story sleep in peace.

You bid me not tell Emily, that your cousin is in love with her: but I think I will. Girls begin very early to look out for admirers. It is better, in order to stay her stomach, to find out one for her, than that she should find out one for herself; especially when the man is among ourselves, as I may say, and both are in our own management, and at distance from each other. Emily is a good girl; but she has susceptibilities already: and though I would not encourage her, as yet, to look out of herself for happiness, yet I would give her consequence with herself, and at the same time let her see, that there could be no mention made of anything that related to *her,* but what she should be acquainted with. Dear girl! I love her as well as you; and I pity her too; for she, as well as somebody else, will have difficulties to contend with, which she will not know easily how to get over; though she can, in a flame so young, generously prefer the interest of a more excellent woman to her own.—There, Harriet, is a grave paragraph: you'll like me for it.

You are a very reflecting girl in mentioning to me, so particularly, your behaviour to your Grevilles, Fenwicks, and Ormes. What is that but saying, See, Charlotte! I am a much more complaisant creature to the men, no one of which I intend to have, than you are to your husband!

What a pious woman, indeed, must be your grandmamma, that she could suspend her joy, her long-absent darling at her feet, till she had first thanked God for restoring her to her arms! but, in this instance, we see the force of habitual piety. Though not so good as I should be myself, I revere those who are so: and that I hope you will own is no bad sign.

Well, but now for ourselves, and those about us.

Lady Olivia has written a letter from Windsor to Lady L——. It is in French; extremely polite. She promises to write to me from Oxford.

Lady Anne S—— made me a visit this morning. She was more concerned than I wished to see her, on my confirming the report she had heard of my brother's being gone abroad. I rallied her a little too freely, as it was before Lord G—— and Lord L——. I never was better rebuked than by her; for she took out her pencil, and on the cover of a letter wrote these lines from Shakespeare, and slid them into my hand:

"And will you rend our ancient love asunder,
To join with *men* in scorning your poor friend?
It is not friendly; 'tis not maidenly:
Our *sex*, as well as I, may chide you for it,
Though I alone do feel the injury."

I never, my dear, told you how freely this lady and I had talked of love: but, freely as we had talked, I was not aware that the matter lay so deep in her heart. I knew not how to tell her that my brother had said, *It could not be.* I could have wept over her when I read this paper; and I owned myself, by a whisper, justly rebuked. She charged me not to let any man see this; particularly not either of those present: and do *you,* Harriet, keep what I have written of Lady Anne to yourself.

My aunt Eleanor has written a congratulatory letter to me from York. Sir Charles, it seems, had acquainted her with Lord G——'s day [Not my day, Harriet! that is not the phrase, I hope!] as soon as he knew it himself; and she writes, supposing that I was actually *offered* on it. Women are victims on these occasions: I hope you'll allow me that. My brother has made it a point of duty to acquaint his father's sister with every matter of consequence to the family; and now, she says, that both her nieces are so well disposed of, she will come to town very quickly to see her new relations and us; and desires we will make room for her. And yet she owns that my brother has informed her of his being obliged to go abroad; and she supposes him gone. As he is the beloved of her heart, I wonder she thinks of making this visit now he is absent: but we shall all be glad to see my aunt Nell. She is a good creature, though an old maid. I hope the old lady has not utterly lost either her invention or memory; and then, between both, I shall be entertained with a great number of love stories of the last age; and perhaps of some dangers and escapes; which may serve for warnings for Emily. Alas! alas! they will come too late for your Charlotte!

I have written already the longest letter that I ever wrote in my life: yet it is prating; and to you, to whom I love to prate. I have not *near* done.

You bid me be good; and you threaten me, if I am not, with the ill opinion of all your friends: but I have such an unaccountable bias for roguery, or what shall I call it? that I believe it is impossible for me to take your advice. I have been examining myself. What a deuce is the matter with me, that I cannot see my honest man in the same advantageous light in which he appears to everybody else? Yet I do not, in my heart, dislike him. On the contrary, I know not, were I to look about me, far and wide, the man I would have wished to have called mine, rather than him. But he is so important about trifles; so nimble, yet so slow: he is so sensible of his own *intention* to please, and has so many antic motions in his obligingness; that I cannot forbear laughing at the very time that I ought perhaps to reward him with a gracious approbation.

I must fool on a little while longer, I believe: permit me, Harriet, so to do, as occasions arise.

AN instance, an instance in point, Harriet. Let me laugh as I write. I did at the time.—What do you laugh at, Charlotte?—Why this poor man, or, as I should rather say, this lord and master of mine, has just left me. He has been making me both a compliment and a present. And what do you think the compliment is? Why, if I please, he will give away to a virtuoso friend, his collection of moths and butterflies: I once, he remembered, rallied him upon them. And by what study, thought I, wilt thou, honest man, supply their place? If thou hast a talent this way, pursue it; since, perhaps, thou wilt not shine in any other. And the *best* anything, you know, Harriet carries with it the appearance of excellence. Nay, he would also part with his collection of shells, if I had no objection.

To whom, my lord?—He had not resolved.—Why then, only as Emily is too little of a child, or you might give them to her. 'Too little of a child, madam!' and a great deal of bustle and importance took possession of his features—let me tell you, madam—I *won't* let you, my lord; and I laughed.

Well, madam, I hope here is something coming up that you will not disdain to accept of yourself.

Up came groaning under the weight, or rather under the *care,* two servants with baskets: A fine set of old Japan china with brown edges, believe me. They set down their baskets, and withdrew.

Would you not have been delighted, Harriet, to see my lord busying himself with taking out, and putting in the windows, one at a time, the cups, plates, jars, and saucers, rejoicing and parading over them, and showing his connoisseurship to his motionless admiring wife, in commending this and the other piece as a beauty? And, when he had done, taking the *liberty,* as he phrased it, half fearful, half resolute, to salute his bride for his reward; and then pacing backwards several steps, with such a strut and a crow—I see him yet!—Indulge me, Harriet! I burst into a hearty laugh; I could not help it: and he, reddening, looked round himself, and round himself, to see if anything was amiss in his garb. The *man,* the *man!* honest friend, I *could* have said (but had too much reverence for my husband), is the oddity! Nothing amiss in the garb. I quickly recollected myself, however, and put him in a good humour, by proper marks of my gracious acceptance. On reflection, I could not bear myself for vexing the honest man when he had meant to oblige me.

How soon I may relapse again, I know not. O Harriet! why did you beseech me to be good? I think in my heart I have the stronger inclination to be bad for it! You call me *perverse.* If you think me so, bid me be saucy, bid me be bad; and I may then, like other good wives, take the contrary course for the sake of dear contradiction.

Show not, however (I in turn beseech *you*) to your grandmamma and aunt, such parts of this letter as would make them despise me. You say, you stand up for me; I have need of your advocateship: never let me want it. And do I not, after all, do a greater credit to my good man, when I can so heartily laugh in the wedded state, than if I were to sit down with my finger in my eye?

I have taken your advice, and presented my sister with my half of the jewels. I desired her to accept them, as they were my mother's, and for her sake. This gave them a value with her, more than equal to their worth: but Lord L—— is uneasy, and declares he will not suffer Lady L—— long to lie under the obligation. Were every one of family in South Britain and North Britain to be as generous and disinterested as Lord L—— and our family, the union of the two parts of the island would be complete.

Lord help this poor obliging man! I wish I don't love him at last. He has taken my hint, and has presented his collection of shells (a very fine one, he says, it is) to Emily; and they two are actually busied (and will be for an hour or two, I doubt not) in admiring them; the one strutting over the beauties, in order to enhance the value of the present; the other courtesying ten times in a minute, to show her gratitude. Poor man! when his virtuoso friend has got his butterflies and moths, I am afraid he must set up a turner's shop for employment. If he loved reading, I could, when our visiting hurries are over, set him to read to me the new things that come out, while I knot or work; and, if he loved writing, to copy the letters which pass between you and me, and those for you which I expect with so much impatience from my brother by means of Dr. Bartlett. I think he spells pretty well, for a lord.

I have no more to say, at present, but compliments, without number or measure, to all you so deservedly love and honour; as well those I have not seen, as those I have.

Only one thing: Reveal to me all the secrets of your heart, and how that heart is from time to time affected; that I may know whether you are capable of that greatness of mind in a love-case, that you show in all others. We will all allow you to love Sir Charles Grandison. Those who do, give honour to themselves, if their eyes stop not at person, *his* having so many advantages. For the same reason, I make no apologies, and never did, for praising my brother, as any other lover of him might do.

Let me know everything how and about your fellows, too. Ah! Harriet, you make not the use of power that I would have done in your situation. I was half sorry when my hurrying brother made me dismiss Sir Walter; and yet, to have but two danglers after one, are poor doings for a fine lady. Poorer still, to have but one!

Here's a letter as long as my arm. Adieu. I was loath to come to the name: but defer it ever so long, I must subscribe, at last,   Charlotte G——.

LETTER XXXIX.

*Miss Jervois to Miss Byron.**

Monday, May 1.

OH my dearest, my honoured Miss Byron, how you have shamed your Emily by sending a letter to her; such a sweet letter too! before I have paid my duty to you, in a letter of thanks for all your love to me, and for all your kind instructions. But I began once, twice, and thrice, and wrote a great deal each time, but could not please myself: you, madam, are *such* a writer, and I am such a *poor thing* at my pen!—But I know you will accept the heart. And so my very diffidence shows pride; since it cannot be expected from me to be a fine writer. And yet this very letter, I foresee, will be the worse for my diffidence, and not the better: for I don't like this beginning neither.—But come, it shall go. Am I not used to your goodness? And do you not bid me prattle to you, in my letters, as I used to do in your dressing-room? Oh, what sweet advice have you, and do you return, for my silly prate! And so I will begin.

And *was* you grieved at parting with your Emily on Saturday morning! I am sure I was very much concerned at parting with you. I could not help crying all the way to town; and Lady G—— shed tears as well as I; and so did Lady L—— several times; and said, You were the loveliest, best young lady in the world. And we all praised likewise your aunt, your cousin Lucy, and young Mr. Selby. How good are all your relations! They must be good. And Lord L——, and Lord G——, for men, were as much concerned as we, at parting with you. Mr. Reeves was *so* dull all the way! —Poor Mr. Reeves, he was very dull. And Mr. Beauchamp, *he* praised you to the very skies; and in such a pretty manner too! Next to my guardian, I think Mr. Beauchamp is a very

---

* The letter to which this is an answer, as well as those written by Miss Byron to her cousin Reeves, Lady L——, &c., and theirs in return, are omitted.

agreeable man. I fancy these noble sisters, if the truth were known, don't like him so well as their brother does: perhaps *that* may be the reason out of jealousy, as I may say, if there be anything in my observation. But they are vastly civil to him, nevertheless; yet they never praise him when his back is turned, as they do others, who can't say half the good things that he says.

Well, but enough of Mr. Beauchamp. My guardian! my gracious, my kind, my indulgent guardian! who, that thinks of him, can praise anybody else?

O madam! where is he now? God protect and guide my guardian, wherever he goes! This is my prayer, first and last, and I can't tell how often in the day. I look for him in every place I have seen him in; [And pray tell me, madam, did not *you* do so when he had left us?] and when I can't find him, I do *so* sigh!—What a pleasure, yet what a pain, is there in sighing, when I think of him! yet I know I am an innocent girl. And this I am sure of, that I wish him to be the husband of but one woman in the whole world; and that is you. But then my next wish is—you know what—ah, my Miss Byron! you must let me live with you and my guardian, if you should ever be Lady Grandison.

But here, madam, are sad doings sometimes between Lord and Lady G——. I am very angry at her often in my heart; yet I cannot help laughing now and then at her out-of-the-way sayings. Is not her character a very new one? Or are there more such young wives? I could not do as she does, were I to be queen of the globe. Every body blames her. She will make my lord not love her, at last. Don't you think so? And then what will she get by her wit?

JUST this moment she came into my closet—Writing, Emily? said she: to whom?—I told her.—Don't tell tales out of school, Emily.—I was *so* afraid that she would have asked to see what I had written: but she did not. To be sure she is very polite, and knows what belongs to herself, and everybody else: to be ungenerous, as you once said, to her husband only, that is a very sad thing to think of.

Anne saw her first, I alighted, and asked her blessing in the shop.

Stothard, del.

Well, and I would give anything to know if you think what I have written tolerable, before I go any farther: but I will go on this way, since I cannot do better. Bad is my best; but you shall have quantity, I warrant, since you bid me write long letters.

But I have seen my mother: it was but yesterday. She was in a mercer's shop in Covent Garden. I was in Lord L——'s chariot; only Anne was with me. Anne saw her first, I alighted, and asked her blessing in the shop: I am sure I did right. She blessed me, and called me dear love. I stayed till she had bought what she wanted, and then I slid down the money, as if it were by her own doing; and glad I was I had so much about me: it came but to four guineas. I begged her, speaking low, to forgive me for so doing: and finding she was to go home as far as Soho, and had thoughts of having a hackney coach called, I gave Anne money for a coach for herself and waited on my mother to her own lodgings; and it being Lord L——'s chariot, she was so good as to dispense with my alighting.

She blessed my guardian all the way, and blessed me. She said, she would not ask me to come to see her, because it might not be thought proper, as my guardian was abroad: but she hoped she might be allowed to come and see me sometimes.—Was she not very good, madam? But my guardian's goodness makes every body good.—Oh that my mamma had been always the same! I should have been but too happy.

God bless my guardian, for putting me on enlarging her power to live handsomely. Only as a coach brings on other charges, and people must live accordingly, or be discredited, instead of credited by it; or I should hope the additional two hundred a-year might afford him one. Yet one does not know but Mr. O'Hara may have been in debt before he married her; and I fancy he has people who hang upon him. But if it pleases God, I will not, when I am at age, and have a coach of my own, suffer my mother to walk on foot. What a blessing is it, to have a guardian that will second every good purpose of one's heart!

Lady Olivia is rambling about: and I suppose she will wait

here in England till Sir Charles's return: but I am sure he never will have her. A wicked wretch, with her poniards! Yet it is pity! She is a fine woman. But I hate her for her expectation, as well as for her poniard. And a woman to leave her own country, to seek for a husband! I could die before I could do so! though to such a man as my guardian. Yet once I thought I could have liked to have lived with her at Florence. She had some good qualities, and is very generous, and in the main well esteemed in her own country; everybody knew she loved my guardian: but I don't know how it is; nobody blamed her for it, vast as the difference in fortune then was. But that is the glory of being a virtuous man; to love him is a credit, instead of a shame. O madam! Who would not be virtuous? And that not only for their own, but for their friends' sakes, if they loved their friends, and wished them to be well thought of?

Lord W—— is very desirous to hasten his wedding.

Mr. Beauchamp says that all the Mansfields (he knows them) bless my guardian every day of their lives; and their enemies tremble. He has commissions from my guardian to inquire and act in their cause, that no time may be lost to do them service, against his return.

We have had another visit from Lady Beauchamp, and have returned it. She is very much pleased with us. You see I say *us*. Indeed my two dear ladies are very good to me; but I have no merit: it is all for their brother's sake.

Mr. Beauchamp tells us, just now, that his mother-in-law has joined with his father, at their own motion, to settle 1000*l.* a year upon him. I am glad of it, with all my heart: Are not you? He is all gratitude upon it. He says that he will redouble his endeavours to oblige her; and that his gratitude to her, as well as his duty to his father, will engage his utmost regard for her.

Mr. Beauchamp, Sir Harry himself, and my lady, are continually blessing my guardian: everybody, in short, blesses him.—But, ah! madam, where is he at this moment? Oh, that I were a bird, that I might hover over his head, and sometimes bring tidings to his friends of his motions and good deeds. I would often flap my wings, dear Miss Byron, at your chamber window, as a signal of his welfare, and then fly back again, and perch as near him as I could.

I am very happy, as I said before, in the favour of Lady and Lord L——, and Lady and Lord G——; but I never shall be so happy as when I had the addition of your charming company. I miss you and my guardian: Oh, how I miss you both! But, dearest Miss Byron, love me not the less, though now I have put pen to paper, and you see what a poor creature I am in my writing. Many a one, I believe, may be thought tolerable in conversation; but when they are so silly as to put pen to paper, they expose themselves; as I have done, in this long piece of scribble. But accept it, nevertheless, for the true love I bear you; and a truer love never flamed in any bosom, to any one most dearly beloved, than does in mine for you.

I am afraid I have written arrant nonsense, because I knew not how to express half the love that is in the heart of your ever obliged and affectionate EMILY JERVOIS.

LETTER XL.

Miss Byron to Lady G——.

Tuesday, May 2.

I HAVE no patience with you, Lady G——. You are ungenerously playful. Thank heaven, if this be wit, that I have none of it. But what signifies expostulating with one who knows herself to be faulty, and will not amend? How many *stripes,* Charlotte, do you deserve?—But you never spared anybody, not even your brother, when the humour was upon you. So make haste; and since you will lay in stores for repentance, fill up your measure as fast as you can.

'Reveal to you the state of my heart!'—Ah, my dear! it is an unmanageable one. 'Greatness of mind!'—I don't know what it is.—All his excellencies, his greatness, his goodness, his modesty, his cheerfulness under such afflictions as would weigh down every other heart that had but half the compassion in it with which his overflows—must not all other men appear little, and less than little, nothing, in my eyes?—It is an instance of patience in me, that I can endure any of them who pretend to regard me out of my own family.

I thought, that when I got down to my dear friends here I should be better enabled, by their prudent counsels, to attain the desirable frame of mind which I had promised myself: but I find myself mistaken. My grandmamma and aunt are such admirers of him, take such a share in the disappointment, that their advice has not the effect I had hoped it would have. Lucy, Nancy, are perpetually reminding me of his excellencies, by calling upon me to tell them something of Sir Charles Grandison; and when I begin, I know not how to leave off. My uncle rallies me, laughs at me, sometimes reminds me of what he calls my former brags. I did not brag, my dear: I only hoped, that respecting as I did *every* man according to his merit, I should never be greatly taken with *any* one, before duty added force to the inclination. Methinks the company of the friends I am with does not satisfy me; yet they never were dearer to me than they now are. I want to have Lord and Lady L——, Lord and Lady G——, Dr. Bartlett, my Emily, with me. To lose you all at once is hard!—There seems to be a strange void in my heart—and so much, as present, for that state of that heart.

I always had reason to think myself greatly obliged to my friends and neighbours all around us: but never, till my return, after these few months' absence, knew how much. So many kind visitors; such unaffected expressions of joy on my return; that had I not a very great counterbalance on my heart, would be enough to make me proud.

My grandmamma went to Shirley Manor on Saturday; on Monday I was with her all day: but she would have it that I should be melancholy if I stayed with her. And she is *so* self-denyingly careful of her Harriet! There never was a more noble heart in woman. But her *solitary* moments, as my uncle calls them, are her moments of joy. And why? Because she then divests herself of all that is either painful or pleasurable to her in this life: for she says that her cares for her Harriet, and especially *now,* are at least a balance for the delight she takes in her.

You command me to acquaint you with what passes between me and the gentlemen of my neighbourhood; in your style, *my fellows.*

Mr. Fenwick invited himself to breakfast with my aunt Selby yesterday morning. I would not avoid him.

I will not trouble you with the particulars: you know well enough what men will say on the subject upon which you will suppose he wanted to talk to me. He was extremely earnest. I besought him to accept my thanks for his good opinion of me, as all the return I could make him for it; and this in so very serious a manner, that my heart was fretted when he declared, with warmth, his determined perseverance.

Mr. Greville made us a tea-visit in the afternoon. My uncle and he joined to rally us poor women, as usual. I left the defence of the sex to my aunt and Lucy. How poor appears to me every conversation now with these men!—But hold, saucy Harriet, was not your uncle Selby one of the ralliers?—But he does not believe all he says, and therefore cannot wish to be so much regarded, on this topic, as he ought to be by me, on others.

After the run of raillery was over, in which Mr. Greville made exceptions favourable to the women present, he applied to every one for their interest with me, and to me, to countenance his address. He set forth his pretensions very pompously, and mentioned a considerable increase of his fortune, which before was a handsome one. He offered our own terms. He declared his love for me above all women, and made his happiness in the next world, as well as in this, depend upon my favour to him.

It was easy to answer all he said, and is equally so for you to guess in what manner I answered him; and he, finding me determined, began to grow vehement, and even affrontive. He hinted to me, that he *knew* what had made me so very resolute. He threw out threatenings against the man, be he who he would, that should stand in the way of his success with me; at the same time intimating saucily, as I may say (for his manner had insult in it), that it was impossible a certain event could ever take place.

My uncle was angry with him; so was my aunt: Lucy was still more angry than they: but I, standing up, said, Pray, my dear friends, take nothing amiss that Mr. Greville has said.— He once told me that he would set spies upon my conduct in town. If, sir, your spies have been just, I fear nothing they can say. But the hints you have thrown out, show such a total want of all delicacy of mind, that you must not wonder if my *heart* rejects you. Yet I am not angry: I reproach you not: every one has his peculiar way. All that is left me to say or to do, is to thank you for your favourable opinion of me, as I have thanked Mr. Fenwick: and to desire that you will allow me to look upon you as my neighbour, and *only* as my neighbour.

I courtesied to him, and withdrew.

But my great difficulty had been before with Mr. Orme.

His sister had desired that I would see her brother. He and she were invited by my aunt to dinner on Tuesday. They came. Poor man! he is not well! I am sorry for it. Poor Mr. Orme is not well! he made me such *honest* compliments, as I may say: his *heart* was too much in his civilities to raise them above the civilities that justice and truth might warrant in favour of a person highly esteemed. Mine was filled with compassion for him; and that compassion would have showed itself in tokens of tenderness, more than once, had I not restrained myself for *his* sake.

How you, my dear Lady G——, can delight in giving pain to an honest heart, I cannot imagine. I would make all God Almighty's creatures happy, if I could; and so would your noble brother. Is he not crossing dangerous seas, and ascending, through almost perpetual snows, those dangerous Alps, which I have heard described with such terror, for the generous end of relieving distress?

I made Mr. Orme sit next me. I was assiduous to help

him; and do to him all the little offices which I thought would light up pleasure in his modest countenance; and he was quite another man. It gave delight to his sister, and to all my friends, to see him smile and look happy.

I think, my dear Lady G——, that when Mr. Orme looks pleasant, and at ease, he resembles a little the good-natured Lord G——. Oh, that you would take half the pains to oblige him, that I do to relieve Mr. Orme!—*Half the pains,* did I say? that you would not take pains to *dis*oblige him; and he would be, of course, obliged. Don't be afraid, my dear, that in such a world as this, things will not happen to make you uneasy without your studying for them.

Excuse my seriousness. I am indeed *too* serious at times.

But when Mr. Orme requested a few minutes' audience of me, as he called it, and I walked with him into the cedar parlour, which you have heard me mention, and with which I hope you will be one day acquainted; he paid, poor man! for his too transient pleasure. Why would he urge a denial that he could not but know I must give?

His sister and I had afterwards a conference. I was greatly affected by it; and at last besought her, if she valued my friendship as I did hers, never more to mention to me a subject which gave me a pain too sensible for my peace.

She requested me to assure her, that neither Mr. Greville, nor Mr. Fenwick, might be the man. They both took upon them, she said, to ridicule her brother for the profound respect, even to reverence, that he bore me; which, if he knew might be attended with consequences: for that her brother, mild and gentle as was his passion for me, had courage to resent any indignities that might be cast upon him by spirits boisterous as were those of the two gentlemen she had named. She never, therefore, told her brother of their scoffs. But it would go to her heart, if either of them should succeed, or have reason but for a distant hope.

I made her heart easy, on that score.

I have just now heard, that Sir Hargrave Pollexfen is come from abroad already. What can be the meaning of it? He is so low-minded, so malicious a man, and I have suffered so much from him—what can be the meaning of this sudden return? I am told that he is actually in London. Pray, my dear Lady G——, inform yourself about him; and whether he thinks of coming into these parts.

Mr. Greville, when he met us at Stoney-Stratford, threw out menaces against Sir Hargrave on my account; and said, it was well he was gone abroad. I told him then, that he had no business, even were Sir Hargrave present, to engage himself in my quarrels.

Mr. Greville is an impetuous man; a man of rough manners; and makes many people afraid of him. He has, I believe, *indeed,* had his spies about me; for he seems to know everything that has befallen me in my absence from Selby House.

He has dared also to threaten Somebody else. Insolent wretch! but he hinted to me yesterday, that he was exceedingly pleased with the news, that a certain gentleman was gone abroad, in order to prosecute a *former amour,* was the light wretch's as light expression. If my indignant eyes could have killed him, he would have fallen dead at my foot.

Let the constant and true respects of all my friends to you and yours, and to my beloved Emily, be always, for the future, considered as very affectionately expressed, whether the variety of other subjects leave room for a particular expression of them, or not, by, my dearest Lady G——, your faithful, and ever obliged   HARRIET BYRON.

LETTER XLI.

Lady G—— to Miss Byron.

Saturday, May 6.

I THANK you, Harriet, for yours. What must your fellows think of you? in this gross age, your delicacy must astonish them. There used to be more of it formerly. But how should men know anything of it, when women have forgot it? Lord be thanked, we females, since we have been admitted into so constant a share of the public diversions, want not courage. We can give the men stare for stare wherever we meet them. The next age, nay, the rising generation, must surely be all heroes and heroines. But whither has this word *delicacy* carried me; me, who it seems, have faults to be corrected for of another sort; and who want not the *courage* for which I congratulate others?

But to other subjects. I could write a vast deal of stuff about my lord and self, and Lord and Lady L——, who assume parts which I know not how to allow them: and sometimes they threaten me with my brother's resentments, sometimes with my Harriet's; so that I must really have leading-strings fastened to my shoulders. Oh, my dear! a fond husband is a surfeiting thing; and yet I believe most women love to be made monkeys of.

But all other subjects must now give way. We have heard *of,* though not *from,* my brother. A particular friend of Mr. Lowther was here with a letter from that gentleman, acquainting us that Sir Charles and he were arrived at Paris.

Mr. Beauchamp was with us when Mr. Lowther's friend came. He borrowed the letter on account of the extraordinary adventure mentioned in it.

Make your heart easy, in the first place, about Sir Hargrave. He is indeed in town; but very ill. He was frightened into England, and intends not ever again to quit it. In all probability, he owes it to my brother that he exists.

Mr. Beauchamp went directly to Cavendish Square, and informed himself there of other particulars relating to the affair, from the very servant who was present, and acting in it; and from those particulars, and Mr. Lowther's letter, wrote one for Dr. Bartlett. Mr. Beauchamp obliged me with the perusal of what he wrote; whence I have extracted the following account: for his letter is long and circumstantial; and I did not ask his leave to take a copy, as he seemed desirous to hasten it to the doctor.

On Wednesday, the 19-30 of April, in the evening, as my brother was pursuing his journey to Paris, and was within two miles of that capital, a servant-man rode up, in visible terror, to his post-chaise, in which were Mr. Lowther and himself, and besought them to hear his dreadful tale. The gentlemen stopt, and he told them that his master, who was an Englishman, and his friend of the same nation, had been but a little while before attacked, and forced out of the road, in their post-chaise, as he doubted not, to be murdered, by no less then seven armed horsemen; and he pointed to a hill, at a distance, called Mont Matre, behind which they were, at that moment, perpetrating their bloody purpose. He had just before, he said, addressed himself to two other gentlemen, and their retinue, who drove on the faster for it.

The servant's greatcoat was open; and Sir Charles observing his livery, asked him if he were not a servant of Sir Hargrave Pollexfen? and was answered in the affirmative.

There are, it seems, trees planted on each side the road from St. Denis to Paris, but which, as France is an open and unenclosed country, would not, but for the hill, have hindered the seeing a great way off, the scuffling of so many men on horseback. There is also a ditch on either hand; but places left for owners to come at their grounds, with their carts, and other carriages. Sir Charles ordered the post-boy to drive to one of those passages; saying, He could not forgive himself if he did not endeavour to save Sir Hargrave and his friend, whose name the man told him was Merceda.

His own servants were three in number, besides one of Mr. Lowther's. My brother made Mr. Lowther's servant dismount; and, getting himself on his horse, ordered the others to follow him. He begged Mr. Lowther to continue in the chaise, bidding the dismounted servant stay, and attend his master, and galloped away towards the hill. His ears were soon pierced with the cries of the poor wretches; and presently he saw two men on horseback holding the horses of four others, who had under them the two gentlemen, struggling, groaning, and crying out for mercy.

Sir Charles, who was a good way a-head of his servants, calling out to spare the gentlemen, and bending his course to relieve the prostrate sufferers, two of the four quitted their prey, and mounting, joined the other two horsemen, and advanced to meet him, with a show of supporting the two men on foot in their violence; who continued laying on the wretches, with the butt-ends of their whips, unmercifully.

As the assailants offered not to fly, and as they had more than time enough to execute their purpose, had it been robbery and murder, Sir Charles concluded it was likely that these men were actuated by a private revenge. He was confirmed in this surmise, when the four men on horseback, though each had his pistol ready drawn, as Sir Charles also had his, demanded a conference; warning Sir Charles how he provoked his fate by his rashness; and declaring, that he was a dead man if he fired.

Forbear, then, said Sir Charles, all further violences to the gentlemen, and I will hear what you have to say.

He then put his pistol into his holster; and one of his servants being come up, and the two others at hand (to whom he called out not to fire till they had his orders), he gave him his horse's reins; bidding him have an eye on the holsters of both, and leapt down; and, drawing his sword, made towards the two men who were so cruelly exercising their whips; and who, on his approach, retired to some little distance, drawing their hangers.

The four men on horseback joined the two on foot, just as they were quitting the objects of their fury; and one of them said, Forbear, for the present, further violence, brother; the gentlemen shall be told the cause of all this.—Murder, sir, said he, is not intended; nor are we robbers: the men whom you are solicitous to save from our vengeance are villains.

Be the cause what it will, answered Sir Charles, you are in a country noted for doing *speedy* justice, upon proper application to the magistrates. In the same instant he raised first one groaning man, then the other. Their heads were all over bloody, and they were so much bruised that they could not extend their arms to reach their wigs and hats, which lay near them, nor put them on without Sir Charles's help.

The men on foot by this time had mounted their horses, and all six stood upon their defence; but one of them was so furious, crying out, that his vengeance should be yet more complete, that two of the others could hardly restrain him.

Sir Charles asked Sir Hargrave and Mr. Merceda whether they had reason to look upon themselves as injured men, or injurers? One of the assailants answered, that they both knew themselves to be villains.

Either from consciousness, or terror, perhaps from both, they could not speak for themselves, but by groans; nor could either of them stand or sit upright.

Just then came up, in the chaise, Mr. Lowther, and his servant, each a pistol in his hand. He quitted the chaise, when he came near the suffering men; and Sir Charles desired him instantly to examine whether the gentlemen were dangerously hurt or not.

The most enraged of the assailants having slipt by the two who were earnest to restrain him, would again have attacked Mr. Merceda; offering a stroke at him with his hanger: but Sir Charles (his drawn sword still in his hand) caught hold of his bridle; and, turning his horse's head aside, diverted a stroke, which, in all probability, would otherwise have been a finishing one.

They all came about Sir Charles, bidding him, at his peril, use his sword upon their friend: and Sir Charles's servants were coming up to their master's support, had there been occasion. At that instant Mr. Lowther, assisted by his own servant, was examining the wounds and bruises of the two terrified men, who had yet no reason to think themselves safe from further violence.

Sir Charles repeatedly commanded his servants not to fire, nor approach nearer, without his orders. The persons, said he, to the assailants, whom you have so cruelly used, are Englishmen of condition. I will protect them. Be the provocation what it will, you *must* know that your attempt upon them is a criminal one; and if my friend last come up, who is a very skilful surgeon, shall pronounce them in danger, you shall find it so.

Still he held the horse of the furious one; and three of them, who seemed to be principals, were beginning to express some resentment at his cavalier treatment, when Mr. Lowther gave his opinion, that there was no apparent danger of death: and then Sir Charles, quitting the man's bridle, and putting himself between the assailants and sufferers, said, That as they had not either offered to fly, or to be guilty of violence to himself, his friend, or servants, he was afraid they had some reason to think themselves ill used by the gentlemen. But, however, as they could not suppose they were at liberty, in a civilised country, to take their revenge on the persons of those who were entitled to the protection of that country, he should expect, that they would hold themselves to be personally answerable for their conduct at a proper tribunal.

The villains, said one of the men, know who we are, and the provocation; which merits a worse treatment than they have hitherto met with. You, sir, proceeded he, seem to be a man of honour, and temper: we are men of honour, as well as you. Our design, as we told you, was not to kill the miscreants; but to give them reason to remember their villany as long as they lived; and to put it out of their power ever to be guilty of the like. They have made a vile attempt, continued he, on a lady's honour at Abbeville; and finding themselves detected and in danger, took roundabout ways, and shifted from one vehicle to another, to escape the vengeance of her friends. The gentleman, whose horse you held, and who has reason to be in a passion, is the husband of the lady. [A Spanish husband, surely, Harriet: not a French one, according to our notions.] *That* gentleman, and *that,* are her brothers. We have been in pursuit of them two days; for they gave out (in order, no doubt, to put us on a wrong scent), that they were to go to Antwerp.

And it seems, my dear, that Sir Hargrave and his colleague had actually sent some of his servants that way; which was the reason that they were themselves attended but by one.

The gentleman told Sir Charles that there was a third villain in their plot. They had hopes, he said, that he would not escape the close pursuit of a manufacturer of Abbeville, whose daughter, a lovely young creature, he had seduced, under promises of marriage. Their government, he observed, were great countenancers of the manufacturers at Abbeville; and he would have reason, if he were laid hold of, to think himself happy, if he came off with being obliged to perform his promises.

This third wretch must be Mr. Bagenhall. The Lord grant, say I, that he may be laid hold of and obliged to make a ruined girl an *honest woman,* as they phrase it in LANCASHIRE. Don't *you* wish so, my dear? And let me add, that had the relations of the injured lady completed their intended vengeance on those two libertines (a very proper punishment, I ween, for all libertines); it might have helped them to pass the rest of their lives with great tranquillity; and honest girls might, for any contrivance of theirs, have passed to and from *masquerades* without molestation.

Sir Hargrave and his companions intended, it seems, at first, to make some resistance; four only, of the seven, stopping the chaise: but when the other three came up, and they saw who they were, and knew their own guilt, their courage failed them.

The seventh man was set over the post-boy, whom he had led about half a mile from the spot they had chosen as a convenient one for their purpose.

Sir Hargrave's servant was secured by them at their first attack; but after they had disarmed him and his masters he found an opportunity to slip from them, and made the best of his way to the road, in hopes of procuring assistance for them.

While Sir Charles was busy in helping the bruised wretches on their feet, the seventh man came up to the others, followed by Sir Hargrave's chaise. The assailants had retired to some distance, and, after a consultation together, they all advanced towards Sir Charles; who, bidding his servants be on their guard, leapt on his horse, with that agility and presence of mind, for which, Mr. Beauchamp says, he excels most men; and leading towards them, Do you advance, gentlemen, said he, as friends, or otherwise?—Mr. Lowther took a pistol in each hand, and held himself ready to support him; and the servants disposed themselves to obey their masters' orders.

Our enmity, answered one of them, is only to these two *inhospitable* villains: murder, as we told you, was not our design. They know where we are to be found; and that they are the vilest of men, and have not been punished equal to their demerits. Let them on their knees ask this gentleman's pardon; pointing to the husband of the insulted lady. We insist upon this satisfaction; and upon their promise, that they never more will come within two leagues of Abbeville; and we will leave them in your protection.

I fancy, Harriet, that these women-frightening heroes need not to have been urged to make this promise.

Sir Charles, turning towards them, said, If you have done wrong, gentlemen, you ought not to scruple asking pardon. If you know yourself to be innocent, though I should be loath to risk the lives of my friends and servants, yet shall not my countrymen make so undue a submission.

The wretches knelt; and the seven men, civilly saluting Sir Charles and Mr. Lowther, rode off to the joy of the two delinquents, who knelt again to their deliverer, and poured forth blessings upon the man, whose life, so lately, one of them sought; and whose preservation he had now so much reason to rejoice in, for the sake of his own safety.

My brother himself could not but be well pleased that he was not obliged to come to extremities, which might have ended fatally on both sides.

By this time Sir Hargrave's post-chaise was come up. He and his colleague were with difficulty lifted into it. My brother and Mr. Lowther went into theirs; and being but a small distance from Paris, they proceeded thither in company; the poor wretches blessing them all the way; and at Paris found their other servants waiting for them.

Sir Charles and Mr. Lowther saw them in bed in the lodgings that had been taken for them. They were so stiff with the bastinado they had met with, that they were unable to help themselves. Mr. Merceda had been more severely (I cannot call it more cruelly) treated than the other; for he, it seems, was the greatest malefactor in the attempt made upon the lady: and he had, besides, two or three gashes, which, but for his struggles, would have been but one.

As you, my dear, always turn pale when the word *masquerade* is mentioned; so, I warrant, will ABBEVILLE be a word of terror to these wretches as long as they live.

Their enemies, it seems, carried off their arms; perhaps, in the true spirit of French chivalry, with a view to lay them, as so many trophies, at the feet of the insulted lady.

Mr. Lowther writes, that my brother and he are lodged in the hotel of a man of quality, a dear friend of the late Mr. Danby, and one of the three whom he has remembered in his will; and that Sir Charles is extremely busy in relation to the executorship; and having not a moment to spare, desired Mr. Lowther to engage his friend, to whom he wrote, to let us know as much: and that he was hastening everything for his journey onwards.

Mr. Beauchamp's narrative of this affair is, as I told you, very circumstantial. I thought to have shortened it more than I have done. I wish I have not made my abstract confused, in several material places: but I have no time to clear it up. —Adieu, my dear. CHARLOTTE G——.

END OF VOL. IV